Contemporary Problems
in Geography

The general editor of *Contemporary Problems in Geography* is Dr. William Birch, who is Director of the Bristol Polytechnic. He was formerly on the staff of the University of Bristol and the Graduate School of Geography at Clark University in the U.S.A. and he has been Chairman of the Department of Geography in the University of Toronto and Professor of Geography at the University of Leeds. He was President of the Institute of British Geographers for 1976.

Alan Wilson is Professor of Regional and Urban Geography at the University of Leeds. After reading machematics at Cambridge he has served as Scientific Officer at the National Institute of Research in Nuclear Science, Research Officer at the Institute of Economics and Statistics. University of Oxford, Mathematical Adviser at the Ministry of Transport, and Assistant Director of the Centre for Environmental Studies. His publications include *Entropy in Urban and Regional Modelling, Papers in Urban and Regional Analysis*, and *Urban and Regional Models in Geography and Planning*.

Michael Kirkby is Professor of Physical Geography at the University of Leeds. He has done research at Cambridge and at the Johns Hopkins University and previously taught at the University of Bristol. In 1972 he published *Hillslope Form and Process* with M. A. Carson.

For Rita, Chris,
and Lucy

Political, Electoral, and Spatial Systems

An Essay in Political Geography

R. J. JOHNSTON

CLARENDON PRESS · OXFORD
1979

Oxford University Press, Walton Street, Oxford OX2 6DP

OXFORD LONDON GLASGOW
NEW YORK TORONTO MELBOURNE WELLINGTON
IBADAN NAIROBI DAR ES SALAAM CAPE TOWN
KUALA LUMPUR SINGAPORE JAKARTA HONG KONG TOKYO
DELHI BOMBAY CALCUTTA MADRAS KARACHI

British Library Cataloguing in Publication Data

Johnston, Ronald John
  Political, electoral and spatial systems. –
  (Contemporary problems in geography).
  1. Geography, Political
  I. Title   II. Series
  320.1′2   JC319   78–40648

  ISBN 0–19–874071–9
  ISBN 0–19–874072–7 Pbk

Filmset in 'Monophoto' Times 10 on 12 pt and
printed in Great Britain by
Richard Clay (The Chaucer Press), Ltd,
Bungay, Suffolk

Preface

This book is presented as a text in political geography. It does not cover the whole of the subject matter of that field, however. Instead, it introduces to the literature of political geography an integration of political, electoral, and spatial systems analysis in a manner which illuminates how geographical analysis can contribute to understanding of the origins and perpetuation of social inequality. As such, it is hoped that the book will be of considerable use to undergraduates and others, in a variety of courses in the wider fields of social geography, indeed of social science.

In preparing this book, my greatest debt is to Pete Taylor, whose conversations and collaboration in other work over two years were a constant stimulus to me in a variety of ways: he is, of course, in no way responsible for the contents of this book. My wife Rita has acted as both devil's advocate and manuscript reader, and I am extremely grateful for her efforts: she may see more influence from the latter of her roles than from the former! The series editor, Bill Birch, and the O.U.P. editor, Andrew Schuller, have both provided most valuable encouragement; Ruth Wells and the staff of the Inter-Library Loan section of the University of Sheffield Library dealt most successfully with a heavy flow of requests for material; Stephen Frampton has produced another excellent set of diagrams; and Joan Dunn has as always worked marvels in producing a final manuscript from my handwriting.

This book is dedicated to a devoted family, to whom I am unable to express the depths of my gratitude.

R. J. JOHNSTON

Contents

Part I
Geography and Government: Some Preliminaries

1 Introduction: Government and the Geography of Social Well-Being

OPINIONS on recent developments in human geography differ. Some observers view them as fundamental, arguing that the 'theoretical and quantitative' innovations of the 1950s and 1960s constituted a revolution involving a complete reorientation of geographical scholarship. Others believe that this period was characterized by evolution rather than revolution, with major methodological changes associated with the adoption of positivist philosophies of science and the widespread acceptance of the need for mathematical and statistical competence, but no basic alterations to the major concerns of geographical research (Chorley and Haggett, 1967; Chisholm, 1975). For both groups, however, there is general agreement that human geography is concerned with spatial patterns in man's occupation of his terrestrial environment.

The present book is not intended as a contribution to that debate. Its purpose is entirely positivist, to display certain aspects of the spatial patterning of the human condition. As such, it sits firmly in the 'areal differentiation' tradition. Its subject matter is of relatively recent interest to human geographers, however, and its main contribution is in the structure which it imposes upon this material. Until the last two decades, most human geography was concerned with human artefacts, with buildings and settlements, roads and railways, hedges and boundaries, factories and shops. The humans themselves were of very minor importance, except in so far as there was much mapping of where they lived (Hooson, 1960; Johnston, 1976d). Because of this, little stimulus was received from the work being done in political science, in which men as decision-makers are a major focus. The emphasis here is very much on political behaviour, however, and by bringing about an integration of the two foci it is part of the increasing tendency to demolish the disciplinary boundaries of the social sciences.

Social well-being and its geography

There has been an explosion in the volume of research data available for analysis by social scientists, much of it as a result of greater activity by governments in data collection during the decades since the social and economic near-collapse of the 1930s. The even more recent development of large, high-speed computers has attenuated the increasing data overload somewhat, but even so the portrayal and then interpretation of order in such material has posed a major task for social scientists seeking to identify the major patterns in society. With their colleagues in other disciplines, geographers have adopted and adapted multivariate statistical methods as ways of identifying the major spatial patterns, developing what has become known as the technology of factorial ecology (Berry, 1971).

The large number of factorial ecologies reported in the research literature provide a mass of evidence on the general patterns of spatial differentiation in such aspects of the human condition as age, sex, occupational and ethnic structures of populations, and the types and conditions of housing which they inhabit. Such work has been subjected to a variety of criticisms, of which two are relevant here. First, the data used are supplied almost entirely by outside bodies (notably census authorities) and so their nature is not determined by the analyst. As such, research is biased towards the data-collection value judgements of others. (It is the theory of governments about what constitutes a crime, for example, which determines the nature of collected data on what crimes occur where.) Secondly, the studies are characterized by theoretical agnosticism. Data were available and so were analysed. 'Explanations' were then sought from the output of the analyses. Attempts to provide a structure for such work, which was in part theoretical, rested on the notions of systems, and these are of importance here, as indicated in the next chapter.

The late 1960s and early 1970s have been a period of considerable unrest in Anglo-Saxon social science, reflecting a similar unease in the parent societies. The Vietnam War; racial and religious intolerance and riots; student unrest; political corruption; the perceived consequences of rapid resource depletion and environmental despoliation: these and many other conditions of society caused a 'taking stock'. One of the obvious facts which was brought to light concerned the immense inequalities within and between societies, at every spatial scale (Coates, Johnston, and Knox, 1977), and the lack of correlation between social conditions in particular instances and economic conditions in general. A social indicators movement thus began, aimed at measuring social conditions—levels of social well-being—within and between social groups in different places. Geographers joined this movement, arguing the need for territorial social indicators and for the collection of specifically designed data sets which would illustrate the spatial variations in social well-being.

In part, this territorial indicators movement replicated the earlier factorial ecology developments, and can be subjected to the same criticisms. Data came first, and although attempts were made to design the collection and analysis within the constraints of some general theory of social well-being (Smith, 1975; Knox, 1974) the results were general maps which again were very much the products of theoretical agnosticism. Like so much human geography of the last decade, they were patterns in search of an explanation. The present book is a small part of that search.

The determinants of social well-being

What determines the spatial variability in social well-being, the objective and subjective conditions within which daily lives are contained and constrained? For many years, the theory of consumer sovereignty, based on the neoclassical economic laws of supply and demand, was used to provide the explanation. Based in the ethic of high capitalism, with origins in social Darwinism and concepts of *laissez-faire* and free competition, allocation of goods and services reflected peaceful competition in the market-place. Critiques of such a view are founded on the writings of Marx and Engels, but these nineteenth-century works have only recently entered the reading lists of human geographers. In them, competition is far from free and the crucial determinant of well-being is economic power, a commodity which is far from equitably distributed.

In this book, the focus of the analysis is one particular use of power to influence, directly or indirectly, the geography of social well-being. The analyses presented here are very much partial, therefore, being set within a general model comprising three sets of interacting influences on the allocation of the various components of social well-being.

The spatial division of labour

Within any society, the major division of the population is into classes, groups which differ in the functions that they perform and the rewards that they obtain. In advanced industrial societies, there are two major such classes—the capitalist class and the working class—between which the differentiating characteristic is relationship to the mode of production. The working class live by selling their labour; the capitalist class 'own' the other factors of production—land and capital—and live by purchasing labour, selling its product, and maintaining as large a portion of the price as possible. This return to the capitalist class is used to obtain power and prevent others from getting control over the organization and operation of society. The working class attempts to obtain more power, however, and to gain larger portions of the economic rewards, thus creating a continual state of inter-class conflict over the distribution of income and wealth.

The return to the capitalist from his investment in labour power is usually known as profit, and the dynamic of capitalism is a never-satisfied quest for greater profits. To achieve these, labour must be made more productive, thereby changing the ratio of costs to price, and the fruits of this greater productivity must then be consumed, at the required price. More efficient methods of production allow the desired productivity increases to be achieved. These involve economies of scale, both internal and external to the firms involved, which in turn depend on greater specialization of roles within the division of labour. Greater consumption is achieved by expansion of markets, either into formerly untapped areas (a mainspring of imperialism) or by increased spending by the working class 'at home'.

A complex division of labour is a major consequence of the pursuit of these capitalist ends, with a multitude of different occupations. This division has led to a concomitant subdivision of the working class, a process encouraged by capitalism which benefits from the replacement of inter-class by intra-class conflict. A major new sub-class so created has been the bourgeoisie; its main functions involve the co-ordination of production, distribution, and consumption and advancement of the causes of the capitalist class by organizing the flows of money and goods. This group, itself a conglomerate of many occupations some of which have been elevated to professional status, is often distinguished not only by the skills of its members, but also frequently by the relatively high rewards which they are accorded to maintain their allegiance to the capitalist cause.

A major determinant of an individual's social well-being is his class position. At the most general level, the capitalist class contains the richest and the working class the poorest members of a society, but the intensification of intra-class conflict in recent decades, especially between elements of the working class and the bourgeoisie, has produced considerable fluidity in the relative status of certain groups (Westergaard and Resler, 1976). Some, notably those in the upper strata of the bourgeoisie and the least skilled working-class occupations, have remained in the same relative positions, whilst absolute levels of rewards have improved for nearly all.

The geographical relevance of this discussion of the class structure in advanced capitalist societies is that to a considerable extent the spatial pattern of levels of social well-being reflects the spatial pattern of the capitalist system. The origins of the current phase of capitalism were in north-western Europe, from whence much of the rest of the world has been colonized. To increase profits, cheap labour—to be exploited by a small bourgeoisie—was sought wherever it was available, and this colonized population also formed part of the growing market for capitalist products. The profits were returned to the European 'heartland', which was later extended with the rise to colonial power status of, in particular, the United States. Thus at the international scale, levels of social well-being reflect the colonial policies of north Atlantic capitalism (Johnston, 1976e).

Although best illustrated at the international scale, the spatial division of labour is just as important within nations. The process of internal colonialism has involved: first, incorporation of peripheral areas into the capitalist system which is focused on a few major social and economic centres; and secondly, the survival of only a relatively few capitalist firms, almost all of which have their control headquarters in those few major centres and which control levels of employment and well-being for much of the population of the peripheral areas (Pred, 1977). Thus within a country areas can be roughly categorized as either 'capitalist control centres' or 'workhouses'. The spatial segregation is far from complete, for some control functions are decentralized to a local bourgeoisie and control centres need some working-class members to service them.

Finally, inter- and intra-class conflict over resources and power is reflected in the intra-urban pattern of residential segregation. In particular, the capitalist class and its attendant bourgeoisie wishes to insulate itself from contact with the working class, thereby ensuring continuation of the system—via education and marriage, for example—and the maintenance of social distance. The result is a mosaic of separate residential areas for the various groups.

Level of social well-being reflects control over resources, which is a function of class position. The different classes live in separate areas of the capitalist map, and so maps of levels of social well-being are produced. This is the major determinant of the patterns recently identified so assiduously by human geographers. Alongside, however, two further important influences can be identified.

Environments

Two types of environment are relevant here—the physical and the proximate. Interactions between human societies and their physical environments have long been a focus of geographical interest, and the nature of these interactions has been the subject of much debate. The merits of neither the environmental determinism nor the possibilism cases are of import here. What is relevant is that certain physical conditions seem more likely to result in certain human responses, such as the relationships between dampness and bronchitis, humidity and debility, water hardness and tooth decay, whereas societies themselves have created social evaluations of physical environments, like the relationship between elevation, views, and 'desirability' of residential areas.

Control over the physical environment is limited, at least by the finiteness of human ingenuity and resources, and so there is conflict over the so-determined 'better' areas, which invariably is won by the richer and more powerful groups. Thus, as John Braine demonstrated in *Room at the Top*, the rich pre-empt the hills around English cities, upwind of the industrial areas. The control centres are in the pleasant places with, if necessary, satellites for the powerful to retreat to either daily (the cocktail belt) or seasonally (the hill station).

The proximate environment concerns a variable which geographers tried to make their own during the 1960s—distance. Most of the facilities used in everyday life are available at certain places only, and travel is necessary to obtain the required components of the level of social well-being. Some people, because of where they live, are closer to parks and precincts, to shops and offices, doctors and dentists, fire and police stations: travel to these costs time and money and the less that has to be spent, the better off people are. All of the facilities used do not produce positive externalities, however; it may be pleasant to live next to a park but not to a sewerage works or to an odorous factory.

Where one lives within the built environment with respect to positive and negative externalities can have a major influence on well-being. Not surprisingly, there is conflict to live in the 'better' areas, and, since this conflict is mediated in the property market where ability to pay is the major determinant of success, the richer and more powerful are able to reserve those better areas for themselves.

Government

During the twentieth century there has been a major change in the morphology of capitalism with the increased involvement of the state, represented by elected members of institutions and a supporting bureaucratic bourgeoisie. This involvement was not a recent invention. The state has always existed to protect the interests of the capitalist class (Miliband, 1969) and it was responsible, in particular, for much of the colonialism which was crucial to capitalist expansion over the last centuries. Nevertheless, its role has now been extended considerably, and in some cases is almost all-embracing. In some countries, notably those of the COMECON Bloc, state capitalism is near-monopolistic. In many others it enters most aspects of daily life, either ideologically through welfare state and liberal humanitarian conceptions of social justice, or pragmatically because of perceptions of what are known as 'market failures' where public must replace private provision of a good or service. Keynesian economics convinced many governments that they had a major role to play in maintaining healthy capitalist economies through manipulation of the demand for labour and nearly everywhere the state plays a major role as mediator in the inter-class conflict, thereby attempting to prevent the self-destruction of capitalism as working and capitalist classes conflict.

Government is perceived in the countries studied here (largely those of the English-speaking world) as rule for the people by the people's elected representatives. The deduction from this definition is that governments should pursue policies in the national interest. To some extent they do. But different groups (especially classes) will have different perceptions of the national interest, in part if not in total, and so control of government is itself a locale for inter- and intra-class conflict. This conflict is played out in the electoral process, when parties representing different groups—notably classes, but not always—compete to form governments (Taylor and Johnston, 1979). Because of its control over resources, the capitalist class is usually able to manipulate governments to its own ends (Miliband, 1969). Within this general syndrome, however, there are many policy variants. Those undertaken are the ones most suited to the particular ends of the groups in power and these, as it is the prime intention of this book to demonstrate, have clear spatial implications for levels of social well-being.

Integration

Three sets of influences have been outlined here as determinants of the geography of social well-being. In the general sense of the positivist scientific method they are independent variables, but in effect they are far from being either independent or equal in their impact. The major set, on which the other two depend, is the spatial division of labour, the map of where social classes live. Within that map, the inter- and intra-class conflicts are played out. One stage for such activity is the operation of government, via the electoral system, and it is investigation of the nature of government which forms the subject matter of the next chapter.

Following this introductory section of the book, the remaining three parts present the detailed analyses of the relationships between, on the one hand, political and electoral geography and, on the other, the geography of social well-being. This is an area of study which has largely been ignored in the literature of what is traditionally known as political geography (Taylor, 1977; Johnston, 1978c). It is hoped that the analyses and arguments presented here will rectify that omission, with a focus on the geographical inputs to levels of social well-being rather than another description of the outputs.

2 Government and Society: A Systems Approach

ALL societies have some form of government. For the smallest and most primitive, it probably involves but a simple set of rules (laws) plus a mechanism—perhaps a plenary meeting—for ensuring their acceptance and operation. The rules enacted are those which the society wants; when they are operated, the mechanism receives the support of the members. If these conditions are broken, however, there may be some form of revolution against the government, and its replacement by a new one, more receptive to the demands of the constituents and so more deserving of their support.

The meeting will need a chairman, and perhaps also an overseer to ensure continued operation of the system. These may be neutral positions but it is more likely that they will be powerful ones, from which individuals, acting either for themselves or as representatives of a group, are able to manipulate the rules to their own benefits. Few societies will have an over-all consensus as to the benefits to be obtained from government, and ability to manipulate the system will allow one or more groups within it to pursue their own particular ends. To maintain support from the others, they will need to meet at least some of their demands, so government involves a process of buying support. (At least in the long term; in the short term it may be imposed by force of arms, but this requires the continued bought support of the army, at least.) Whilst doing this, ruling groups may impose their permanent control, by, for example, establishing ruling dynasties.

At the other end of the spectrum from the small, primitive society is the large and complex capitalist system. In this, there are more groups with different ends, and more resources to be contested in the political arena. In such situations, governmental power is great. How has it grown, and how does it operate? These questions are the focus of the present chapter, which sets the scene for the rest of the book in the context of the important systems analysis contributions to political theory by David Easton (1965a, 1965b).

The growth of government
In the context of this book, government involves rule over a population in a defined territory by a separate, identifiable group from within society, supported by a bureaucracy. For the former too, such rule will be a full-time occupation. The first group probably originated with the genesis of urban settlements, from which they could impose their rule over the inhabitants of a surrounding hinterland, obtaining tribute from them by a combination of military force and religious persuasion (Johnston, 1977d). Many such

attempts to rule others undoubtedly failed. Those which succeeded were characterized by growth, as the ruling group sought to extend their power and improve their level of social well-being. They achieved the latter by creating new occupations involving workers whose functions were to provide goods and services for élite consumption; to maintain these workers, more tribute was needed from agriculturalists, and in turn more employees were needed to collect this. And so the multiplier continued, with every new division or demand creating greater demands on the primary producers.

More tribute could be obtained by prevailing on the local, subservient agriculturalists to be more productive, in which task they were perhaps aided by technological developments (better seeds, breeds, and tools, etc.); in turn, the provision of technology required more dependent non-agriculturalists. Alternatively, the area under the élite hegemony could be extended—the initial stage of colonialism. To maintain power over a larger area, more administrators and soldiers were needed—all of them making demands on the agriculturalists —as were more transport workers. Growth demanded a more complex division of labour, therefore, and a much more complicated organizational structure.

At some stage a hierarchical spatial system emerged because of the greater power of some ruling élites who 'bought' the tolerance of subservient groups. Each area has a ruling household which extracts tribute from the local proletariat, but in turn pays some of that tribute to a higher-level élite which, by greater efficiency, has been able to extend its empire and encapsulate those of its neighbours, using the latter to run its new 'colonies' for it. Such co-option rather than removal of the local rulers was necessary because of the difficulties of controlling large areas with primitive means of transport; co-option brought with it privileges for the lower-level élite whilst the higher-level rulers offered protection from others of equal standing (generally by using the proletariat being protected!).

Extraction of tribute through a system of ranks was replaced by a superior organization that allowed a similar end without so much demand for supporting armies. Instead of demanding tribute, and offering inducements to those who would collect it, the élite instituted a trading system, buying the tribute with goods of inferior quality. To organize this, a merchant class was developed, along with a currency system. The merchants were allowed profits—selling goods at more than they bought them for—and these were used as investments in more productive agriculture and manufacture. They came to equal the landowners in power, and the latter joined the market system by substituting a system of rents for tribute.

Merchant capitalists wanted to be more powerful and wealthy, to expand their investments and obtain greater profits. Competition developed between them, for existing markets and for new ones, and in this they were encouraged by the landlords, particularly the higher-level rulers. Mercantile expansion needed armies to protect markets and to conquer new ones, and a new alliance was forged. Finance for the needed armies and navies came from the taxpayers—the same class as the earlier providers of tribute.

As mercantilism grew, so did the demands for 'colonial' administrators and armies, especially in periods of conflict. Rents and profits were sometimes insufficient to finance major adventures—or defences—and more tax-raising was necessary. To legitimize this activity, the merchant class and their landlord allies needed widespread support, and such legitimation was achieved by agreeing to allow the major contributors a say in the rule—in government. Initially this say was an infrequently convened Parliament of all major landowners. Later this became a body which met more frequently and was comprised of elected representatives of the landlord and merchant classes. In this way, elected government—based on a very limited franchise of property ownership—began.

Modern government

Industrial capitalism developed out of mercantile capitalism. Increasingly profits and rents were reinvested, not in trade ventures—in ways of getting more goods, especially primary goods, cheaply—but in production—in ways of making more goods, especially secondary manufactures, more cheaply. Labour was put to work in factories, thereby producing more efficiently and increasing the rate of profit. (Efficiency here involves the difference between the unit cost of production and the price received by the seller.) Expansion of this new system created a 'new rich', the industrial capitalists, who contributed to the general wealth of the nation. They too needed the support of the state, and so were allied with landlords and merchants in government, although the interests of all three did not always coincide. (Merchants, for example, benefited from free trade whereas industrialists, especially new ones, preferred protection.)

Alliance of the state with industrial as well as merchant capitalism introduced many new functions for government, well beyond its original role as the provider of protection for the élite. Trade regulation through customs and tariffs became crucial, as did investment in the necessary infrastructure for industrial capitalist success. (Such as railways; Britain is an exception in having a railway system whose development was financed entirely through the private sector, although this was 'regulated' by government.) The income from some of these functions—for example, customs duties—was sufficient to pay for all government activities in some cases, but eventually it proved insufficient, especially as wars became larger, if not necessarily more frequent. Larger, more regular supplies of finance for government were needed; they were provided by a taxation system.

The industrial capitalist system crowded people into towns, in order to reap the economies of scale from the factory mode of production. The living and working conditions of the new urban working class were the cause of some altruistic concern. Alleviation of their distress was not altogether altruistic, however. Instead, government was used to provide the social infrastructure necessary for a healthy and reproducing proletariat, and to prevent disease spreading to the élite themselves (Offe, 1975). Public health and factory regulation became government functions. Furthermore, an increasing proportion of the working class needed some education in order that they could perform their tasks, and again government was expected to provide this service to capitalism. And so from its protective role for the landlord and merchant capitalist classes government evolved into a productive role for the industrial capitalist class. To support this expansion, it needed a large, regular income, which it obtained by taxation, of property, then of income, and then of expenditure.

The spatial concentration of the working class, their importance to the success of industrial capitalism, and then their taxation, heightened the inter-class conflict. Government needed to mediate in this, to ensure the continuance of the system, and the capitalist class was forced to yield some apparent concessions to the proletariat, one of whose demands concerned representation in the process of government. And so the franchise was slowly extended. The working class became more involved in political life; and the need to foster intra-class divisions, thereby forestalling their takeover of capitalism from the capitalists, was realized.

From being the property of one major class, therefore, government has become the property of all, and a stage for acting out the main conflicts within society. The working class has been incorporated, not through altruism or any willing redistribution of wealth from the rich by the rich, but rather by the use of grants of fear (Boulding, 1973) made to the working class in the hope that this will obtain their acquiescence to capitalist policies and, by giving them a cake to fight over, divert them from the true extent of their 'exploitation'. At the same time, government has become a major element in the industrial system, as a purchaser, in particular, of military products. Other groups lobby not for purchase but for infrastructure: the motor-car industry wants more motorways, for example, and the construction industry more housing loans; the service professions want their areas expanded—more schools, more universities, more hospitals, more social work; and the government bureaucracy itself is strongly committed to its own growth.

Government in advanced capitalist societies is a major employer, therefore, a large body at the centre of all conflicts in society. Because it is permanent, it has its own *raison d'être*. The elected representatives want to keep their posts, and extend their power; the bureaucrats employed by government want to extend their influence. Some of the actions of both are not surprisingly aimed at maintaining and extending this power and influence, and so the policies of modern governments are as likely as those in earlier centuries to be determined by the self-interests of the governors.

The Welfare State

When the state expanded its role beyond that of the purely protective function, it undertook two new types of task. The first involved the sale of services to residents—water, sewerage disposal, etc; the second was the relief of indigence: both, as will be indicated in the next chapter, were provided by local governments. With the second of these types came the origin of what is now known widely as the welfare state; the first was more what is termed the mixed economy: both are now often confused into one function.

There are four types of welfare policy (Gilbert, 1975): (1) the relief of dependency, especially poverty; (2) the mitigation of insecurity and risk; (3) the public provision of social services, income surrogates and market regulation; and (4) income redistribution. Most countries have developed policies proceeding through this sequence, although not all have the same commitment to the final two stages and in many there are political parties which clearly differ in their views on the necessity of such policies. Thus the United States mainly operates the first two types, with some policies in the third stage (such as the provision of public education). The United Kingdom, on the other hand, is much more firmly in the final two types. Its Labour Party, in particular, is strongly committed to the use of welfare policy for income redistribution, although the success of its attempts in this direction has not been great (Kincaid, 1973; Westergaard and Resler, 1976; Field, Meacher, and Pond, 1977).

Welfare policy in Britain originated with the Poor Laws, by which local governments—the parishes—were required to provide for their resident indigents, by the provision of work (Bruce, 1961). In the nineteenth century, following the rapid industrialization and urbanization, initial attitudes of those with power focused on the positive qualities of hard work and argued that poverty was to a large degree self-inflicted. Later in the century attitudes changed, however, which (Sleeman, 1973, p. 14)

included intellectual trends, such as utilitarianism; experience of the pressing dangers to public health arising out of conditions in the growing towns; the needs of an industrial society for some degree of education; the pressures of political democracy as the franchise was extended; experience of the inadequacies of the market to provide for urgent social needs, and realization of the continued wide extent of poverty among the unskilled masses at a time of generally rising prosperity.

Although there was some altruistic concern for the plight of men involved in these changes, most of them were imposed on governments by agitation from the powerless or newly enfranchised, particularly (as in other countries, such as New Zealand) after periods of depression when poverty expanded 'upwards' through the social ranks. The depression of the 1930s produced the major change, with the election in 1945 of a majority Labour government which introduced much of what is now widely recognized as the 'welfare state'.

Although many of the former British dominions developed welfare state policies similar to Britain's—indeed, in some cases they preceded their 'mother country' with such innovations—the United States did not. Until the New Deal governments of Roosevelt's in the 1930s, American welfare policy was very much of the Poor Law type; this was altered by the 1935 Social Security Act, which took the country into the second type enumerated above. Despite the growing realization that poverty was not merely a consequence of indolence, and the rapid expansion of public expenditure (see below), there has been relatively little redistribution of income from rich to poor. Industrial capitalism is even stronger in the United States than in the United Kingdom and, as Gilbert (1975, p. 125) points out,

That the poor fare poorly in welfare politics is hardly surprising. In pluralist terms they lack the requisite social and economic resources for group influence. In populist terms they are not only a small numerical minority but they carry the heavy burden of unpopularity.

The working class in the United States is not politically as organized and represented as its counterpart in Britain and the former dominions.

Quantification of government's role

Governments are major employers and spenders within advanced capitalist societies. Their spending has the twin functions of providing a major support for capitalism and reducing conflict between the capitalist and working classes. Their employment covers not only the parliamentarians and their supporting bureaucracies, but also the workers in a variety of 'industries' (postal, health, education, etc.); their spending includes not only the redistribution of real and money income from rich (by taxation) to poor (via benefits, direct and otherwise) but also the purchase of a wide range of consumables—notably defence weapons—and investment in the necessary infrastructure (research and development, various facilities and utilities) for capitalist success.

The rapid growth of this expenditure, as a percentage of Gross National Product, is illustrated in Fig. 2.1 for the U.K. and the U.S.A. By 1953, governments in the two countries were spending 32 and 28 per cent respectively of G.N.P. (Else, 1976); in 1970, the percentages were 35 and 33. In 1974 British governments were spending 56 per cent of G.N.P., compared to 50 per cent in 1970, according to another estimate (Sandford, 1977).

Of this great volume of government expenditure, there is a relatively even split between consumption and transfer payments (which include debt interest and repayments). Thus between 1965 and 1968, 56 per cent of British government expenditure was on the consumption of goods and services; one-third of it was on defence and the remainder on general administration, justice and police, etc. (Else, 1976). The United States federal government spent $275 billion in 1974, nearly 30 per cent of it on defence and a further 30 per cent on

FIG. 2.1   The growth of government expenditure in the U.K. and the U.S.A. Source: Musgrave (1969, p.94–5).

income security programmes (U.S. Department of Commerce, 1974). It employed 2·6 million people—one million of them on the Department of Defense pay-roll—while in addition state and local governments spent just over $100 000 m. (excluding transfers from the federal exchequer) and employed over 11 million out of a total national work-force of about 91 millions.

These American data indicate very clearly that in discussing the role of government within a society it is necessary to consider the two separate, yet very closely linked, levels—national and local. Most countries have a plethora of administrative bodies forming the second of these levels, some performing but a single function and others operating over a wider range of welfare and other policies. The majority of these local governments, and particularly the larger units, are politicized; indeed in Britain the political role of local government elections is such that they provide an excellent index of the popularity of the party in power at the national level.

The political system: a systems approach

The brief discussion so far has indicated the extent of the function of government in an advanced capitalist society and shown that this function is performed at two major levels—local and national. The present section presents a framework for the analysis of these functions by political geographers, within the over-all context of studies of the geography of social well-being.

Easton's model

The concept of the system is one which has been adopted as an organizing framework for a number of social sciences in recent years. In its most basic form a system comprises three sets of components: (1) the elements, or the parts; (2) the interactions, or the relationships between the parts; and (3) the environment, from which the system derives inputs and to which it sends outputs. Thus an internal combustion engine is a system comprising interacting parts; the input from its environment is fuel and its outputs are those which pass through its exhausts. The engine is so structured that it responds to the stimulus of fuel input in a certain way.

In the social sciences, the systems are the institutions which make up society and which react to stimuli by producing certain outputs. They may be 'programmed', so that the same stimulus always produces the same response, but in most cases the interacting elements are human decision-makers, who are usually neither as stereotyped nor as predictable in their responses as the internal combustion engine is. The task of the social scientist, therefore, is to identify how humans work within such systems.

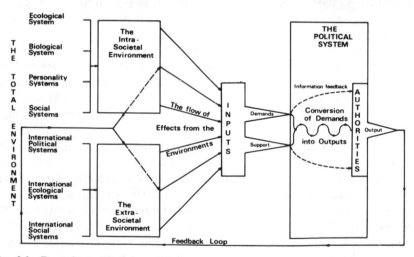

FIG. 2.2   Easton's model of the political system. Source: Easton (1965b, p. 110).

An example of the use of the systems concept in political analysis has been provided by David Easton (1965a, 1965b), whose basic model is given in Fig. 2.2. Central in this analysis is the political system, which is the whole organization of government, and its associated bureaucracy, that processes the inputs and produces the outputs, the policies which are a response to societal demands. These inputs, as the diagram shows, are the product of environmental forces, both those operating locally (the intra-societal environment) and those of the wider world (the extra-societal environment).

The members of the society process these inputs and out of them fashion demands from their government, saying, in effect, that if the government accedes to these demands it will receive their support. The political system then reacts to these demands (in effect, of course, the generation of and reaction to demands is a continuous process) and produces policy outputs which flow into the environment. As a result of these outputs, members of society adjust their demands and alter their level of support for the members of the political system.

Since governments in the advanced capitalist societies discussed here are elected, the main index of their level of support is given in the regular, and usually frequent, expressions of democratic views at the ballot box. An elected government will wish to be re-elected, and so its policies will be directed—at least in part and especially at the time of an election—towards maintaining and if possible extending its support among the electorate. The latter are aware of this, of course, and so phrase their demands accordingly, whilst politicians currently not in the government will attempt to change the support pattern by offering to meet the demands in a better way. (These alternatives are offered by parties, groups of individuals forming an alliance which, if successful at an election, will have a majority of the power-holders and so be able to form a government.)

In an extremely simple society, the members may be unanimous in their demands, the politicans will react to these, and support will be complete. Few, if any, societies are characterized by such a consensus, however, and instead comprise groups with conflicting demands. The discussion so far in this book has suggested that there are two such opposing groups—the capitalist class and the working class—but these are subdivided into many tributary groups which, although they may agree on certain basic issues, are competing among themselves.

To cater for these conflicting demands, Easton's model has been modified in Fig. 2.3 to incorporate several competing groups. Those in the political system are then aware that, except in particular circumstances such as a war when the vast majority of the population are agreed on certain demands, they will be unable to satisfy all of the various claimants. Their task is to decide which to react to, which policies to enact for which demands. They form coalitions of supporters (voters) who will, they hope, re-elect them. At the same time, they must not entirely disabuse the others, or else their lack of support may become open rebellion. The political system must produce outputs which, in some senses, are all things to all men.

How are these conflicting objectives achieved? One major way is through consensus politics via the creation of false conciousnesses. In a society typified by a capitalist versus working class conflict, each will have its own political party wanting power to meet the demands of its supporters. In order to be able to meet those demands the working-class party—unless it intends an

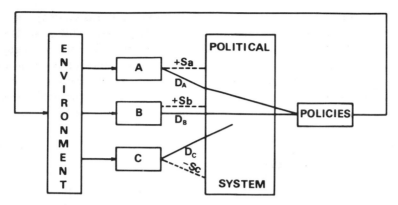

FIG. 2.3   A simplification of Easton's model with the population divided into three classes, A, B, and C. Of the demands from these classes—D_A, D_B, and D_C—which are processed by the political system only those from A and B are represented in policies. The support from A and B for the system is positive, therefore, whereas it is negative from C.

economic and social revolution—must ensure a healthy capitalist operation. A capitalist-class party, on the other hand, must convince the working class that its policies are for their benefit. Thus, as indicated in Chapters 5 and 6, parties have created a mass of 'middle-of-the-road' voters prepared to vote for either; the contest for power is in terms of alternative policies, but the alternatives are muted.

Getting one's own way is easiest if there is no opposition. In the present context this is best achieved by establishing independent territories containing members of a certain class only. As already indicated, the classes are spatially separated, at a variety of scales, so that within a nation each local group can, through use of the local government system, gain some autonomy by having no opposition.

Politics, territories, elections, and well-being

The salience of government as a regulator and allocator within society makes conflict for governmental power a crucial issue in a political economy. As indicated, the outline of this conflict involves the two major classes, but in addition to the inter-class competition and bargaining there is much intra-class conflict as well, between a great plethora of interest groups, large and small, narrow and wide. Some of these groups compete for power through the electoral process; others support contenders for electoral success; others again lobby governments of any persuasion. At the centre of all this activity are the overt political actors, the groups which combine as political parties in the search for the power to direct the affairs of a territory and its populace. It is this contest for power, and its consequences for the geography of social well-being, that forms the focus of the present book in which attention is directed to the geographical inputs to and outputs from the political system.

Two aspects of these inputs and outputs have been chosen for analysis here. The first concerns the operations of local governments as means of articulating the demands in Easton's model and as producers of varying levels of well-being as consequences of the system's operation. The second concerns the electoral process itself—the means by which governments come to power—stressing again the important geographical inputs and their effects on the outputs.

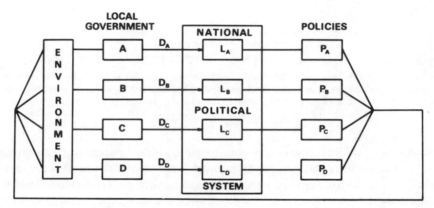

FIG. 2.4   Easton's model modified to allow for a population divided into four local government areas (A ... D) the demands from which (D_A ... D_D) are processed by the four local political systems (L_A ... L_D), set within the national system, which produce distinct sets of policies (P_A ... P_D) for their respective electorates.

The local government system

Study of the operations of local governments is organized within a further modification of Easton's model (Fig. 2.4). The separate groups with their own demands and support occupy separate parts of the national space. Each group attempts to influence the policy outputs through its local governments, so that the spatial variability in outputs reflects the spatial variability in demands. The local governments are not autonomous, however; what they can and cannot do is almost always prescribed by a higher-level government, and so each separate unit in Fig. 2.4 is set in the over-all matrix of the national government.

In the short term, the system operates as a simple stimulus–response mechanism, with each local government reacting to the demands made on it, producing the requisite outputs, and receiving political support, at elections and in general. In the long term, however, this process may not operate to the best interests of some of those involved, and they will attempt to change it, in order to further their interests more efficiently. Such changes can be of a wide variety. Alterations in population distributions (where the classes live) between territories will change the demands, the elected politician decision-makers, and the outputs. More easily achieved, however, is changing the pattern of local government areas, thereby better meeting the various demands, or at least those of the groups able to institute such changes. Thus local government 'reform' is part of the conflict between and within classes, with the map of administrative areas being reconstructed for political/economic ends.

The electoral process

The political system is fuelled in democratic countries by elections, participation in which is one element of societal support for its operations. Each national government (Fig. 2.2) and local government (Fig. 2.4) is elected by the enfranchised population (all adults over the age of eighteen in the countries studied here). Elections are fought between groups (parties) which want to form governments, and it is the need to win elections which makes governments responsive to the demands made of them. Thus the electoral process is a sub-system of the larger political system, a component of the total set of operations which converts inputs to outputs.

There are numerous types of electoral system: that discussed here involves a parliament or equivalent elected body within which decisions are made on the basis of majority agreements (votes). Parties compete in the elections to form permanent majorities in the parliament, and thus to have a complete hold on political power in the sub-system. Until the next election, assuming that the party does not split and there is no action from a higher-level government to override it, a party with an elected majority becomes the decision-making 'box' of Fig. 2.2.

The electoral system is depicted in Fig. 2.5 as comprising four sets of inputs and one output—the latter is the power to make decisions. Of the inputs, the first is the *electoral law* which governs all aspects of the conduct of an election—who can vote; how votes are cast; how representation is determined; when elections are held; how campaigning can proceed, etc. In at least one of the countries analysed here—New Zealand—the electoral law is in effect the constitution (Jackson, 1973).

The second input is a set of *constituencies*, the areas which send the representatives to the parliament, and whose nature (size, etc.) is determined by the electoral law. Some countries, notably Israel, do not use constituencies, but they are an integral part of the electoral process at all levels of government in the countries studied here. They are laid out over a further map, that of the *distribution of voters*, which provides the third input to the system. As indicated in Chapter 1, there is a spatial division of labour producing the residential separation of various social and economic groups at all scales. Much of this separation relates to the bases for political conflict, whether

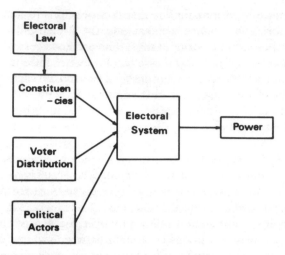

FIG. 2.5   A systems model of the electoral process.

between social classes or between religious groups (Ulster), racial and linguistic groups (Canada and the United States), or others which lead to different political viewpoints. These various groups are located in differing strengths in the different constituencies.

Finally in this list of inputs comes the *political actors*, who comprise three types. The overt actors are those who actually contest the elections—the parties and their candidates—whereas the covert actors are those who support

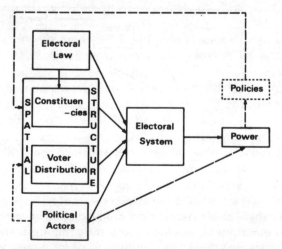

FIG. 2.6   The short-term operation of the electoral process showing—by the dashed lines—how some political actors use their power to 'campaign' in the spatial structure (via policies), whereas others 'campaign' directly because they are powerless.

the first type, usually by making financial contributions to their campaigns. Finally, there is a group of overt actors who are not candidates for elected office but who aim to influence both those who are and those who are voting for them. These are the political lobbies and pressure groups.

The interaction of these four inputs within the electoral system produces the output, political power for an elected government. Having obtained power, a governing party will wish to retain it next time, as will its individual members, whereas defeated opponents will strive for success next time. For the former, this involves *policies* (feedback outputs) designed to win votes, from where they matter; for the latter, the striving involves similar *promised policies*. Thus the short-term operation of the system (Fig. 2.6) involves the use of power by the political actors in electioneering within the spatial structure of the inputs (the constituencies and the voter distributions). In the long term, outputs may be devised to change the inputs, so as to further the demands of one group over those of another. This may involve changing the electoral law, changing the constituencies (with or without a change in the law), or changing the distribution of voters (Fig. 2.7).

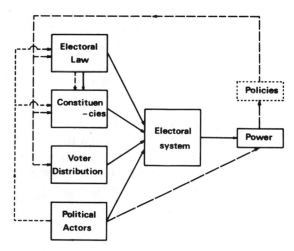

FIG. 2.7   The long-term operation of the electoral process showing—by the dashed lines—how political actors manipulate the inputs to the electoral system, for their own ends.

Conclusions

Two aspects of the political system have been identified for analysis here: the pattern of local governments and the services which they provide in response to resident demands; and the electoral process by which power is achieved. At any one time each of these components exists and is operating, providing the short-term or static context for analysis. Over time, however, the components are changed to meet new political demands, providing a dynamic analytical context.

The preceding paragraph provides an outline for the rest of the book, which is divided into three further parts, each containing one chapter for each of the two components. In Part II, the two components are described, with one chapter on the nature of local government and another on the conduct of elections. Then in Part III the focus is shifted to the static operations of the components: Chapter 5 analyses variability between local governments in their outputs (how much governments spend) as responses to local demands, and Chapter 6 looks at spatial patterns of spending within individual government territories (where governments spend) as reactions to the electoral process. Finally, in Part IV the dynamics of the components are investigated, with chapters on local government 'reform' and electoral 'reform'.

Throughout the book, although all the topics dealt with are related to politics and elections, the fundamental concern is with the outputs, with the contributions of governments to the geography of social well-being. As such, the book represents an attempt to integrate political and electoral geography with mainstream human geography. The geographical inputs which help to drive the political system, and the political outputs which feed back to the wider environment are thus seen in their full interrelation, rather than as separate components of an academic field which seems now to have as many impervious intra-disciplinary boundaries as there are similar interdisciplinary demarcations.

The potential subject matter of such a book is immense. It is made manageable here by confining attention to but a few countries—the United Kingdom and the United States in particular, but with some reference to other countries (notably the ex-dominions of the British Empire) with similar political and electoral systems. There is little doubt, however, that the general patterns identified here apply even more widely.

Part II
The Two Systems

3 Local Governments

ALTHOUGH it is at the level of the nation-state that most of the important decisions influencing livelihood are made, the various layers of local government within each state are parts of a decision-making apparatus that have considerable influence on the variations in levels of social well-being. This chapter outlines the nature of those layers. Particular attention is paid to the United Kingdom and the United States, the two countries which are the major foci of the rest of the book; however, although there are differences of detail, in most countries the pattern of local government conforms with either that of the centralized state (U.K.) or the federation (U.S.A.), so that the two examples used here have wider relevance. The first part deals with the factual basis; the second is concerned with some basic themes in the study of local governments.

The functions of local government

The pattern and character of local government must be such as to enable it to do four things: to perform efficiently a wide range of profoundly important tasks concerned with the safety, health and well-being, both material and cultural, of people in different localities; to attract and hold the interest of its citizens; to develop enough inherent strength to deal with national authorities in a valid partnership; and to adapt itself without disruption to the present unprecedented process of change in the way people live, work, move, shop and enjoy themselves (Royal Commission on Local Government in England, 1969a, p. 1).

This is a typical statement about the functions of local governments. Sharpe (1976), for example, recognizes three major functions for local governments. The first is the *liberty function,* with a strong local government system providing a division of power and responsibility and preventing the growth of a centralized autocracy. Secondly there is the *participation function*, with local government allowing individuals to participate in local democracy—often as a training-ground for later service in higher levels of government—and diffusing power amongst the populace. Finally, there is the *efficient provision of services function.* Certain services are local in scope, being concerned with local consumers only, and are best provided by local governments.

Of these three, Sharpe favours the third as the most important. Local government may be a check against centralized autocracy, but since local government itself can be maladministered and most individuals are not free to live wherever they will, the liberty function is less real than apparent. Similarly, participation may be important as a form of political self-education and as a means of breeding harmonious local commitment. But, according to

Sharpe (see also Hill, 1974), it is the efficient provision of services which is most important because: services should be organized near to the point of delivery; local governments can promote local demands; local, small groups are easier to mobilize to support their demands; local governments are publicly accountable at elections, and so superior to public corporations, which are not; local governments can better respond to local changes in needs; and 'local authorities provide a bulwark against the growth of the autonomy of professional groups in government' (p. 220).

Many of these views are repeated by others—see, for example, Blair (1964) on American local government. In plural societies, with many competing value systems, local government allows the various 'atoms of democracy' to produce 'government of, for, and by the people'. Particular emphasis is laid, however, on governments as providers of services, and this, rather than the more philosophical issues of liberty and participation, will be the focus here.

The origins of local government

Local government areas may be produced by one of two opposing processes. The first is a residual from the amalgamation of formerly separate, if not independent, territories into larger units. Especially if such amalgamations are voluntary, as in several federations such as the U.S.A., and the E.E.C., the members may retain to themselves certain functions, as are enshrined, for example, in the American Constitution. Alternatively, subordinate territories may be created within larger units in order to operate certain legislative powers at a more local level. This may be to gain economic or democratic efficiency; it may be the result of central governments transferring potentially contentious issues to another body.

The British local government system to 1974

British local government originally had three units. Most important of these was the *county*, land granted to an earl by the monarch in return for certain obligations. Later, direct rule was imposed via the monarch's representative— the Lord Lieutenant, who may also have been the feudal earl—who was responsible for law and order and for bridges and prisons (Richards, 1968).

Within each county was a mosaic of *parishes*, initially ecclesiastical units but later with secular functions involving four people—the overseer, the surveyor, the constable, and the churchwarden—in the provision and upkeep of roads and the maintenance of the poor. Separate from the parishes were the *boroughs*, urban areas with royal charters giving them the right to appoint their own justices, to hold their own courts, to hold markets, and to have representation alongside the counties in parliament.

This tripartite system was extended after the Industrial Revolution to include three new types of unit. *Turnpike trusts* were established by Act of Parliament to raise money by tolls for the maintenance and improvement of roads, thereby transferring the costs to the users from those who happened to live on a certain route. *The Poor Law Unions* also took a responsibility from the parishes, for oversight of the relief of the poor in groups of parishes. Finally, *Improvement Commissions* were established to raise taxes and provide facilities (lighting, streets, etc.) in the new industrial towns which lacked borough status.

The first major reform of this system occurred in the 1830s when Poor Law Unions were established to cover the whole country—they were non-obligatory before—and fixed rules were established for their operations. Boroughs were reformed too, in terms of their financial powers, but their governments were given much greater flexibility in how they operated. Later legislation expanded their functions with regard to the oversight of public health, and in the 1870s a system of separate Rural and Urban Sanitary Districts for the whole country was established.

The system which was used for the first three-quarters of the twentieth century was established by three acts passed between 1888 and 1899. Its main features in England and Wales (Scotland was treated similarly) were:

(1) 62 counties, whose main functions related to roads and the administration of police and justice.

(2) 61 independent county boroughs, with all the functions of a county. With few exceptions, these were the urban places with more than 50 000 inhabitants to which a further 23 were added by 1922 and three more thereafter.

(3) 28 metropolitan boroughs within the jurisdiction of the London County Council, which were responsible for local public health, libraries, housing, and recreation.

(4) The urban and rural districts within the counties. There were two types of urban area: the urban districts, of which there were 785 in 1927 (Freeman, 1968) and the municipal boroughs, the larger towns without C.B. status (255 in 1927), which had wider powers devolved to them from the counties. In addition, there were 650 rural districts, reduced in 1929 to 477 (U.D.s were reduced to 573 at the same time).

Numerous extra functions were handed over to these local governments during the twentieth century, perhaps the most important being the public education system which was formerly operated by *ad hoc* boards. Some functions were removed—that of the former Poor Law Unions was centralized into the welfare state in the 1930s and hospitals were taken over by the National Health Service in 1948—but in 1968 Richards enumerated 121 different functions, powers, and duties of the various types of local authority.

The inefficiency of this system was widely recognized, and several abortive attempts were made to reform it. In general, however, the only changes made were piecemeal patching-up, although the 1958 Local Government

Commission did recognize the existence of urban regions known as conurbations, which were defined prior to the 1961 census. It was the number of separate authorities and the range of their sizes that caused most concern, however, with regard to efficient operation: the largest county had 2·4 million residents and the smallest 30 000; the largest county borough had 1 million and the smallest 33 000. Change was not instituted until the 1960s and 1970s, however, so most of the analyses reported here relate to the pre-1974 system.

The British local government system today

The main criticisms of the system just described were concerned with the administrative division of town and country, which failed to recognize their economic and social interdependence; the separation of powers between county councils and their county borough enclaves, which made many functions difficult to carry out; the small size of most authorities relative to estimates of the size for efficient units; and the need for many services to be provided by central government because of these deficiencies. The timing, extent, and nature of reform were political issues which are analysed in Chapter 7. The outcome for England (again parallel systems were introduced in Scotland and Wales) was:

(1) Six metropolitan counties, divided into a small number of metropolitan districts. The latter provide local services—refuse collection, sewerage disposal, education, personal social services, development planning; the former are responsible for strategic planning, for highways and transport services, and for fire, police, and ambulance services.
(2) Thirty-nine counties, divided into 296 district councils: the latter are solely responsible for only one major service—housing.
(3) A Greater London Council responsible for strategic planning and metropolitan roads, divided into 32 metropolitan boroughs with responsibility for development planning, housing, and health and welfare services. In the area of the former London County Council, education was handed to an *ad hoc* Inner London Education Authority; in the outer suburbs it was to be a borough function.

The American local government system

The general structure of the nineteenth-century British local government system was imposed in most of the dominions and colonies of the Empire, including the U.S.A., so most of the countries considered here are characterized by similar features; rural and urban areas generally have separate governments, for example. There are variations, many of them reflecting the lower population densities in many parts of the 'new world' but, as detailed here, the American system has many similarities with the British except, of course, for the much greater independence of the states.

In the American domestic economy, the state governments are more important spenders than the federal government. Excluding defence, foreign relations, the space programme, and repayment of the national debt (much of it related to earlier defence expenditure) the states spend $1.63 for every federal $1.00 spent on domestic programmes. One-third of this non-federal expenditure is on education, and states are also responsible for highways, justice, public welfare, police, health, and recreational facilities, albeit often with considerable federal financial aid. Thus, as Dye (1969, pp. 3–4) expresses it, 'Despite the glamour of national politics, states and communities carry on the greatest volume of public business, settle the greatest number of political conflicts, make the majority of public decisions, and direct the bulk of public programs.' The first states were separate colonies (Simmons, 1976) with certain proprietary rights, and the later additions follow that mould, the autonomy of states in many areas being written into the federal constitution. Each state has its own constitution, subordinate to the federal, and a similar tripartite system of government of executive, legislature, and judiciary. (Nebraska deviates slightly with a unicameral legislature only.) These constitutions are generally strong with regard to financial matters. In most cases, the powers of governments to tax, and also to borrow money, are very limited, reflecting the anti-government, pro-*laissez-faire* powerful interest groups that were active around the turn of the century (Penniman, 1971; Sharkansky, 1969).

The independence of the states is written into Amendment X of the federal constitution, which constrains the Washington government by stating (Vile, 1976, p. 293), 'The powers not delegated to the United States by the Constitution, nor prohibited by it to the States, are reserved to the States respectively, or to the people.' Thus the federal government cannot legislate on housing, health, safety, welfare, and morals. But it can raise either taxes or loans and spend money on those areas by offering grants to the states, as Dye (1969, p. 45) explains.

Congress cannot outlaw billboards on highways, because billboard regulation is not among the enumerated powers of Congress in the U.S. Constitution. But the federal government, through its power to tax and spend, can provide financial assistance to the states to build highways and then pass a law threatening to withdraw financial aid, if the states do not outlaw billboards themselves.

Using this power, the federal government now provides more than 15 per cent of all moneys spent by state and local governments.

Local governments are subsidiary to state governments and their forms and functions, responsibilities and limitations are laid down in the state constitutions. The two original types, from which others have developed, reflect differences between the original colonies. In New England, closely settled areas with nucleated settlements were governed by direct democracy— a town meeting—with powers similar to those of the English Poor Law

Unions. In the dispersed rural economy of the South, on the other hand, there was a system of counties, with each divided into subsidiary parishes (Blair, 1964). Counties were later introduced to New England, as a superior form above the level of the township.

The county and township were adopted generally, and formed the matrix for the survey and layout of the newly settled lands west of the Appalachians. With the growth of towns, a third category was introduced—the municipality—and then a fourth, the special district, was conceived to provide for *ad hoc*, single-purpose territorial authorities. Some states vary slightly from this fourfold typology (Rhode Island has no counties, for example, and only 21 states have township government). The general pattern is a common one, however, and provides one government unit for approximately every 2700 people (Table 3.1); there is one elected official for approximately every 400 residents.

Table 3.1
Local government units in the U.S.A., 1942–1972

	County	Township	Municipality	Type of unit Special district School	Other
1942	3050	18 919	16 220	108 579	8299
1952	3052	17 202	16 807	67 355	12 340
1957	3050	17 198	17 215	50 454	14 424
1962	3043	17 142	18 000	34 678	18 322
1967	3049	17 165	18 048	21 782	21 264
1972	3044	16 991	18 517	15 781	23 885

Source: relevant issues of the *Census of Governments*.

Counties form the basic units. Their functions vary according to their population density (Blair, 1964). The *rural counties*, usually lacking nucleated settlement of any size, provide the legal minimum in government services, and county government is very much an administrative arm of the state, involved in maintenance of law and order and of roads, the supervision of public health, and the organization of public welfare. The more densely peopled *semi-rural counties* may have services additional to the minimum, such as libraries, whereas in the *semi-urban counties*, usually integuments of metropolitan areas, services such as street lighting, sewerage disposal, and garbage collection are required and there is need for greater control over the physical and built environments. These areas will probably be characterized by active political conflicts, as will the *urban counties*, which often need facilities such as airports.

Municipalities (cities, towns, boroughs, villages) are areas incorporated by the state governments for some form of local administration: incorporation usually involves a petition from local residents and then a poll after which, if 25 per cent of residents vote and a majority are in favour, the urban government is created. The municipal functions are laid out in the relevant charter, which may be peculiar to the place or may refer to all municipalities in the state within a certain population range. Most, particularly the largest, are general-purpose governments, supplementing, replacing, sometimes duplicating the functions of their encompassing counties.

Townships are small rural settlements, usually with less than 2500 residents and few administrative functions. They are not incorporated, so are not politically or financially independent of the counties. Most of their functions involve local administration for the county government. In Michigan, for example, they provide cemeteries, street lights, volunteer fire departments, and water supplies; in Illinois their responsibilities cover property assessment for taxation purposes, the maintenance of roads, and the support of indigents.

Finally there are the *special districts*, the most numerous units of local government. Until recently, as Table 3.1 shows, more than half of these have been *school districts, ad hoc* authorities with a great degree of independence over all educational matters. (School districts are entirely independent in 23 states; semi-independent in 16; and partially independent in 7: only five states have no school districts but rather a centralized educational system. Nebraska alone had 3264 school districts in 1960.) The districts are run by elected school boards, with powers over syllabus, teacher salaries and numbers, etc., and administered by supervisors. *Non-school special districts* similarly have elected boards. They cover a very wide range of functions. In 1967, for example, Michigan had only 110 such districts, but Illinois had 2313, including 704 Fire Protection Districts and 811 Drainage Districts, plus unique units such as the Carbondale Railroad Relocation Authority: in Cook County alone, in addition to the City of Chicago there were 196 special districts in 1972, 93 of them supervising parks and 72 providing fire services (Stetzer, 1975).

Special districts reflect the ultimate in local, independent control of the provision of services, illustrating the ethos of privatism described by Berry (1976, p. 27) as 'a preference for governmental fragmentation and for interest-group politics under presumed conditions of democratic pluralism'. They have become so numerous, according to Stetzer (1975, pp. 26–36), because of a number of interacting factors: (1) the constitutional limitations on taxing and spending by local governments, which make a new unit preferable to expanding the functions of an existing one; (2) the inability of local governments to levy differential taxes in areas of high demand for certain services, again operating against the notion of large, general-purpose units; (3) the lack of spatial conformity in the demands for various services; (4) the desire for business-like management through user charges; (5) general public acceptance of privatism and user charges rather than redistributive taxation;

(6) the ease of getting federal aid for certain functions—e.g. airports and natural resource conservation; (7) the influence of special interest groups with their desire for independence; and (8) remnants of the past, as with volunteer fire departments.

As a result of the liberal rules operating in most states for the incorporation of special districts, many of which are virtually invisible and are very difficult to research, there is an amazingly complex pattern of governments, especially in and around the metropolitan areas. Thus Wood (1961, p. 1) described New York as 'A vigorous metropolitan area, the economic capital of the nation [which] governs itself by 1467 different political entities (at latest count), each having its own power to raise and spend the public treasure, and each operating in a jurisdiction determined more by chance than design'. To many commentators, this system of a multiplicity of special districts is an effective way of both minimizing political conflict and providing services efficiently within the context of local demands (Stetzer, 1975, pp. 156–7). Their efficiency is very variable, however, as pointed out in the rest of this chapter, which highlights some major themes in the geography of local government that are relevant to later chapters.

Separate and independent

That local governments are not only separate territorial authorities but also in some respects are independent from their superior parent bodies is important, since it allows resident interest groups to use the system to advance their particular causes. These various groups—occupational and life-style, ethnic and cultural, etc.—are spatially separated one from another, if not entirely segregated, at a variety of scales. Within the United States, for example, settlers from different parts of Europe are concentrated in different regions (Sharkansky, 1970a), and the Mormon religious group moved to Utah to establish its own territory. Within most cities, income and occupational, age and ethnic groups are all markedly segregated, by a combination of choice and constraint. During the last century or so, the availability of rapid transport, especially to the affluent, has encouraged such segregation. The well-to-do have moved from the congested inner cities to their semi-rural Utopias of suburbia, where they have incorporated municipalities. The poor, the elderly, and the low economic status groups have been denied access to such areas until recently (Guterbock, 1976), and although this has changed somewhat, blacks, for example, are still very much under-represented in American suburbia (Berry et al., 1976). In the United Kingdom, incorporation laws have been much less liberal. Nevertheless, separate urban districts were established in the suburbs of most large cities, many of them around pre-existing small country towns.

The separate powers of local governments allow their residents to obtain services consonant with their own value systems, and, especially for the smaller districts, remove the need to provide services for other groups living elsewhere beyond the boundaries. The American school district system illustrates this very well. Racial integration of schools has long been anathema to very many whites, who perceive great dangers in having their children educated alongside blacks. Suburban residence, in a small municipality and a small school district—the two may relate to the same area—offers a way of avoiding the sort of integration being imposed by the courts in the larger cities with large populations of blacks (Zoloth, 1976).

Zoning as a territorial power

A major benefit of independent government status in the United States—and in Britain to a lesser extent—is that it gives the residents the power to control land use patterns in the area through zoning procedures. In this way, the local governments act as articulators of local democracy, but not necessarily as efficient providers of services. Zoning in the United States is explicit in the way it can be used to define not only the allowable use in an area, but also the quality of the user, by setting prescribed densities, building standards, etc. Thus suburban middle-class municipal governments have zoned to exclude relatively cheap, lower-status developments through setting minimum densities; 64 per cent of suburban Philadelphia, for example, is zoned for occupation at not less than one acre per dwelling. Elsewhere, children may be zoned out (hysterectomy zoning) by, for example, specifying the maximum number of rooms allowed in individual apartments (Muller, 1976).

This practice of exclusionary zoning, largely aimed at keeping blacks and poor families out of 'desirable' suburbia, has been challenged in recent years in two ways. First, action groups have tried to get more liberal zoning laws passed by the municipalities, usually with little success (Danielson, 1976). If they do win, the rich usually retreat into new fastnesses, especially to escape the integration of schools. Racial composition of local schools is considered by many Americans as an index of neighbourhood quality (Clotfelter, 1975a), so that in Atlanta, for example, the prices of residential property rose most rapidly during the 1970s in those areas least affected by school integration (Clotfelter, 1975b). Attempted desegregation in one area, it seems, merely leads to segregation in another.

The other method of fighting exclusionary zoning involves use of the courts and the Fourteenth Amendment, which states (Vile, 1977, p. 294): 'No State shall make or enforce any law which shall abridge the privileges or immunities of citizens of the United States.' Thus in a case in New Jersey, for example, it was held that exclusionary zoning is in the interest of special groups only and not the general interests of all citizens of a metropolitan area, an argument upheld by the Supreme Court in the 1975 decision on *Southern Burlington County NAACP* v. *Township of Mt. Laurel.* Not all decisions have followed the same line, however, and a recent one regarding Petaluma (in the

San Francisco area) allowed zoning by the local municipality to restrict development there despite the general, area-wide pressure for more building land (Muller, 1976). Indeed, the issue of exclusionary zoning remains open, but if it is eventually ruled against it may be, as Babcock (1973, p. 319) points out in discussing a Pennsylvania decision that a municipality 'could not totally exclude apartments', that 'Philadelphia suburbs with ordinances that forbid apartments will have to zone the town dump for apartments'.

The Courts have also been used to contest the use of special district boundaries to avoid the integration of schools in suburban areas. In many cities in recent years, court orders have led to the institution of busing to integrate the schools within a single district, but during the period 1974–6 a series of cases was heard which resulted in a court decision that the eleven school districts in New Castle County, Delaware must be integrated, with at least 10–35 per cent minority group pupils in each high school by 1977 (Raffel, 1977). This is likely to involve the busing of more than 15 000 pupils in the county (which covers the Wilmington metropolitan area) and, if followed by further decisions, could lead to an end to the use of school districts to maintain middle-class white 'racial separateness'. Thus use of the Courts by political actors in the U.S.A. is increasingly becoming a way of achieving social goals by circumventing the local government system described in this and the previous chapter.

Whatever the final outcome of the current legal struggles, the independent status of municipalities and other local governments has had a major impact on the morphology of American society, particularly on the edges of metropolitan areas. Although this independence has been exploited by the high-income groups, others have occasionally used it. An interesting example is the City of Vernon on the eastern fringe of metropolitan Los Angeles, which used its powers to zone, licence, and tax to develop as a sports and entertainment centre serving adjacent suburbs during the first decade of this century. Thus (Nelson, 1952, p. 188),

When the bars in Los Angeles closed at 10 p.m., Vernon's saloons opened until dawn. When Los Angeles limited drinks to light wines and beer, the self-styled 'longest bar in the world' was built in Vernon. When prize fighting was illegal in many cities, Vernon was holding championship bouts in a coliseum seating 11 000 persons. When Sunday baseball was 'blue-lawed' out of Los Angeles, the Vernon Tigers were playing Sunday morning in their home park.

These advantages were temporary, as more liberal laws were passed elsewhere. Vernon then developed as an industrial city, and by the 1950s nearly 75 per cent of its land area was used for industries employing about 60 000 people. Vernon's population was then only 417 residents. Extra industrial land has been annexed (in 1926 an annexation of 300 acres was unanimously voted for by the two residents) and meanwhile the number of residents has declined. By zoning for industry only the city does not have to provide libraries, parks, sidewalks, etc. for the resident population, thereby allowing the industrialists to extract more of the surplus labour value from their workers than is the case in 'mixed' areas: in 1949 Vernon's tax rate on property was the lowest in California at $0.10 per $100 value. A similar manipulation of the zoning laws was operated nearby in the 1950s, when three cities of Dairy Valley, Dairyland, and Cypress were incorporated (Fielding, 1962). In each the land was entirely zoned for dairy farming, protecting the farmers from 'invasion' of their land by subdividers, until they were ready to yield.

Government finance and fiscal effort

Many local governments raise their revenues as rates/taxes on the value of properties within their jurisdictions, and so although, as indicated later, other sources are now provided, the various independent units have different resources available from which to finance the provision of services. This means that, in effect, the income structure of a local government area is crucial as an influence on its ability to spend.

Table 3.2

The fiscal resources of two hypothetical local governments

		Values		
	<£10 000	£10 000– 15 000	£15 000– 20 000	£20 000– 25 000
I Property Values				
Mean Value in Group	£7500	£12 500	£17 500	£22 500
Mean Annual Income of Occupants	£1000	£2000	£3500	£6000
Properties in those Groups in				
A	200	200	100	0
B	50	50	100	300
Total Value of Properties in				
A	£1 500 000	£2 500 000	£1 750 000	0
B	£ 375 000	£ 625 000	£1 750 000	£6 750 000
II Property Taxes to pay for Education				
Total Cost per Unit in				
A	£260·87	£434·78	£608·69	—
B	£157·89	£263·16	£368·42	£473·68
Cost as a Percentage of Income in				
A	26·1	21·7	17·4	—
B	15·8	13·2	10·5	2·1

Such differences are illustrated in Table 3.2. Two districts, A and B, are shown as having different distributions of property values. Properties are classified into four groups according to their values and the incomes of their owners; as indicated, B is a high-value area and A is characterized by low-value homes. Assume that it costs £1000 annually to finance a child's education, and that each area has a school population of 200. The total cost is thus £200 000 annually in each area; in A, this works out as £1 for every £28·75 of property values, whereas in B it is £1 for every £47·50. The costs per property, and as percentages of owners' incomes, are thus as indicated in panel II of Table 3.2. From them, the following conclusions can be drawn: (1) in both communities the relatively poor pay relatively more, suggesting that property taxes are regressive rather than progressive; (2) to provide the same sum for education (which may or may not be the same as the same standard of education) costs relatively more in poor communities; (3) in richer communities the cost to the rich is less than it is to people with the same incomes in poor communities, since in the former case they do not have to 'subsidize' their poorer co-residents; and (4) because of the high relative costs, low-income communities are likely to be able to afford only inferior educational facilities to those in high-income areas, with probable consequences for spatial variations in the quality of education.

The figures used in Table 3.2 are hypothetical but they are not entirely divorced from reality. Thus within American states the variations between school districts in the average value of property per pupil are as high as 183 times greater in one district than another (in Kansas) with an average over the 49 states which use property taxes to raise school finance (the exception is Hawaii) of 17·3 (Bergman, 1976, p. 71). The result of such differentials is that poorer communities have to make greater demands on residents' incomes (these are known as greater fiscal efforts) to provide basic services. One attempt to measure such differences has been provided by Akin and Auten (1976) for the state of New York. Their data show Fiscal Capacity ($ *per capita* as a function of property values and incomes), Fiscal Needs, Aid Received from the Federal Government, and Fiscal Residual, defined as Needs less (Capacity + Aid). A positive residual indicates that all of the Fiscal Capacity is not being drawn on—a low Fiscal Effort is being made—and the summary statistics in Table 3.3 indicate that it is the suburban areas which are in this favoured position.

Table 3.3
The average fiscal situation of New York school districts ($)

Community	Fiscal capacity	Aid	Fiscal needs	Fiscal residual
New York	309	273	711	− 124
Five Large Cities	268	142	414	− 4
Independent Cities	213	212	454	− 29
Rural	244	268	505	+ 7
New York Suburbs	392	183	455	+ 120
Five Large City Suburbs	278	189	421	+ 46

Source: Akin and Auten (1976, pp. 461–3).

That these differences between school districts in their ability to finance education for all at the same standard breaks the anti-discriminatory Fourteenth Amendment to the Constitution has been raised recently in the American Courts. On the basis of data such as those in Table 3.4 (compare with Table 3.2), the Texas court ruled in 1971 that discrimination had been proved in the case of *Rodriguez* v. *San Antonio Independent School District*, thereby destroying much of the rationale for local as against state-wide, or even nation-wide, provision of education. The Supreme Court overturned the Texan decision on appeal in 1973, however, ruling that the disparities in Table 3.4 did not violate the equal protection clause (Dye, 1975, p. 159).

Table 3.4

Fiscal differentials between Texan school districts

Market value of taxable property per pupil in district	Tax rate per $100	Tax yield per pupil	Number of districts
$100 000 <	$0.31	$585	10
$100 000–50 000	$0.38	$262	26
$50 000–30 000	$0.55	$213	30
$30 000–10 000	$0.72	$162	40
$10 000 >	$0.70	$ 60	4

Source: Lineberry and Sharkansky (1974, p. 233).

Central city versus suburb

Within a metropolitan area, differences between local government units are largely those between the central city and the suburbs, and these are the usual focus in studies of differentials, although variations at other scales may well be important too. In the mid-1960s, for example, property in New York state was valued at a total of $3200 per resident and that in California at $2748, whereas it was only $1250 in Alabama and $900 in Mississippi. Both costs and needs may vary from place to place, but usually needs are greatest where resources (incomes) are poorest so that, for example, state tax burdens are highest in the United States in such relatively low-income states as North and South Dakota, Montana, Kansas, and Louisiana (Dye, 1969, p. 455), and in England and Wales the poorest counties in terms of rateable value *per capita* (Durham, Cumbria, West Glamorgan, and Mid Glamorgan) include some of those with the most pressing needs.

Focusing on the central-city/suburban differences, it is generally assumed that the latter areas contain the higher status, richer populations with high fiscal capacity but relatively few needs for welfare expenditure by local government. Analyses of 1960 and 1970 American Census data (Schnore, 1965, 1972; Schnore, Andre, and Sharp, 1976) show that this is not always so. In general, the older the metropolitan area, the more likely it is that the well-to-do have fled the congested city centre and colonized the suburbs, so that to a considerable extent suburbs in western states are not as exclusively for the rich as are those in the north-east. In the United Kingdom, all metropoli are 'old' and, despite central city gentrification and the restraints on urban sprawl provided by planning policy (Hall *et al.*, 1973), the suburbs are where the rich are to be found.

Table 3.5
Fiscal capacity and effort in Greater Manchester, 1973–1974

| District | Value of property per domestic ratepayer (£) | | Rate poundage | Average rate bill (£) |
	Domestic	Non-domestic		
Manchester	59·65	107·22	1·020	60·84
Stockport	61·79	57·68	0·855	52·83
Stretford	63·41	135·20	0·895	56·75
Urmston	74·97	132·23	0·798	59·83
Sale	81·72	30·50	0·900	73·54
Altrincham	74·02	62·14	0·950	60·24
Hale	115·37	23·37	0·995	114·79
Wilmslow	96·49	48·47	0·905	87·32
Alderley Edge	109·33	36·50	0·960	104·96
Cheadle and Gatley	96·22	36·90	0·875	84·19
Hazel Grove	110·23	44·60	0·870	95·90
Marple	81·59	22·03	0·895	73·02
Bowdon	118·79	28·24	0·925	109·88

Source: Department of Environment: Rates and Rateable Values in England and Wales, 1973–4.

City–suburban differences in the United Kingdom are illustrated in Table 3.5 with data for the southern part of the Manchester conurbation, prior to the 1974 local government reform. Four pieces of information are provided for each area: the value of domestic property per domestic ratepayer; the value of non-domestic property per domestic ratepayer; the rate poundage in 1973–4; and the average rate bill per domestic ratepayer in that year. Three types of area are shown: the central city—Manchester; industrial suburbs—Stockport, Stretford, and Urmston; and high-status residential suburbs. The first two clearly have much more valuable non-domestic property to 'subsidize' the domestic ratepayer, but their domestic properties are in general much less valuable than are those in the third type. Because of the relative concentration of needs there, the central city has the greatest rate poundage (£1·02 for every £1 of property value; British values are based on an assumed rental, not the market price, as in the U.S.A.). Rate bills for householders are on average lower in Manchester and the industrial suburbs, because of the 'subsidizing' from non-domestic properties. In no suburban area is the rate bill twice that of Manchester, however, and so, assuming that average incomes in the suburbs are at least twice those of the central city, suburban fiscal effort is relatively low.

The extent of the central-city/suburban differences has been illustrated in the United States recently by the financial plight of the City of New York which has a large concentration of population in need but the resources of the wealthy suburbanites are denied to it. Thus within a metropolitan area separate and independent can mean hardship in one area and plenty in another, with income inequalities exaggerated by the local government system. This was demonstrated by Nathan and Adams (1976) who compiled a separate hardship index for the central city and the suburban ring for each of 55 metropolitan areas. (Hardship was a composite of unemployment, dependency—population under 18 and over 65—income, education, crowding, and family poverty.) A central-city hardship ratio was then devised, which had a value of 100 if city and suburb had the same index, and the greater the value above 100, the greater the concentration of social and economic problems in the central city. The largest ratio was 422, for Newark: 14 of the 55 metropoli had ratios exceeding 200 and only ten less than 100 (i.e. suburbs worse than central cities). In general, the better the city, the less the difference between it and its suburbs, so that there is a concentration of problems in certain metropolitan areas, in which the suburbs are much more 'gilded ghettos'.

Externalities, free riders, and spillovers

If they cannot get them free, most people want goods and services as cheaply as possible, even if this involves them being somewhat parasitic on others. In technical terms, such benefiting from the actions of others is known as a positive externality; the reverse is a negative externality, when somebody else benefits at your cost. Externalities have clear spatial expressions (Cox, 1973). A shopkeeper may get more trade without any effort because of a successful advertising campaign by his neighbour; a householder may suffer a negative externality, perhaps reducing the value of his property, if a dogs' home is opened next door.

Spatial externalities come about because of the overlapping of continuous and discontinuous distributions and the permeability of the latter's boundaries. Pollution diminishes at a given rate with distance from its source, for example, but homes are discontinuous territories over whose boundaries the pollution flows. Thus, according to Carey and Greenberg (1974; see also Mumphrey and Wolpert, 1973), one gets a geography of hypocritical decision-making: territorial communities will overlook those costs—ecological or otherwise—which they impose on others while trying to benefit from expenditures elsewhere. Their best strategy is to maximize the negative externalities of their own actions (make others pay the costs) as well as to maximize also on the positive externalities of the actions of others.

Political fragmentation, especially in densely peopled metropolitan areas, encourages externality effects. Suburban residents, for example, may use a park in a local city, provided free for the use of its residents out of its revenues. Because entry to the park is not policed the suburbanites use freely something others are paying for. They are free riders. Measurement of the extent of this free-rider problem is extremely difficult. Most conclude, or assume, with Hawley (1951, p. 107) that the suburbanites are the free riders, and that central city rate- and taxpayers are 'carrying the financial burden of an elaborate and costly service installation, i.e. the central city, which is used daily by a non-contributing population in some instances more than twice the size of the contributing population'. In particular, this suggests that suburban commuters to central cities are free riders, but others counter by saying that spending by commuters in the city increases prosperity there directly (in the business establishments patronized) and indirectly (in higher property values and so more city resources), thereby more than compensating for the costs imposed on city governments.

Table 3.6
Suburban–central city exploitation: Detroit

Municipality	Per Capita property value ($)	Median family income ($)	Per Capita benefits from Detroit ($)	Per Capita payments to Detroit ($)	Per Capita benefits– payments ($)
Allen Park	2943	9420	9.86	3.34	6.52
Birmingham	4077	12850	18.22	5.64	12.58
Dearborn	6438	8500	9.25	2.53	6.72
Grosse Pointe Park	4103	13250	16.53	9.75	6.78
Highland Park	4525	5620	3.96	2.23	1.73
Roseville	2378	7870	13.09	3.32	9.77

Source: Neenan (1973, various tables).

To evaluate these conflicting claims, Neenan (1973) studied in detail the use made of Detroit by residents of six suburban municipalities (Table 3.6). Three sections of the economy were studied: (1) the use of Detroit-provided facilities (Library, Art Museum, Zoo, etc.) by suburban residents as a percentage of all users—they were then allocated the same percentage of the costs, on a user-pays basis; (2) the expenditures on public welfare made by Detroit city, the costs of which are avoided by suburban residents; and (3) facilities provided by Detroit which suburbanites use (hospitals, universities, and freeways).

Account was also taken of the Michigan taxes (sales and motor vehicle licences/gasoline) paid by suburban residents which are redistributed to local governments according to population, producing a net inflow to Detroit.

The accounts do not balance (Table 3.6); in every case the suburban residents on average receive more benefits from Detroit than they make contributions to the costs of running Detroit; in Neenan's terms, the suburbs are exploiting the central city. The sums may seem small; they total $2 037 029, less than $8.50 per Detroit resident per annum and below one per cent of that city's annual budget. But the suburbs studied account for only 10·6 per cent of the total suburban population; if they are a representative sample of the whole, then the total exploitation comes to about 6·5 per cent of Detroit's budget, or more than $80 per Detroit resident per annum (Neenan, 1972).

A more detailed study involving the exploitation thesis has been reported for Washington, D.C. (Greene, Neenan, and Scott, 1974), with three major conclusions. First, the suburban populations of Maryland and Virginia free ride on the Washington taxpayer to the extent of $120 per person each year. Secondly, there is no exploitation by commuters, who cost Washington $15.7 m. per annum but who contribute $15.5 m. in sales taxes and parking fines plus an unknown sum to property valuations. Finally, because of the peculiar position of the District of Columbia with regard to federal aid which exceeds the volume of exploitation, there is 'a net fiscal advantage from living in the District of Columbia for every income class except the very highest' (Greene, Neenan, and Scott, 1974, p. 180).

Not all of the evidence favours the suburban free-rider thesis, however. In part this reflects differences between studies in what they analyse, and it also indicates the difficulty of evaluating many of those costs and benefits, assuming that all can be expressed in monetary terms. An example of a different type of analysis to Neenan's is given by work on Clayton School District in Missouri (Hirsch, 1970); Clayton is a suburb of St. Louis. In this, the costs include the alternative uses to which money could be put if not invested in education—i.e. consumption foregone; benefits include the long-term, extra income which students receive as a consequence of their educational attainments; and the balance sheet takes account of migrations—the extent to which Clayton benefits from immigrants the costs of whose education were met elsewhere, and loses because those whose education it pays for then leave. In this way, spillovers were subdivided into spillins (benefits or positive externalities) and spillouts (costs or negative externalities).

The balance sheet was drawn up between Clayton and five other areas (Table 3.7), and the results show that the spillouts exceeded the spillins. Clayton School District's taxpayers were subsidizing the rest of the United States in 1959–60, so that (Hirsch, 1970, p. 220) 'because of spillovers the $933,000 net benefit Clayton would have realized from its own education in a closed, migrationless economy was turned into a net cost of $1.5m.'. Clayton is a high-income area, however, as Table 3.7 shows. If income is held constant, then Clayton is seen to subsidize the rest of Missouri, except St. Louis County.

Table 3.7
Interjurisdictional spillovers: Clayton school district

				Area			
	Clayton S.D.	Rest of St. Louis County	City of St. Louis	Rest of S.M.S.A.	Rest of Missouri	Rest of U.S.A.	Total
By Location of Benefits from Clayton's Education: Costs to Clayton							
Benefits ($m.)	2·979	0·024	0·021	0·007	0·044	0·738	3·813
Costs ($m.)	1·647	0·568	0·084	0·057	0·115	0·409	2·880
Net Benefits ($m.)	1·332	−0·544	−0·063	−0·050	−0·071	0·329	0·933
By Location of Costs from other Places' Education: Benefits to Clayton							
Benefits ($m.)	2·979	0·038	0·029	0·018	0·086	1·353	4·503
Costs ($m.)	1·647	0·574	0·481	0·245	1·031	2·037	6·015
Net Benefits ($m.)	1·332	−0·536	−0·452	−0·227	−0·945	−0·684	−1·512
Net Spillover to Clayton							
Spillover ($m.)		0·038	−0·389	−0·177	−0·874	−1·013	−2·445
Median *Per Capita* Income							
1959 Income ($)	8391	5317	3289	3888	2912	3667	
Ratio of Income to Clayton Income		0·63	0·39	0·46	0·35	0·44	
Education Gains to Clayton as a Ratio of Losses (Spillins/Spillouts)		1·01	0·23	0·30	0·19	0·63	

Source: Hirsch (1970, pp. 269–72). Copyright © 1970 by McGraw-Hill, Inc., and used with their permission.

In his seminal paper on a 'pure theory of public expenditures' Tiebout (1956) suggested that people are aware of the sorts of differentials discussed here and locate their homes so as to maximize the benefits which they receive from their tax payments. One deduction from this is that, if location is a contest for externalities, then local governments will tend to underprovide services, since, according to Mills (1972, p. 234), their residents are not inclined to pay for services to be exploited by 'outsiders'. Adams (1965) tested this hypothesis and suggested that indeed 'balkanization' of local governments does produce inefficient services, but a later study by Isserman (1976) has contradicted the conclusion, showing no relationship between number of governments and level of source provision. As in so much of this type of work, evaluation of the externality hypotheses is extremely difficult and the exact nature of 'exploitation' very hard to determine.

The problem of finance

The two preceding themes of 'separate and independent' and 'externalities' indicate major differences between local governments in their resources to tackle the tasks, many obligatory, which they must undertake. The problem of local resources relative to needs is acute and has led to much debate on the best way to finance the efficient operation of local governments.

The major issue concerns the degree to which local governments should be forced to rely on the local resource base, within the centrally imposed constraints on money-raising, thereby producing the sort of differentials illustrated by the Texan school districts (Table 3.4). In general, it seems to be agreed that welfare policy requires some redistribution of resources from rich to poor areas, which implies greater central control over expenditure. This has been taken furthest in Great Britain. In the 1920s, about one-quarter of local government revenues came from the central Exchequer, mainly as grants to pay for the education system (Rhodes, 1976)—today about 60 per cent is centrally provided. Local governments want more, to relieve the burden on the ratepayers (and so make the governments themselves electorally popular) and in 1928 a system of weighted grants according to population was agreed. In 1948 a new system was devised, aimed at meeting differences in resources and needs and equalizing the resource base of all areas. Many problems were encountered, however, including the non-rating of agricultural land and the burden on domestic ratepayers in areas with little non-domestic land use (see Table 3.5).

A new system was introduced in 1966 by which the Exchequer makes grants to local authorities on three grounds—needs, resources, and domestic. The last of these was introduced as 'an ingenious device for giving relief from rates to householders, politically the most important group of ratepayers' (Rhodes, 1976, p. 152); in effect, domestic ratepayers now pay a slightly lower rate poundage than do neighbouring non-domestic ratepayers. The resources element is intended to bring all local governments to the same level (in 1975–6, an average rateable value of £176 per resident) and one-quarter of the current Rate Support Grant total is used in this way (the domestic element takes up 9 per cent of the total cost): this is a similar procedure to that used in federal countries such as Canada and Australia to equalize the fiscal capacity of states and provinces (Dawson, 1973).

Finally, the needs element reflects the fact that different populations make different demands on resources, and so sums are allocated according to population structures. The sums to be paid are based on regression estimates of spending on various services in earlier years, and Table 3.8 shows the resulting scale of payments in 1975–6. Clearly, British local governments spend much on the young and the old, so that areas with many in these categories receive more in their Rate Support Grant.

The Rate Support Grant (R.S.G.) system removes much freedom of action from local governments, since if they decide to spend more than directed the total extra cost must be met from local rates. Thus in 1975–6 the R.S.G. was set at 65·5 per cent of what the central government thought local governments should be spending, so that the grant was being used as part of national financial policy. In 1976–7, the R.S.G. order indicated that there would have to be increases in both council house rents and public transport fares. Separate and independent?

Table 3.8

The needs element in the British rate support grant, 1975–1976

Item	Amount received (£)
Per resident person	1·36
Per education unit above 205/1000 population (education units are pupils weighted by level of schooling)	132·03
Per acreage per head in excess of 1·5—per acre	2·18
Population decline 1970–5 (divided by 1000)—per unit	0·037
New buildings 1975–6—per building	363·20
Persons of pensionable age in excess of 20/1000—per unit	177·29
Persons living at more than 1½ persons per room, in excess of 10/1000—per unit	67·83
Persons in households lacking basic amenities, in excess of 10/1000—per unit	14·68
Lone parent families with dependent children in excess of 5/1000—per family unit	530·08

Local governments are much less constrained in the United States, in particular because of the constitutional restrictions on the activities of the federal government. Since the 1930s, however, increasing federal direction if not control over state and local spending has evolved with the grants-in-aid policies by which (Porter, 1976, p. 94) federal agencies set minimum levels of payment, write the eligibility standards, and provide some of the money for welfare programmes, whereas the local governments decide on the total payments to be made and rule on the eligibility of each applicant. According to Nathan (1976), this system fulfils five aims: (1) local government retains some power, so that centralized autocracy is avoided; (2) local needs are met by federal redistribution; (3) there is an equalization of fiscal capacity between areas, since grant formulae are progressive, giving more to states with relatively low-income populations; (4) pressure is taken off property and sales taxes, which are non-progressive, especially in the hardest-hit central cities (Riew, 1970); and (5) a greater proportion of the welfare programme is met from the progressive income tax collected by the federal government than was the case when there were no grants. (The first income tax was in fact levied by a state—Wisconsin, in 1911; the federal government followed in 1913 and now gets about 44 per cent of its revenue from that source: 16 states still have no local income tax.)

The growth of federal aid to local governments (including states) has been very rapid during this century. In 1902, the federal government raised 38·5 per cent of all government revenues, and in 1932 only 28·6 per cent; under wartime conditions, it was the destination for 80·3 per cent of all revenues in 1950, and today it raises about 59 per cent of the total. As a consequence, the state and local governments are much less independent financially. In 1902, only 1·6 per cent of their receipts were from the federal exchequer, but today central funds provide about 17 per cent of moneys for local spending.

There are now more than 200 federal grant-in-aid programmes, with the most expensive covering public welfare, education, and highway construction. The formulae used do not ensure any large redistribution effect which reduces the fiscal effort of the relatively low-income states, however, and to some local governments grants-in-aid are not the best means of obtaining extra revenue (Porter *et al.*, 1973).

In recent years there has been considerable discussion of more liberal federal aid programmes, with larger sums granted and fewer strings attached. This has become known as General Revenue Sharing, which was introduced in the State and Local Fiscal Assistance Act, 1972. Approximately $5 billion was to be disbursed annually—one-third of it to states and the rest to local governments—according to a formula comprising three variables— population, fiscal effort, and income level—which would give most to the poorest, most heavily taxed districts (Dye, 1975, p. 213). The initial (Heller- Pechman) proposals were that eventually 10 per cent of federal income tax revenue should be distributed in this way (Hirsch, 1970, p. 122), so that over the period 1972–7 some $30.2 billion should be allocated. Five restrictions were placed on use of this money (Lineberry and Sharkansky, 1974, p. 120): (1) it must be spent on priority areas; (2) there should be no discrimination by race, colour, origin, or sex; (3) it should not be spent in certain areas—e.g. education, public welfare—for which there are other federal programmes; (4) any workers employed with these funds must be paid the operative local wages; and (5) plans and accounts must be published. Although not a 'no strings' situation, therefore, general revenue sharing invites much more local political conflict over these resources than do the fixed grants-in-aid.

Political variations

Two themes developed in this and the preceding chapter are that: (1) much political activity—beliefs, values, voting, etc.—is class-based; and (2) that classes are spatially segregated, being concentrated into different adminis- trative areas, at a variety of scales. From these it is a relatively straightforward deduction that those elected to power in local governments will reflect this spatial variability in political beliefs, so that the values expressed by governments (in terms of the parties or interest groups which control them) are spatially variable too. The administrative map is thus also a political map.

The validity of this deduction can be identified in most situations. Smallwood (1965), for example, showed that in Greater London before the reorganization of 1964 there were two clear types of boroughs and urban districts according to the socio-economic status of their residents and the political affiliations of their governments. Of the 38 areas inhabited by relatively low-status populations, every one was administered in 1962 by the Labour Party whose main electoral appeal is to the working-class voter, whereas of the 45 higher-status areas 43 had an elected council dominated by Conservatives, Liberals, or Independents, all of whom make their main policy initiatives towards the capitalist and 'middle' classes. Many local councils were dominated by a single party. In the ten east London boroughs of the old London County Council area, Labour won 514 of the 534 seats, including every seat in five boroughs; opposing this eastern Labour hegemony, the Conservatives won at least 70 per cent of the seats in five of the west London metropolitan boroughs.

The larger the local government unit—in population rather than area—the less likely it is that political beliefs will be so concentrated on one party. Because of its great size, London is more likely to show such polarization than are smaller metropoli, but to some extent it disappeared after the 1964 reorganization which produced much larger boroughs; many of these amalgamated districts of different persuasions, producing more balanced councils. Camden Borough, for example, is an amalgam of the former independent boroughs of St. Pancras, Holborn, and Hampstead. In its first election, Labour won 27 seats to the Conservative 3 in the former St. Pancras, but lost 6–0 in Holborn and 17–7 in Hampstead, producing a council with a Labour : Conservative ratio of 34 : 26 (Wistrich, 1972).

Somewhat similar patterns are repeated throughout Britain. In general, the urban areas, particularly those dominated by manufacturing industries, elect Labour-majority councils whereas suburban and rural areas prefer the Conservative party. (Some rural counties—increasingly a smaller number—return non-partisan independents, whose general ethos is more in line with Conservative than with Labour policies.) Voter turn-out at British local government elections is generally low, however, and abstention is often used as a protest vote against the policies of the party in power at the national level. As a consequence, control of local government may change between parties, which could reflect changed voter preferences for certain local policies (as, for example, over council house rents in Sheffield: Hampton, 1970) but is more likely to represent dissatisfaction with national policies. Since the local government reform of the 1960s and 1970s, this has resulted in greater variability in the political party control of the larger units.

Political polarization between local government areas is also very marked in the United States, but although the Democrat party has, since the 1930s, been more aligned with the working-class urban areas and the Republican party with affluent suburbia and the rural areas, political loyalties are not as class-based as in the United Kingdom (Alford, 1963). The extent of other influences is best demonstrated at the state level, with the Democrat hegemony in the South. After the Civil War, the white population united in the Democrat party in the states of the former Confederacy to defeat attempts by their northern opponents to politicize the newly liberated blacks. As a consequence, the Democrats became the only party of the South; the main elections were intra-party—at the primaries—and in some states Democrats won every seat in both houses of the legislature (Key, 1949).

This major electoral pattern has been summarized by Ranney (1965, 1971) in a classification of states according to electoral competitiveness. For the period studied he used four variables: (1) the proportion of votes in the state gubernatorial elections won by the Democrats; (2) the proportion of seats in the state lower houses won by the Democrats; (3) the proportion of the seats in the state senates won by the Democrats; and (4) the proportion of the time period when Democrats held the governorship plus a majority of seats in both houses. The resulting index varied from 0·0 to 1·0; the former value indicates complete Republican hegemony and the latter absolute Democrat control. Four classes of states were then identified:

(1) One-Party Democrat: indices exceeding 0·90—no competition to Democrat rule;
(2) Modified One-Party Democrat: indices of 0·70–0·90—some competition but no real threat to Democrat rule;
(3) Competitive: indices between 0·30 and 0·70—the parties are balanced and one could well wrench power from the other at an election; and
(4) Modified One-Party Republican: indices of 0·10–0·30—some competition but no real threat to Republican rule.

There are no one-party Republican states. Figure 3.1A shows the clear Democrat control of the South and its borders, with the Republican strength in northern New England and the Midwest. Recently, as Fig. 3.1B suggests, the polarization has decreased somewhat, largely through Republican gains in the South (in part because of north-to-south migration, notably to Florida): the South is traditionally conservative and has used the Democrat party to express this, but with the current party realignment (Ladd and Hadley, 1976) southerners have been more prepared to vote for Republicans (such as Nixon) rather than liberal Democrats (such as McGovern). Complete change from the pattern in Fig. 3.1 is not yet suggested, however.

Since the New Deal coalition was forged by Roosevelt, the cities have traditionally voted Democrat in the U.S.A., and the suburbs Republican. This does not represent clear ideological differences between their populations, however, since the party label has been used as a means of gaining power rather than as an expression of policies. Urban politics in particular have been dominated for many decades by political machines which merely use the party title and involve (Dye, 1969, p. 256) 'a style of politics in which ideologies and issues are secondary and personal friendships, favors, jobs, and material rewards are primary'. Machine politics involve a business-like organization,

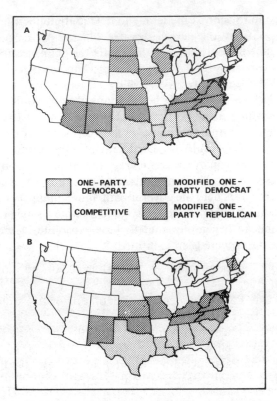

FIG. 3.1   Ranney's classification of state political complexions in the U.S.A.: A pre-1965; B pre-1970.

trading public services and political patronage for votes. Recipients of the patronage are often the poor and the immigrants 'who identified with their ethnic group, their families, their neighborhood, and their ward' (Greer and Greer, 1976, p. 210) and so with the party which dominated those social networks. Many machines had a charismatic leader, such as Mayor Daley of Chicago, of whom it was said (Dye, 1969, p. 260), 'Few others understand so well the labyrinths of formal and informal power, the complex structure of federal, state, and local government and public opinion.' The Democrat organization in Chicago and Cook County, indeed in the whole of Illinois, was very much dominated by this one man for two decades.

Reform and non-partisan politics in the U.S.A.

Self-interest of the voters—the petty patronage and jobs that they can get (Frost, 1961)—provided the votes for the machine bosses, but this self-interest did not extend to policy preferences. The voting which resulted was what became known as 'private regarding' and was considered by some to be socially divisive and not in the best interests of the public at large. Thus the alliance of machine bosses, the immigrants and the poor from whom they 'bought' votes, and the businessmen to whom they 'sold' government contracts, was countered by a middle-class 'reform' movement, dedicated to the development of 'public regarding' voting, to the ideals of local democracy in small units, and to government as an efficient provider of services in the general public interest.

The ethos of the reform movement was anti partisan politics and in favour of 'good' government for all. It had four main aims (Banfield and Wilson, 1963, pp. 140–1): (1) obtaining greater power for the electorate through wider use of referendum and the initiative (a petitioned-for referendum); (2) more information for voters and simpler voting procedures; (3) checking the takeover of politics by immigrant machines; and (4) segregating local government—which is a business for providing services—from state and national government, which is political in content. Patronage was to be replaced by a civil service; mayors were to serve longer terms as stronger executives; parties were to be eliminated; management of departments was to be by appointed businessmen not political hacks; and elections were to be at large, so as to remove socially divisive local representation.

Reform was an upper-middle-class movement and its successes were in the conservative, small suburban municipalities (in Canada as well: Massam, 1973; Mercer, 1974). Three alternative forms of municipal governments are now available as a result of the movement: (1) the traditional *mayor–council system* in which all officials are elected; (2) the *city commission* in which a small body of elected commissioners (one per major department) is responsible for administration; and (3) *council–manager* in which a small, elected council oversees the work of an appointed manager. (Counties, too, have been affected, with many now run by a council–manager equivalent: Blair, 1964.)

In general, the largest and the smallest cities have retained the mayor–council form of government (Kessel, 1962), the former because of the diversity of interests in their areas for which politicians and parties act as brokers and the latter (those with 10 000 inhabitants or less) because they lack the resources to employ a professional management (Dye, 1969). The other two types dominate in suburbia (Schnore, 1965), where most municipalities have homogeneous populations and single interests to which commissioners or managers can respond.

The non-partisan elections typical of 'reformed' municipalities (Lineberry and Fowler, 1968) do not necessarily mean a non-political environment, of course. Indeed, the whole ethos of reform is political, reflecting the view of the middle class that business-like local government best represents their interests. Elections are clearly fought by partisan groups on some occasions (Adrian, 1959), though this can also occur in 'non-reformed' situations outside America (Forrest, Marjoribanks, and Johnston, 1977). In general, however, the non-partisan election, and also the at-large contest, are ways of ensuring the dominance of the majority viewpoint in an area.

Conclusions

Local governments are, according to theorists, commentators, and those operating the system, primarily vehicles for providing services in line with local demands. These demands are articulated through local elections, and are met out of local resources (at least in part). Demands, resources, and political affiliations all vary between local government areas, as illustrated here, with potential consequences for the geography of social well-being. Such spatial outputs of this component of the political system are discussed in Chapter 6; attempts to change the system so as to change the outputs are the focus of Chapter 8.

4 Elections: Translating Votes into Seats

THE purpose of an election is to produce a Parliament or equivalent body of representatives, and the electoral law defines the mechanism whereby votes are translated into seats in the Parliament. The elections studied here are fought by parties, groups of like-minded individuals who contest seats on a predetermined policy; their aim is to win as many seats as possible in the Parliament. In the present discussion of how electoral systems work (Fig. 2.5), therefore, attention is very much on the parties rather than on the individual candidates.

Under most electoral laws, the translation of votes into seats is not directly proportional: there is usually some mis-match so that the percentage of seats allocated to a party is not the same as its percentage of the votes cast. Occasionally, as in Britain in 1951 and in February 1974, the party with most votes does not get most seats. Such an occurrence is relatively rare, but quite frequently the two percentages disagree considerably, as at the British October 1974 general election when the Liberal Party won 20 per cent of the votes but only 1·5 per cent of the seats. Such non-proportional representation is of interest here, not simply as a feature of the electoral geography of a territory but also because it is a function of certain aspects of electoral laws which can be manipulated by those in power. The present chapter outlines the basis for such manipulations.

Electoral bias

The mis-match between votes and seats—often termed the electoral bias of a system—comes about because of the use of constituencies. Detailed analysis of the characteristics of such bias has been presented by Rae (1971), who studied the results of all national general elections in twenty countries during the period 1945–65. His conclusions included the following, which are of importance to the arguments presented here.

(1) Parties with a large share of the votes tend to get an even larger share of the seats. Regressing a party's percentage of the seats (S) against its percentage of the votes (V) gave the equation

$$S = -2·38 + 1·13\ V.$$

From this, it can be calculated that there is a 'breaking point' where V is about 20; below that level, parties get less seats than votes, with the converse above 20 per cent.

(2) The largest party in terms of votes almost always receives an even larger

share of the seats. This is a development of the previous conclusion, and is based on the results in 106 of 117 of the elections studied (the exceptions were for Scandinavia, where a system designed to produce proportional representation is used, and the French 1951 election, at which the Communists won most votes but not most seats—see p. 187).

(3) Representation in parliament is frequently denied to small parties, which get less than 20 per cent of the votes and no seats.

(4) Most parliamentary majorities are manufactured, in that parties winning over half of the seats rarely also win more than half of the votes. Of the 117 elections studied, 43 resulted in a parliamentary majority for one party but in only 16 of these was that an 'earned parliamentary majority'; in 63 per cent of the elections, an absolute parliamentary majority was 'manufactured' by the electoral system.

Types of electoral system

Rae's results suggest that virtually all elections produce biased results. Some are more open to bias than others, however, depending on the nature of the system (Loosemore and Hanby, 1971). There is a great variety of electoral systems used to translate votes into seats, but they have three major distinguishing characteristics: (1) the number of votes for each elector; (2) the way in which these are cast and translated into seats; and (3) the number of representatives per constituency. Combinations of these produce the following types of system (for a more detailed discussion see Taylor and Johnston, 1979, Chapter 2; Lakeman, 1974; Birke, 1961).

The plurality system in single-member constituencies

This system, used in Great Britain, New Zealand, Canada, South Africa, and the United States for all national elections, is the simplest to operate. Each elector is presented with the list of candidates for the relevant constituency (increasingly, the party affiliation is indicated) and selects one: the votes are tallied and the candidate receiving most, irrespective of whether they form a majority of all those cast, is declared elected.

The plurality system in multi-member constituencies

This variant of the previous system operates in the same way: n candidates are to be elected so the n receiving most votes are the winners. The number of votes available to each elector may be the same as the number of seats to be filled. In some cases, however, electors are given fewer votes in order to reduce the possible bias. (If, in a five-member constituency, party A received 60 per cent of the support from the electors, then if each elector had 5 votes all five party A candidates would come at the top of the poll. The 40 per cent voting for other parties would gain no representation.) Thus, in Japan, each elector has one vote only irrespective of the number of seats to be filled.

In some elections the multi-member constituency is the whole territory, so that there are no representatives from separate areas. Such elections are often known as 'at large' contests. In some, the elector may have as many votes as there are places to be filled; in others he may get less.

The weighted plurality system

In this type, a single contest is fought across a number of constituencies, each of which has a different weight in the amalgamation of votes. The best example is the Electoral College used in the contests for the United States' presidency. The constituencies are the 50 States plus the District of Columbia, each of which is represented in the College by a number of Electors equivalent to its Congressional Representation (two Senators plus at least one of the 435 Representatives who are allocated to the states on a population basis). In each state, the presidential candidate winning most votes—again irrespective of whether they form a majority—receives all of the state's Electoral College votes, so that a narrow victory in a large state can bring considerable electoral rewards (as when Kennedy defeated Nixon in 1960 in Illinois by 8858 votes out of 4·75 m., thereby winning all 27 Illinois Electoral College votes). In the Electoral College, the winner must receive a majority of the votes, otherwise the election is transferred to the House of Representatives.

Preferential voting in single-member constituencies

Under the plurality system in single-member constituencies, the winning candidate (party) may receive only a minority of the votes. To avoid such minority victories, the Alternative Vote (AV) system was designed in Australia (Graham, 1962). Each elector, instead of indicating only his first choice for representative, rank orders all candidates. If no candidate receives a majority of first preferences, the second choices of the bottom candidates on the list are added to the first preferences. If a candidate then receives a majority he is elected; if not, the bottom-but-one candidate is eliminated and his second preferences are allocated: the procedure continues until one candidate receives a majority of the votes.

A variation of this, known as the double-ballot system, is currently employed in France. If no candidate wins a majority of votes in a constituency, a second ballot is held a week later. All those receiving less than 5 per cent of the available votes in the first contest must withdraw from the second; others may withdraw, perhaps forming an alliance with a remaining candidate. At the second ballot, the single-member plurality system operates.

Preferential voting in multi-member constituencies

This system, used in the Republic of Ireland since 1922, is based on liberal notions of giving voters as much choice as possible. Electors rank order all candidates, as in the AV system, and candidates must gain a certain number of votes (the electoral quota, equivalent to a majority in that the n elected members win the most votes) for election. To ensure that as many votes are used as possible (i.e. all electors' preferences are taken into account), if a candidate wins more votes than needed for victory, the extra are transferred (hence the system is known as the Single Transferable Vote or STV system) to his supporters' lower preferences. The procedure of finding the winners under STV is tedious, therefore, especially in large constituencies returning ten members (as to the Australian Senate) or more, but the system both allows wide voter choice and produces relatively little electoral bias.

List systems in multi-member constituencies
This system, which is used in many European countries, involves the elector casting a single vote for the party of his choice. Seats are then allocated to parties by constituencies, according to their percentages of the votes. Completely proportional representation is rare, because whereas a party's percentage of the votes can be any number between 0 and 100, only a few fixed percentages of the seats are available—with 5 seats, 0, 20, 40, 60, 80, and 100. In some countries, electors can indicate which of a party's candidates they prefer: in others, which candidates are elected from the list is determined by the party organization alone.

Electoral systems and electoral bias
Rae's analyses indicate that electoral bias is a feature of all systems of translating votes into seats. Some systems produce more bias than others, however, as he showed by comparing Plurality–Majority elections (PM—those held in Canada, France, Great Britain, New Zealand, and the United States) with those held using either list or preferential (STV) electoral laws (LP). Among his conclusions were the following:

(1) The bias towards the larger parties is greater under PM than under LP systems. Separate regressions of S on V show

for PM systems $S = -6\cdot3 + 1\cdot20\ V$

for LP systems $S = -0\cdot84 + 1\cdot07\ V$

so that in the former all parties with less than 32·5 per cent of the votes over the territory as a whole tend to get fewer seats than votes, whereas in LP systems such bias operates only against those parties with less than 12 per cent of the votes.

(2) The bias between percentage of seats and percentage of votes for the largest party is greater under PM systems. The average difference between the two percentages was 8·12 points for PM systems and 1·24 points for LP systems.

(3) PM systems deny any representation at all to more parties than do LP

systems. The average number of parties (excluding independents and 'nonsense' candidates) winning votes but no seats was: PM systems, 2·34; LP systems, 0·79.

(4) Parliaments elected by PM systems are more likely to have only two parties represented there. Of the 107 elections studied in this part of the analysis, 30 used PM systems and 23 produced only two parties with at least 5 per cent of the seats; under LP systems, such a result occurred in only 4 of the 77 cases. Under PM systems, therefore, minority parties rarely fare well unless, as in Canada, they are strong in certain places (see Taylor and Johnston, 1979, Chapter 7).

(5) The average number of parties needed to provide a parliamentary majority is less under PM (1·15) than under LP systems (1·96), suggesting that manufactured majorities are more likely and inter-party coalitions less frequent in the former case.

(6) PM systems magnify changes in party support between elections more than LP systems do. If VS is the difference between the percentage of the votes won by a party at two successive elections, and SS the difference in seat percentages, then

	PM	LP
Average VS	3·24	2·58
Average SS	6·86	2·68
SS/VS	2·11	1·04

Under PM systems, therefore, changes in public preferences are very much magnified in the allocation of seats to parties.

Rae provides conclusive evidence, therefore, that PM systems produce most electoral bias. The extent of this bias has been stressed by Tufte (1973), who fitted the equation

$$S = a + bV$$

to election results from several territories using PM. He found b values (the degree of magnification of votes into seats) of 3·65 for New Jersey state elections (V is percentage of votes to Democrat) and 2·83 for British general elections (V is percentage of votes for Labour). Further, he found that the bias was not symmetrical, in that all parties were not equally affected. If there were no bias, then when V is 50 S should also be 50: for the New Jersey Democrats S was 50 when V was 61·3, indicating that Republicans had an 11·3 percentage point bias in their favour over the Democrats; for the British Labour Party, the similar bias to Conservative was 0·2.

The plurality electoral system is favoured in the countries studied here and, as demonstrated in the present section, such a system produces marked electoral biases. As background to a study of the electoral and political impact of such biases, the remainder of this chapter outlines their causes, looking first at non-partisan bias, which is inherent in the system, and then partisan bias, which may affect parties differentially.

Non-partisan bias

In PM elections, held using single-member constituencies and with only two major parties contesting the seats (Democrat and Republican in the United States; Conservative and Labour in Great Britain; etc.), some electoral bias is almost certain, even if there is no manipulation of the constituency pattern for political ends. This bias can be accounted for in a simple statistical model, which has been known of since early in the present century.

The cube law

According to this 'law', which is in effect an observed empirical regularity over many election results, the relationship of seats won by a party to its votes is expressed as

$$\frac{S_{ij}}{1 - S_{ij}} = \left(\frac{V_{ij}}{1 - V_{ij}}\right)^3$$

where S_{ij} is the proportion of the seats won by party i at election j and $1 - S_{ij}$ is the proportion won by the opposition party (remembering that only two parties are being considered); V_{ij} is the corresponding proportion of votes won by party i at election j. Rewritten as a linear function, this becomes

$$\log_e \frac{S_{ij}}{1 - S_{ij}} = 3 \log_e \frac{V_{ij}}{1 - V_{ij}}$$

and in regression form for testing

$$\log_e \frac{S_{ij}}{1 - S_{ij}} = a + b \log_e \frac{V_{ij}}{1 - V_{ij}}$$

where a should be 0·0 and b 3·0.

Two questions arise with regard to this law: why is there any bias? and why is the ratio of seats to votes cubic? The answer to the first is easily demonstrated. Take a country divided into 100 constituencies with 100 voters in each. Elections are contested by parties A and B, each of which wins half of the votes in the country as a whole (5000 votes) but not in each of the constituencies. Instead, on average A wins 0·5 of the votes in each constituency, with a standard deviation of 0·137. The 100 constituencies are distributed according to a normal curve (Fig. 4.1). From it

$$\frac{S_{ij}}{1 - S_{ij}} = \left(\frac{V_{ij}}{1 - V_{ij}}\right)^3 \quad \text{becomes} \quad \frac{0·50}{0·50} = \left(\frac{0·50}{0·50}\right)^{-3} = 1^3 = 1$$

so that A wins half of the votes and half of the seats (all those to the right of 0·5 in Fig. 4.1).

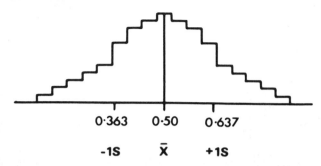

FIG. 4.1   Normal distribution of proportion of the vote for A in 100 hypothetical constituencies: $X_A = 0.50$; $S_A = 0.137$.

Now assume that A wins 0·55 of the votes, so that from the cube law

$$\frac{S_{ij}}{1 - S_{ij}} = \left(\frac{0.55}{0.45}\right)^3 = 1.22^3 = 1.82 \quad \text{so} \quad S_{ij} = 0.65.$$

With 0·55 (55 per cent) of the votes, therefore, A gets 0·65 of the seats. Fig. 4.2 shows how this comes about, on the assumption that, relative to the result shown in Fig. 4.1 there is a swing of 10 per cent (0·5 to 0·55) to A in each constituency so that the normal curve remains with $X_A = 0.55$. A now wins all the seats to the right of the 0·50 position. With $X_A = 0.50$ and $S_A = 0.137$, 0·50 as a Z-deviate is

$$Z_{0.50} = \frac{0.50 - 0.55}{0.137} = \frac{-0.05}{0.137} = -0.365$$

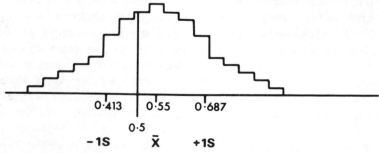

FIG. 4.2   The normal distribution of Fig. 4.1 shifted to the right so that $X_A = 0.55$.

and tables of the normal distribution show that approximately 65 per cent of all values lie to the right of this point. The bias then results because the proportion of the curve lying to the right of 0·50 (indicating the proportion of the seats won by A) is greater than the proportion of the votes won by A (indicated by the mean value).

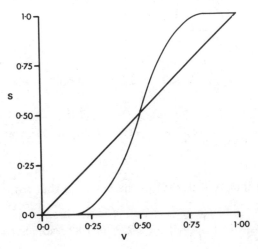

Fig. 4.3   The relationship between S and V according to the cube law.

From the cube law, therefore, the proportion of seats won by a party can be predicted from its votes, and the relationship between the two is S-shaped, indicating pronounced biases where the chance of them is greatest (Fig. 4.3. There can be no bias when $V_{ij} = 0·50$; when $V_{ij} = 0·90$, there can be little bias, since S_{ij} cannot be greater than 1.0.) The validity of this law rests on a series of assumptions, however: that voting is for two parties only; that the distribution of votes for a party over the constituencies has a normal form, with a certain standard deviation; and that the swing of votes from one party to another is uniform across all constituencies. The extent to which these are realistic assumptions varies from place to place and time to time. A distribution very close to normal was shown for the 1950 British general election in Kendall and Stuart's (1950) classic paper on the cube law (Fig. 4.4), for example, and Butler and Stokes (1969) have shown that the uniform swing is generally valid for general elections in Britain, although there are individual and groups of constituencies which vary from this for particular reasons (Taylor and Johnston, 1979, Chapter 6).

Having answered the first question with regard to bias, it is now necessary to ask why the standard deviation of the normal curve is 0·137, producing a cubic relationship between S and V. No reason can be given for the precise value of the standard deviation; the general explanation lies in the spatial division of

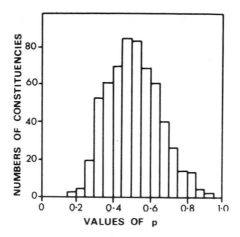

FIG. 4.4 The distribution of votes for Labour at the 1950 British general election in the 607 constituencies contested by both Labour and Conservative. Source: Kendall and Stuart (1950, p. 194). By permission of Routledge and Kegan Paul.

labour and the concentration of certain socio-economic classes, and hence the supporters of a particular party, in certain constituencies.

Assume the same 100 constituencies with 100 voters in each, and A getting 0·5 of the votes. Over all, the probability of any voter supporting A is 0·5 so that, assuming a random allocation of voters to constituencies, the binomial theorem could be used to predict the number of constituencies where A = 0·45, 0·49, etc. The resulting frequency distribution would be very 'peaked', with a standard deviation much lower than 0·137, and most constituencies would be similar to the over-all pattern. Because of the spatial division of labour, however, the distribution of A's supporters is not random; if one voter is selected at random from constituency x and proves to be a supporter of A, the likelihood of another voter in that constituency also supporting A will be much greater than 0·5—0·8 perhaps. In other words, supporters of a particular party tend to be spatially clustered, so that instead of comprising 10 000 individual voters, the geography of the 100 hypothetical constituencies is more likely to be made up of 1000 clusters of 10 voters, with all voters within each voter cluster supporting the same party. If these clusters are distributed randomly, then some constituencies may have most of their clusters containing all A supporters, giving an over-all value for A of perhaps 0·8; others may have few A supporters, giving a constituency proportion of 0·2; most will have a relatively even balance of A and non-A clusters, producing the peak around the mean in Fig. 4.1.

Testing the cube law

The cube law come about, it is suggested, because of a regularity in the distribution of the various population groups (usually socio-economic classes, but not always) that support the major parties. But how good is it as a description of election results? According to the earlier discussion, when fitted as a regression equation the values of a and b in the cube law should be 0·0 and 3·0 respectively.

Tufte's (1973) results show a very close fit only in the case of the British general elections. For the others, the value of b is less than 3, indicating that the geography of support for the relevant party does not produce a normal distribution of votes with a standard deviation of 0·137.

Table 4.1

The parameters of the cube law regression

Elections	a	b
Great Britain—general elections 1945–1970 (Labour)	−0·02	2·88
New Zealand—general elections 1946–1969 (Labour)	−0·12	2·31
United States—general elections 1868–1970 (Democrat)	0·09	2·52
United States—general elections 1900–1970 (Democrat)	0·17	2·20
Michigan—state elections 1950–1968 (Democrat)	−0·17	2·19
New Jersey—state elections 1946–1969 (Democrat)	−0·77	2·09
New York—state elections 1934–1966 (Democrat)	−0·23	1·33

Source: Tufte (1973, p. 546)

Variability of the value of b can be related to the kurtosis of the distribution of constituency values of A; the greater the degree of variation around $\bar{X}_A$, the smaller the value of b, because fewer seats will change hands with a given swing. This is illustrated by Fig. 4.5. With a very peaked, or leptokurtic, distribution of votes around a mean of approximately 0·5, a slight change produces many more seats; in Fig. 4.5A, therefore, $\bar{X}_A$ is 0·50 with a standard deviation of 0·050 and A wins 0·50 of the seats; with a slight shift to the right, so that $\bar{X}_A$ is 0·52, A wins 0·66 of the seats (Fig. 4.5B). The seat : vote relationship with such a distribution produces very marked biases (Fig. 4.5C).

With a platykurtic, or very broad, distribution having a relatively large standard deviation, the swing of votes is not magnified as much in the allocation of seats. Thus in Fig. 4.5D $\bar{X}_A$ is 0·5 and S_A is 0·150; A wins 0·5 of the seats. With a swing so that $\bar{X}_A$ is 0·52, A wins 0·55 of the seats (Fig. 4.5E) and the bias in the seats : votes relationship is much less pronounced (Fig. 4.5F).

Variations in the value of b, or the strength of the cube law effect, can be accounted for by variations in the underlying geography of the votes. Tufte also found that the value of a was not equal to 0, however, suggesting that the cube law operated differentially on the parties. To account for this variability it is necessary to turn to partisan bias in a constituency system, which again is built on the underlying geography of votes.

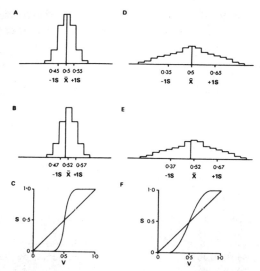

FIG. 4.5   The operation of the cube law with different standard deviations.

Partisan bias

Partisan bias comes about because certain of the assumptions on which the cube law is based are not relevant in 'real' situations. Three sources are identified here: the first refers to the normal distribution; the second concerns the size of constituencies; and the third relates to competition from other parties (plus non-voting). To understand the operation of the biases in these contexts, however, a simple classification of votes is introduced.

Types of votes in single-member plurality systems

A constituency in a single-member plurality system is won by the party getting most votes. If there are 100 seats in a constituency, therefore, 51 are sufficient for victory, if there are two parties involved; any more are of no value, since they bring no extra seats for the party, whereas fewer than 50 are of no use at all, since they bring no representation. A party may win 600 votes over ten constituencies of 100 voters each, therefore, but not necessarily win 0·6 of the seats, because of where those 600 votes are located.

To indicate the variable importance of votes according to their location, they can be classified in the following way, by party (Gudgin and Taylor, 1974):

(1) Wasted votes. These are the votes which bring no seats, because they are won in constituencies which the party loses.

(2) Excess votes. These too bring no seats to the party, since they are extra to the number needed to win the constituencies in which it is successful.

(3) Effective votes. These win constituencies, and are calculated as one

more than the total won by the opposition. (Effective votes may be defined as one more than half of the number of votes cast; the relative differences are unchanged.)

Table 4.2 illustrates the calculations involved in this classification, for a simple, hypothetical ten-constituency system. In it, A and B get equal numbers of votes in each class.

Table 4.2

Wasted, excess, and efficient votes in ten hypothetical constituencies

	Votes for			Votes in constituencies won by					
					A			*B*	
Constituency	*A*	*B*	Winner	*W*	*E*	*F*	*W*	*E*	*F*
1	55	45	A		9	46	45		
2	40	60	B	40				19	41
3	51	49	A		1	50	49		
4	54	46	A		7	47	46		
5	45	55	B	45				9	46
6	46	54	B	46				7	47
7	49	51	B	49				1	50
8	60	40	A		19	41	40		
9	65	35	A		29	36	35		
10	35	65	B	35				29	36
Total	500	500	A 5 B 5	215	65	220	215	65	220
Averages									
Per seat won					13	44		13	44
Per seat lost				43			43		

*Key to votes: *W*—wasted; *E*—excess; *F*—effective.

Skewness and the differential concentration of party supporters

Close inspection of the distribution of Labour votes at the British 1950 general election (Fig. 4.4) shows that this in fact is not quite normal; it is slightly skewed to the right. There are more observations in the right-hand tail—the constituencies with large proportions of Labour votes—than there are in the comparable left-hand tail: in other words, there were more 'very safe' Labour constituencies—with large numbers of excess votes—than 'very safe' Conservative constituencies, with consequences for the seats: votes relationship.

A normal distribution is symmetrical, with the mean value the same as the median. With a skewed distribution, however, the mean lies to the right of the median, if the skew is positive, and to the left if it is negative; the greater the deviation between these two values, the greater the skew. With a skewed distribution, in either direction, the cube law does not predict the seat allocation precisely; in general, if the distribution of seat proportions for a party is positively skewed, it will suffer a bias against it in terms of seats.

To illustrate this effect of a skewed distribution, take the ten constituencies with 100 votes each again. The distribution of proportions for party A is

$$0.30, \ 0.35, \ 0.40, \ 0.45, \ 0.45, \ 0.45, \ 0.55, \ 0.55, \ 0.70, \ 0.80.$$

Over all, A wins 500, or 0.50, of the votes but because the distribution is positively skewed, its median proportion is only 0.45. It wins only 4 (0.40) of the 10 seats. For the opposing party—B—on the other hand, the vote proportions are

$$0.70, \ 0.65, \ 0.60, \ 0.55, \ 0.55, \ 0.55, \ 0.45, \ 0.45, \ 0.30, \ 0.20.$$

B gets 0.50 of the total votes cast, but its median proportion is 0.55 and it wins 0.60 of the seats. This bias towards B comes about because it has relatively few wasted votes in the seats it loses, compared to its opponent, and also relatively few excess votes in the seats that it wins (Table 4.3). The bias against A results from it winning seat 10 by a large majority (larger than any in the seats won by B) and losing 3 seats narrowly to B's two.

Table 4.3

The effect of skewness on vote distributions

| | Votes for | | | Votes in constituencies won by | | | | | |
| | | | | | A | | | B | |
Constituency	A	B	Winner	W	E	F	W	E	F
1	30	70	B	30				39	31
2	35	65	B	35				29	36
3	40	60	B	40				19	41
4	45	55	B	45				9	46
5	45	55	B	45				9	46
6	45	55	B	45				9	46
7	55	45	A		9	46	45		
8	55	45	A		9	46	45		
9	70	30	A		39	31	30		
10	80	20	A		59	21	20		
Total	500	500	A 4	240	116	144	140	114	246
			B 6						
Averages									
Per seat won					39	36		19	41
Per seat lost				40			35		

*Key to votes: W—wasted; E—excess; F—effective.

The type of partisan bias illustrated in Table 4.3 results from the differential concentration of majorities: the more very safe seats a party has, the more excess votes it amasses; the more marginal seats it loses, the more wasted votes it amasses. To measure the extent of this bias, Soper and Rydon (1958) have suggested the use of a simple statistical measure of skewness (Blalock, 1960, p. 74).

$$MD_A - \bar{X}_A = DM_A$$

where MD_A is the median vote proportion for party A; $\bar{X}_A$ is the mean vote proportion for party A; and DM_A is the bias coefficient for party A resulting from the differential concentration of majorities.

Thus, from Table 4.3

$$MD_A - \bar{X}_A = 0.45 - 0.50 \qquad\qquad DM_A = -0.05$$

$$MD_B - \bar{X}_B = 0.55 - 0.50 \qquad\qquad DM_B = +0.05$$

so that there is a negative bias against A of 0.05, balanced by a positive bias to B of a similar magnitude.

The implication from this discussion is that a positive skew produces a negative bias (fewer seats than votes) and vice versa. This is not always the case, however (Gudgin and Taylor, 1974). If a party wins 0.90 of the votes, then the nature of their distribution across the constituencies is irrelevant; it will win all of the seats, so a positive skew will produce no bias relative to the non-partisan predictions of the cube law: similarly, if it wins only 0.10 of the votes it will lose all of the seats, as would be predicted. With about 0.50 of the votes, a positive skew will produce a negative bias of fewer seats either than votes or than seats predicted by the cube law. At intermediate levels (where V—proportion of the votes—is about 0.30 or 0.60) a positive skew is associated with a positive bias, as indicated in Fig. 4.6B and C. In Fig. 4.6B, because of the short left-hand tail, the party with the positively skewed distribution wins virtually all of the seats, whereas in Fig. 4.6C, the long right-

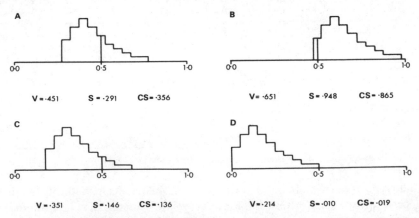

Fig. 4.6   Votes (V) and seats (S), relative to predicted number of seats according to the cube law (CS), for a party whose vote distribution is positively skewed, at different levels of V.

hand tail brings more seats than would be predicted for a normal distribution (i.e. by the cube law) when $V = 0.351$. In most two-party contests, however, it is rare for one party to get more than 0.60 of the votes, so a positive skew is usually associated with many excess votes and a negative bias. (Conversely, of course, a negative skew is associated with few excess votes and positive bias.) To perform very well in certain constituencies only is not the best use of votes, therefore.

Constituency size differences

So far, it has been assumed that all constituencies contain the same number of voters. If this is not the case, however, further bias can arise, since fewer votes are needed to win a small than a large constituency. Table 4.4 illustrates this point. As before, there are ten constituencies and 1000 votes in all, but the ten vary in their size.

Table 4.4

The effect of constituency size on vote distributions

Constituency	Votes for A	Votes for B	Winner	Votes in constituencies won by A — W	A — E	A — F	B — W	B — E	B — F
1	21 (0·30)	49 (0·70)	B	21				27	22
2	28 (0·35)	52 (0·65)	B	28				23	29
3	36 (0·40)	54 (0·60)	B	36				17	37
4	41 (0·45)	49 (0·55)	B	41				7	42
5	41 (0·45)	49 (0·55)	B	41				7	42
6	40 (0·45)	50 (0·55)	B	40				9	41
7	55 (0·55)	45 (0·45)	A		9	46	45		
8	77 (0·55)	63 (0·45)	A		13	64	63		
9	84 (0·70)	36 (0·30)	A		47	37	36		
10	104 (0·80)	26 (0·20)	A		77	27	26		
Total	527 (0·527)	473 (0·473)	A 4 B 6	207	146	174	170	90	213
Averages Per seat won					36·5	43·5		15	35·5
Per seat lost				34·5			42·5		

*Key to votes: *W*—wasted; *E*—excess; *F*—effective.

In the set of constituencies of Table 4.3, there were 100 votes cast in each so that, where $\bar{V}_A$ is the average number of votes in seats won by A, etc.,

$$\bar{V}_A = \bar{V}_B = 100.$$

In the unequal-sized constituencies of Table 4.4, however,

$$\bar{V}_A = 122.5 \qquad \bar{V}_B = 85.0.$$

Party A's strength is in the larger constituencies, therefore, which are harder to win in terms of votes; as a consequence A has a larger average number of effective votes $(\bar{F}_A)$ in the constituencies won than does B; the latter's total votes are stretched further, and it has fewer excess votes per seat won.

To measure this second type of electoral bias, due to differential sizes, Soper and Rydon (1958) suggest using

$$\bar{X}_A - P_A = SD_A$$

where P_A is the over-all proportion of the votes won by A; $\bar{X}_A$ is the mean proportion of the votes won by A; and SD is the size differential bias for A. If all constituencies were the same size then $P_A = \bar{X}_A$ as it would be if the constituencies won by A were a random sample of all constituency sizes; if, on the other hand, A's votes are concentrated in the small constituencies, then $P_A < \bar{X}_A$ (as indicated for party B in Table 4.4), whereas if A's votes are concentrated in the large constituencies, $P_A > \bar{X}_A$. For Table 4.4,

$$\bar{X}_A - P_A = 0{\cdot}500 - 0{\cdot}527 \qquad SD_A = -0{\cdot}027$$

$$\bar{X}_B - P_B = 0{\cdot}500 - 0{\cdot}473 \qquad SD_B = +0{\cdot}027$$

indicating a negative bias against A; with 0·5 of the votes, it wins only 0·4 of the seats.

Differential majorities, constituency sizes, and total bias

The discussion so far has focused on these two types of bias separately when clearly both operate together. To obtain an index of over-all bias, therefore, the two separate measures should be summed, giving

$$DM_A + SD_A = TB_A$$

where TB_A is the total bias for party A. Substituting,

$$TB_A = (MD_A - \bar{X}_A) + (\bar{X}_A - P_A) = MD_A - P_A.$$

Returning to Table 4.4, therefore,

$$P_A = 0{\cdot}527 \qquad \bar{X}_A = 0{\cdot}5 \qquad MD_A = 0{\cdot}45$$

$$DM_A = 0{\cdot}45 - 0{\cdot}5 = -0{\cdot}05$$

$$SD_A = 0{\cdot}5 - 0{\cdot}527 = -0{\cdot}027$$

$$TB_A = 0{\cdot}45 - 0{\cdot}527 = -0{\cdot}077$$

The bias against party A is 0·077, or 7·7 per cent, of which 65 per cent $(-0{\cdot}05/-0{\cdot}077) \times 100$ results from the differential concentration of majorities and the remaining 35 per cent from constituency size differences. The nature of the interaction between population distributions and the constituency network means that party A is discriminated against in the allocation of seats because it tends to win the big seats by big majorities; B is favoured because its strength is in the small constituencies, which it wins by relatively narrow margins.

Table 4.5

*Components of the electoral bias: New Zealand general elections**

Election	P_N	$\bar{X}_N$	MD_N	DM_N	SD_N	TB_N	Seats won
1957	0·486	0·491	0·507	0·016	0·005	0·021	39/76
1960	0·531	0·537	0·552	0·015	0·006	0·021	46/76
1963	0·526	0·533	0·563	0·030	0·007	0·037	45/76
1966	0·522	0·532	0·536	0·004	0·010	0·014	44/76
1969	0·516	0·520	0·525	0·005	0·004	0·009	45/80
1972	0·472	0·474	0·467	−0·008	0·002	−0·005	32/83
1975	0·557	0·558	0·552	−0·006	0·001	−0·005	55/83

* All figures refer to the National Party

To illustrate the use of these various measures in a 'real' situation, Table 4.5 gives the various bias indices for the National Party (equivalent to the British Conservative Party) at each New Zealand general election during the period 1957–75. These indices refer to the European electorates only (the opposition Labour Party won all four Maori electorates each time) and are calculated using the votes for the two main parties only (which never fell below 0·85 of the total). For the elections of 1957 to 1969 inclusive, that party clearly benefitted from winning both the smaller (rural) constituencies and also from not having the largest 'safe' seats. At the last two elections following the 1972 redistribution of seats, however, the total bias swung against the party, which retained a slight advantage in the smaller constituencies but was now suffering from a differential concentration of its supporters.

Third parties and abstentions

In the analyses so far, it has been assumed: (1) that only two parties contest each constituency, and (2) that all eligible electors cast votes. Neither assumption is generally tenable. Some elections do involve only two parties and in some systems (for example, Australia) voting is compulsory and so there are very few abstentions. More usually, however, the two main parties have to face other contestants and must counter the possibility of abstentions.

The distributions of third-party strength and of abstentions can produce bias in the relationships of seats to votes for the two main parties. It has already been shown that smaller constituencies require less votes to win them, so that parties with strengths there make more effective use of their votes. The effects of third parties and abstainers are exactly the same, in that they reduce the number of votes needed to win a constituency. Take, for example, a constituency with 100 voters, in which party A needs 51 votes to be sure of defeating party B. If there were a party C as well, and both B and C got 30 votes, only 31 would be needed by A to win. Similarly, if only A and B contested the seat, but 10 of the electors abstained, then only 46 votes would be needed for victory by A. The more votes that are not involved in the competition between the two main parties, therefore, the fewer effective votes needed to win the constituency and the better the return to the party which tends to win where such a condition exists.

Table 4.6
The effect of third party on vote distributions

| | | Votes for | | | Votes in constituencies won by | | | | | |
| | | | | | | A | | | B | |
Constituency	A	B	C	Winner	W	E	F	W	E	F
1	54	43	3	A		10	44	43		
2	38	50	12	B	38				10	39
3	50	48	2	A		1	49	48		
4	53	43	4	A		9	44	43		
5	46	47	7	B	46				0	47
6	43	45	12	B	43				1	44
7	46	47	7	B	46				0	47
8	60	38	2	A		21	39	38		
9	64	32	4	A		31	33	32		
10	35	55	10	B	35				19	36
Total	489	448	63	A 5	208	72	209	204	31	213
				B 5						
Averages										
Per seat won						14·4	41·8		6·2	42·6
Per seat lost					41·6			40·8		

* Key to votes: *W*—wasted; *E*—excess; *F*—effective.

Table 4.6 illustrates these effects, using the same set of ten equal-sized constituencies as in Table 4.2. The new element in Table 4.6 is a third party, C, which wins 0·063 of the 1000 votes. Its vote-winning power is not evenly distributed over the ten constituencies, however: in those won by A it averages 0·030 only, whereas in those won by B its average is 0·096. As a result, B needs fewer votes on average to win its five constituencies so that, despite getting 41 votes fewer than A over-all, it wins the same number of seats. This is shown by the figures for the average number of excess votes per constituency won; B's votes are more efficiently distributed than A's.

The role of abstentions can also be illustrated by Table 4.6 if party C is replaced by abstentions: again B benefits because there are more abstainers in the constituencies which it wins than there are in those held by A. In effect, therefore, party C is changing the distribution of constituency sizes. In Table 4.2, where all votes were cast for either A or B, the average number of votes cast in constituencies won by the two parties was $\bar{V}_A = \bar{V}_B = 100$: in Table 4.6, however, the average numbers of votes cast for the two main parties was 97 in those won by A and 90·4 in those won by B.

Further detailed examples showing the interaction of all components of partisan bias—differential majorities, constituency sizes, third parties, and abstentions—are not represented here, since the purpose of the analysis has been to demonstrate how these various components work and not to provide illustrations of their import from several countries. One final point about third party and abstention effects should be noted, however: whereas the influence of abstentions is linear, that of third parties is not. The more abstentions there are, the less the votes needed to win a constituency, and so the more efficiently a party's votes may be distributed. More third party votes above a certain level in a constituency may make it harder to win, however; that level is the number of votes held by the losing 'major' party. For the latter component, therefore, the sort of analysis presented here is only valid if the third party is not likely to win seats.

Conclusions

Various aspects of the bias involved in the translation of votes into seats in a two-party plurality electoral system have been presented here. One of these components, the non-partisan bias of the cube law, affects both parties equally; the others are to one party's advantage and another's disadvantage.

Various methods of analysing these biases have been presented in the literature (e.g. Brookes, 1959, 1960; Johnston, 1976f, 1976g; Gudgin and Taylor, 1978) and have indicated how certain political parties, usually those of the 'left', have suffered the partisan biases. Parties of the 'right' benefit frequently from the large volumes of excess votes built up by their opponents in their safe seats, and by the variations in constituency size which also tend to operate against the interests of the 'left'. As a consequence, parties of the left often lose elections despite winning most votes, as happened in Britain in 1951 (but not in February 1974 because the size, gerrymander, and abstentions components were all strongly in Labour's favour then: Johnston, 1976g); it would have happened in New Zealand in 1957 (Table 4.5) when National won less than half of the European votes but 39 of the 76 seats, if Labour had not won all four Maori seats.

The purpose of the present chapter is not to give empirical detail on electoral bias, however, but to indicate how it occurs. In particular, the aim has been to identify those components which can be manipulated by those in power (Fig. 2.7) and those which cannot. The first group—the non-manipulable—contains the non-partisan bias illustrated by the cube law, and also the biases introduced through third party and abstention effects. It may be possible for a major party somehow to manipulate voter reactions to both their main opponent and a third party in order to obtain a positive bias, but this is unlikely, and so for the purpose of this book there are only two partisan bias components open to manipulation: the differential majorities and the constituency size differences. Both are a consequence of the way in which the network of constituencies can be laid over the distribution of voters and invite development of an electoral cartography for partisan ends.

Although this brief chapter has been concerned very largely with bias in a two-party plurality system (for more detail, see Gudgin and Taylor, 1978, and Taylor and Johnston, 1979) it should be remembered that, according to Rae's findings discussed earlier, virtually all constituency-based electoral systems produce some bias. Thus it may be in the interests of the party in power to change the electoral system. Since the countries focused on in this book all use some form of the plurality system, no discussion has been presented here on the types of biases in other systems. Proponents of electoral reform in Britain and elsewhere argue for alternative systems, however, so some examples of possible effects of such changes are included in Chapter 8.

Manipulation of the electoral system to partisan benefit clearly should be feasible, given the effects of constituency size and differential majorities outlined here. In the short term, however, parties must operate within existing systems, and in countries using the plurality procedure vote distributions such as that in Fig. 4.4 are quite usual. The spatial pattern of clusters of like-minded voters produces relatively few constituencies which are strongly oriented to one party or another. Most constituencies are fairly evenly balanced between the two, and these are where elections are fought, won and lost.

**Part III
The Systems in Operation**

5 Variations in Local Government Spending

THE level and nature of spending by a local government should reflect the demands and needs of the inhabitants of its territory, as indicated by the political dispositions of the parties they return to power. Some parties are elected on the basis of campaigns which involve spending promises, whereas others seek votes on manifestos which promise to reduce government expenditure, or at least not to increase it significantly. Why should parties differ in this way, producing local governments with different policies on taxing and spending?

Local governments are not independent agents, but rather are constrained in how much they can spend, and what on, by the higher-level bodies to which they are subservient. These constraints should be more severe in a centralized system, such as Britain's, than in a federal state on the American model, but an investigation by Boaden (1970) has suggested that British local governments vary considerably in the discretion they exercise on spending.

Table 5.1

Variations in spending: County Boroughs in England and Wales, 1965–1966

	Welfare	Children	Service Health	Education	Library
Mean expenditure per 1000 population (£)	1044	748	2200	23970	689
Standard deviation	263	211	373	2100	150
Spending by twenty smallest C.B.s					
Number in highest quartile	5	3	5	6	5
Number in lowest quartile	4	9	5	6	3
Spending by sixteen poorest C.B.s					
Number in highest quartile	6	3	8	5	3
Number in lowest quartile	3	4	3	2	2

Source: from Boaden (1971, pp. 14–18).

Using the 82 County Boroughs of England and Wales during the mid-1960s, Boaden showed considerable differences in their spending *per capita* on five different services (Table 5.1). He then hypothesized that perhaps it was the smallest and the poorest authorities which were most likely to conform to central direction, since they were politically weak (because of small size) and most dependent on central finance through the Rate Support Grant (see p. 45). He tested this idea by dividing the C.B.s into quartiles according to their *per capita* spending, expecting that if the hypothesis were valid none of the poorest and smallest would deviate markedly from the over-all average. The data did not support his hypothesis. On welfare services, for example, five of the smallest authorities were in the upper quartile on spending, and four were in the lowest (Table 5.1).

Boaden concluded (1971, p. 19) that 'Central control is less apparent in policy outcomes than might have been supposed'. British local authorities, it would seem, are as flexible as their American counterparts. There, also in the 1960s, the state governments differed very considerably in how much they spent *per capita* on various welfare programmes (Table 5.2). Furthermore, the states which were big spenders on one programme tended to be big spenders on the others, too. Thus on the six listed in Table 5.2, the average ranking for Wisconsin over the 48 conterminous states was 5·33 and for New York it was 7·33; by contrast, for Pennsylvania it was 25·5 (the 'average' state) and for Alabama and Mississippi it was 44·0 and 45·3 respectively.

Table 5.2
State welfare spending in the United States, 1961

		Average Payment per Recipient in Program ($)				
	Aid to Dependent Children	*Old Age Assistance*	*Aid to the Blind*	*Aid to the Disabled*	*General Assistance*	*Un-employment Insurance*
Average (48 states)	116.68	67.85	73.36	68.19	65.13	33.84
Highest Value	178.57	96.51	126.45	132.90	110.76	42.32
Upper Quartile	148.75	82.11	87.42	81.54	65.11	34.92
Lower Quartile	93.03	57.70	61.21	54.64	30.70	26.97
Lowest Value	36.38	35.40	38.43	34.85	12.89	21.24

Source: derived from Dawson and Robinson (1965, pp. 388–9). Copyright © 1965 by Little, Brown and Company, Inc.

Given such wide variations between territorial authorities in both countries, some attempt is needed to account for this important aspect of state involvement in the geography of social well-being. The next section provides a simple, verbal and diagrammatic model on which such an explanation can be based, and it is followed by a discussion of empirical studies whose findings can be used as 'tests' of the model.

A model of how much governments spend

A number of models (perhaps 'explanation sketches' would be a better descriptive term) have been proposed to account for the sorts of variations illustrated in Tables 5.1 and 5.2. Most emphasize, in one form or another, the three independent variables advanced by Boaden (1971), and the present model is based upon them too.

Needs

'From each according to his abilities, to each according to his needs' is a common slogan derived from the works of Marx. Most welfare programmes have been devised to meet particular needs. The assessment of need is extremely difficult, of course (Harvey, 1973, pp. 101–5), and in general only coarse indicators of how much is wanted, by whom, and where, are available. Nevertheless, because of the spatial division of labour, it is clear that the residents of some local governments have more need of some services than do those of other, perhaps neighbouring, territories.

In general, therefore, it can be suggested that the greater the volume of need in an area, the greater the spending on the services relevant to its alleviation. Thus, for example, Hull would have spent £27 105 per 1000 residents on education services in 1965–6 whereas Eastbourne spent only £19 548, because 26 per cent of Hull's population were aged under 15 compared to only 16 per cent of Eastbourne's. But needs cannot account for all of the variations indicated in Table 5.2. The cost of living may be higher in Massachusetts than in Mississippi, but it is very unlikely that $126.45 per month in the former was only meeting the same needs as $38.43 per month in the latter. Needs will account for some of the geographical variations in spending, therefore, but not all of them.

Resources

As indicated in Chapter 2, because of the spatial division of labour some local governments are much richer than others; the resources available to be taxed, *per capita*, vary extensively as a result so that the fiscal effort required to meet certain needs will vary also. Thus an area with low *per capita* property values may be unable to raise sufficient revenue from its residents to finance the liberal welfare policies which its government favours, whilst in another, with relatively rich residents, such liberal policies could be financed without making much demand on the taxpayers' wallets.

Regarding resources, therefore, it can be hypothesized that the greater the resources available to a local government, the greater the spending on needs. Fig. 5.1 illustrates the general validity of this explanation for one of the data sets summarized in Table 5.2; the richer a state's population, the more generous was its government in the payments made to the unemployed. Nevertheless, there is considerable variability around the general trend indicated in the figure so that available resources, like needs, is insufficient as a variable to account for all of the inter-state differences in government spending.

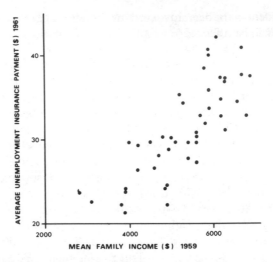

F IG. 5.1   The relationship between resources (median family income) and welfare payments
(unemployment insurance per recipient) in the United States.

Dispositions

In addition to producing inter-governmental variations in needs and
resources, the spatial division of labour also results in differences between
local governments in the political attitudes of their residents, and hence of
their elected representatives also. Since many political ideologies and attitudes
are crystallized around the issue of government spending, it can be
hypothesized that the attitudes and dispositions of the elected decision-
makers are significant influences on spending levels. Boaden (1971) suggests
that these dispositions are affected by three elements:

(1) The decision-makers' perceptions both of needs and of the standards at
    which they should be met. For much public spending there are
    nationally determined criteria and guidelines, but these usually specify
    minima above which local officials are free to range within their money-
    raising powers.

(2) The distribution of need among the electorate relative to the origins of
    the decision-makers. If a majority of the latter come from a certain
    section of the community which is in a particular need—particularly if
    they represent that section through a constituency-based electoral
    system—they are more likely to know of and be prepared to react to that
    need than are representatives from other sections.

(3) Attitudes towards the role of government. Many public services (fire
    brigades, police, recreation, education, health, etc.) could be, and to
    some degree are, provided by the private sector. Different groups in

society differ in the degree to which they support public sector provision, and this will be reflected in the attitudes of their elected representatives.

Together, these three elements indicate why locally elected politicians will differ in their operation of various policies, given the spatial division of labour.

Two major sets of constraints circumscribe the flexibility within which local politicians can operate. The first concerns the already-mentioned externally defined rules. Thus Hansen and Kjellberg (1976) have suggested a fourfold classification of flexibility for Norwegian municipal governments.

	Degree of Local Autonomy in Defining Policy Goals	
Degree of Local Autonomy in Financing and Spending Decisions	High	Low
High	Cultural Activity	Education
Low	Social Welfare	Natural Insurance Contributions

The representative policies refer to Norway, but the general schema has wider applicability. In Britain, for example, local governments have no discretion on either axis in the operation of various licensing schemes—they act as administrators for a nationally uniform service—but they have great flexibility in the operation of other services, such as family planning.

The second set of constraints concerns the ability of politicians to operate policies to benefit certain groups—their constituents, presumably—over others. Some services are broad in scope and can only be provided for everybody, whereas others are narrower in scope and can be aimed at particular groups (Boaden, 1971, p. 39). The latter include many of the major spending programmes in a welfare state, over which local governments perhaps have relatively little flexibility of control. The former are more generally available, such as fire services, libraries, museums, art galleries, and parks. Nevertheless, although available to all, they may be so provided as to benefit certain groups. Admission to a park may be free, but the further a family lives from it, the less use it is likely to make of it, because of the time and cost involved in getting there (Massam, 1975). Because of 'frictions of distance', therefore, almost all policies can be made socially selective if they are capable of being spatially selective (see Chapter 6).

There are many examples of inter-government variations in public policies which reflect the influence of dispositions. The introduction of comprehensive secondary education by British local authorities, reacting to both local demands and a central government directive of 1965, was far from uniform, for example. By July 1966, of the County Boroughs 64 per cent of those with a

Labour-dominated council had submitted plans for comprehensive reorganization compared to 26 per cent of those lacking such political rulers (Boaden and Alford, 1969). Eleven years later, the recalcitrant authorities still resisting the demand for such reorganization were characterized by their non-Labour councils. (Most non-Labour councils were no longer recalcitrant, however, indicating that dispositions were not the only determining factor.)

Political parties in the United States are less ideological and local branches are much more pragmatic in their reactions to their social environments than is the case in Britain. Thus, in accounting for why several Southern states spent less than half of the expected sum on a new Anti-Poverty Program (which in part was federally financed), Cowart (1969, p. 235) suggested that

Perhaps the explosive political nature of welfare spending in the South, coupled with a perception that Negroes are the principal beneficiaries, influences political leaders to respond with similar caution and delay to new, functionally similar programs. The perception by Southern whites that AFDC is a federal welfare program which substantially benefits Negroes and increases illegitimacy rates among them may caution restraint in the acceptance of new federal programs directed towards similar clientele groups.

Such attitudes are typical of the regional variability in dispositions towards welfare policies in the U.S.A., which Sharkansky (1970a) associates with the spatial pattern of immigrants from different origins.

Table 5.3

Cost and benefits of the Medicaid programme: selected regional averages, 1968

	States	With Medicaid	Average Benefit per Household	Net Benefit per Household ($3000>)
New England	6	6	+$ 7.12	+$447.44
Mid-Atlantic	5	4	−$ 8.46	+$353.57
Upper Midwest	4	4	+$18.05	+$399.55
Mountain	5	4	−$ 8.87	+$ 88.30
South	10	3	−$13.21	+$ 25.76

Source: computed from data in Sharkansky (1970b) and Stuart (1972).

The Medicaid programme, by which the costs of medical purchases by those on public welfare are met out of state/federal funds, was introduced in 1965. (The higher the average income of families in a state, the smaller the proportion of the total cost met from the federal grant-in-aid: Tresch, 1975.) By 1968, 14 states (including the District of Columbia) were not operating the programme (Stuart, 1972; Johnston, 1978b). From Cowart and Sharkansky's findings it might be suggested that such states were mainly in the South, as indeed seven were (Table 5.3). As a result, residents in some states were benefiting from the taxes of others, whereas in some states Medicaid was being paid for in federal taxes but no benefits were received. Thus, as Table 5.3 shows, poor families in New England, where all states operated Medicaid at relatively high payment levels, received a net benefit of $447.44 in 1968 whereas their contemporaries in the South received only one-twentieth of that amount. Thus although (Stuart, 1972, p. 167) 'The program was designed to reduce inequities in the distribution of welfare payments among states ... After two and a half years of Medicaid these differences have become more, not less, pronounced'. And so, in 1970 four states (New York, California, Pennsylvania, and Massachusetts) with 27 per cent of the nation's population and only 17 per cent of the families earning less than $3000 annually obtained 56 per cent of all the Medicaid grants from the federal exchequer.

The model summarized

The fragmentary evidence presented in this section supports the general hypotheses that levels of government spending are influenced by three independent variables: needs, resources, and dispositions. These three are unlikely to be entirely independent, however. The less the resources in an area, the greater the needs for certain welfare services are likely to be, for example, and the more disposed the politicians towards liberal public spending to meet such demands. Detailed evaluation of the interactions between the variables requires sophisticated analysis, therefore.

The focus of the present book is on the influence of political dispositions, within the context of needs and resources. To further the analysis of this variable it is necessary to inquire more deeply into the possible relationships between environments, dispositions, and policies.

Politicians, voters, and policies

Politicians may enter local government for altruistic reasons, for the satisfaction of serving part or the whole of the electorate; others aim to advance their own political careers, via the party organizations. Many combine these functions, serving the community, advancing certain group causes, and promoting self-interest. Over time, it would seem, the altruistic purposes have declined: as local politics have become 'nationalized' and the business of local government more voluminous, so parties and interest groups have taken over from the 'community servant'. Local government operations can thus be seen as part of a more general process of politics, which should be amenable to theoretical explanation.

The Downs model

The model to be used here was developed by Downs (1957) out of earlier classical work in location theory (Hotelling, 1929; Alonso, 1964). It is based on the simple axiom that, in politics as in other aspects of life, self-interest rules and men make rational decisions based upon their selfish attitudes and what they perceive as the best ways of fulfilling their goals.

There are two deductions from this axiom, one for the political parties and the other for the voters. For the parties and their members (Down, 1957, p. 28), 'politicians ... treat policies purely as means to the attainment of their private ends, which they can reach only by being elected', leading to the hypothesis (pp. 28–31) that 'parties formulate policies in order to win elections, rather than win elections in order to formulate policies ... such behaviour implies that the government party is aware of some definite relationship between its policies and the way people vote'. Similarly (p. 36), the voter 'casts his vote for the party he believes will provide him with more benefits than any other'. Putting parties and voters together, Downs argues that parties encourage the development of certain ideologies among voters— sets of attitudes about how society should be organized and governed. Such ideologies cannot be too different, or this would create an unstable society, as in Ulster in the 1970s (Laver, 1976). There must be general consensus over many issues—a property-owning democracy, perhaps—and the ideological differences are of degree rather than kind, about means rather than ends.

Societal attitudes develop towards politics, therefore, so that most people are in general agreement about the fundamentals. It is then possible to hypothesize an attitude scale on which most voters can be placed. The majority will be in the centre, reflecting the general consensus; there will be relatively few at the extremes of the scale, holding strongly opposed views and being unable to compromise their fundamental differences. There can, of course, be many of these scales, one for each major political issue. Downs assumes that there is only one issue ('how much government intervention in the economy should there be'—p. 116), on the grounds that most elections are fought on single issues such as this: in any case, his major arguments hold for any number of scales.

Once the voters have been located on this scale, the parties then develop policies relevant to the issue(s) defining the scale, so as to win the election. Over the long term parties may seek to alter attitudes, perhaps fundamentally, to ensure voter support, but over the short term the desire for power *now* means that parties accommodate policies to existing attitudes. They do this in the same way that shops locate according to the profit-maximization notions of classical location theory; they seek to be as close to as many voters as possible, thereby winning the support of the rational populace who pursue their self-interest with the party most likely to fulfil it.

Like Hotelling's retailers, the two parties in Downs's model converge at the centre of the population distribution, as Fig. 5.2 illustrates. A normally distributed population of voters along the ideological continuum is assumed. (Any distribution will produce the same result if, as propounded here,

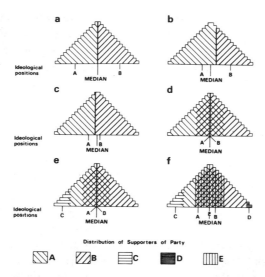

FIG. 5.2   Evolution of party locations on the ideological scale of voter attitudes. The various shaded areas show the locations of each party's supporters: in d, e, and f parties A and B get equal support from voters in the modal area.

consensus politics prevail.) Initially, the two parties—A and B—perceive that there is a left wing and a right wing to the ideological scale, and each emerges to serve one such wing. Thus in Fig. 5.2a, the two parties are equidistant from the centre and the extreme ideological position; each is closest to half of the voters, and so wins half of the votes. To counter the stalemate, A changes its policy package, locating itself closer to the centre (Fig. 5.2b): it now has the support of more than half of the voters, and would win an election. B must then react by moving even closer to the median (Fig. 5.2c), thereby capturing more than half of the votes.

This changing of party policy proposals to win votes should eventually lead to the disappearance of any differences between the parties, as they converge at the median (Fig. 5.2d). By doing this, however, parties risk losing support from their wings to 'protest' third parties (e.g. Fig. 5.2e), and other, 'centre' parties may try to force them apart (Fig. 5.2f). In reality, of course, the equilibrium in Fig. 5.2d will never occur, for a variety of reasons. The composition of the voting population is always changing, which will lead to shifts in the detailed morphology of the distribution (Butler and Stokes, 1969); like economic decision-makers (Pred, 1967), neither the voters nor the parties are perfect—some voters may support parties other than those closest to them, because of misperceptions, misinformation, or even sheer cussedness, whereas parties may misread the distribution of voters on the scale and produce unattractive policies.

Many caveats, riders, and exceptions can be made when treating Downs's model in detail, but its general predictions remain simple and are valid for the present purpose. In a two-party system, each party will design a package of policies aimed at the median voters, without whom no electoral majority is possible, while at the same time also focusing on one particular wing of the voter distribution, to avoid protest groups capturing votes (Fig. 5.2e) and giving some clear party attitudinal identity (see Nie, Verba, and Petrocik, 1976, Chapter 17 and Laver, 1976). In policy terms, therefore, there should be two major parties, both accepting many of the consensus, middle-of-the-road attitudes of the voters but each aiming at one of the two wings of the distribution.

Local government and the Downs model

Every local government area will have its own distribution of voters along the ideological continuum. Few, because of the spatial division of labour and the consequent pattern of political differences noted in Chapter 3, will conform to the national distribution, whatever it may be. Rather, there is likely to be a variety of distributional types, as indicated in Fig. 5.3, ranging from the extreme left-wing (b) through the marginal left-wing (d) and the stereotype national (a) to the marginal right-wing (e) and the extreme right-wing (c).

If local government areas were politically independent of each other, then each would have its unique set of political parties whose policies were tailored to the local attitudes. Thus in Fig. 5.3b, there would presumably be two parties

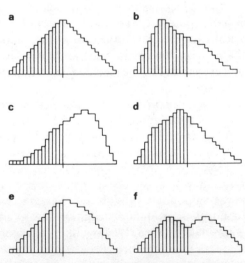

FIG. 5.3   Various distributions of voters on the ideological scale in hypothetical local government areas. The shaded portions indicate those voters to the left of the median voter in the national distribution (a).

both with left-wing attitudes, whereas in Fig. 5.3a the two parties would both be middle-of-the-road. Because of the nationalization of politics, however, a party which is to the right nationally cannot move very far to the left in an area such as in Fig. 5.3b; instead, while trying to attract some of the 'left-wing' voters, it must accept what is virtually permanent minority or opposition status there. As Robertson (1975, p. 51) suggests, for a party 'To allow a man who will otherwise lose to buck the party line may cost it the election of others ... Democratic politics requires high internal party discipline.' Thus some local government areas will be safe for one of the two main parties, and others will be more competitive, in which small changes in either or both of voter attitudes and party policy proposals could cause an election to be won or lost.

The Downs model and government spending

As developed here, political power in local government is contested by two national parties, but because local government areas differ in the political attitudes of their voters, the nature of the contest varies spatially. The present section develops from this position, presenting two major models of how the pattern of government spending might reflect the geography of the contests.

The adversary model

Each party has a base in one of the wings of the ideological attitude scale of the Downs model, and its policies will reflect that base. In part, the operation of such policies would seem to be self-defeating since, for example, left-wing policies might alienate centre as well as right-wing voters, producing defeat at the next election, a situation which Finer (1975) suggests is currently typical of the British electoral system. Furthermore, many voters in the centre are relatively apathetic towards local political issues unless their own self-interests are seriously affected, as suggested by their turn-out at elections. Parties can hope to carry sufficient of these voters, when necessary, and perhaps convince them that what they are doing is for the general good. Thus we have a *mandated adversary model*, in which a party proceeds to introduce its policies, whatever the margin of its electoral victory.

The *careful adversary model*, on the other hand, suggests that parties elected on narrow electoral margins in certain areas will not be as likely to push policies reflecting their 'wing' as will those having large majorities. Whereas once elected the mandated adversary party of the left might proceed with large programmes of public spending, therefore, the careful adversary party of the left might move much more cautiously, preferring to be judged as neither a squanderer nor a miser in its use of local taxes; good government is careful government.

Both alternatives of this model might be relevant in different situations, depending on the local and national environments. Mandated adversary policies might be applied for certain programmes, perhaps, especially if they are not too costly or do not impinge greatly on the public consciousness, whereas careful adversary policies might be more relevant in other budgetary sectors. Evaluation of the model must take account of particular, local circumstances (in space and time), therefore, rather than rely on general hypotheses.

The vote-buying model

Assume two local government areas with voter distributions like those in Fig. 5.3b and d. Both are ruled by the party of the left. In the former, the party has a very safe hold on the electorate, and it would take a major shift of attitudes to the right for the party to be in any danger of electoral defeat. In the latter (Fig. 5.3d), however, its hold on power is much more marginal. How will the party differ in its policies between these areas?

In the former area—the safe left-wing territory—its general policy could well be one of benign neglect, except with regard to issues which are central to the party's ideology and which its supporters require it to operate. But there is no need for great activity by the party in wooing voter support, since it has plenty to ensure continued electoral success. If the voters feel strongly about an issue they can, in Hirschman's (1970) terminology, use the *voice* option, articulating demands to which the government will respond. With no apparent *exit* option for voters, however, there is no general call for an active government, since voters have no available alternative.

In the more marginal local government areas, on the other hand, there is an obvious *exit* option available—a vote for the other party could well contribute to the incumbent's defeat. The government in this case must buy *loyalty* by responding to perceived and voiced needs. The more marginal the electoral situation, the more responsive the government will be in operating policies which will buy votes—Boulding's (1973) grants of fear.

According to this model, then, the more marginal the electoral situation facing a government the more it will spend to the benefit of those it hopes will vote for it. (This hypothesis assumes that both needs and resources are held constant.) Which voters it will focus its spending on will depend on the nature of the local electorate. In general, however, it has usually been argued that such vote-buying concentrates on the relatively poor. Government, it is assumed, is allied with, if not in the hands of, the capitalist class, and will only tax its supporters further in order to pay for welfare policies which are of much more benefit to the working class if such taxation helps to win power, and so is in the interests of the ruling group. Vote-buying, then, should involve relatively high levels of spending on welfare state policies.

Local governments: adversaries or vote buyers?

Which of these models is likely to be most relevant, in which situations? Local governments are responsible for a wide range of services relevant to the welfare state, and where they have freedom in deciding how much to spend on various services, it may well be that the vote-buying model is the most relevant, so that

$$E = f(N, R, M)$$

where E is expenditure *per capita*; N is needs; R is resources; and M is electoral marginality. In addition, however, parties differ in their dispositions towards spending. This is particularly the case in Britain with the clear difference between the Labour and Conservative parties in attitudes to levels of public expenditure. American parties are not as ideological and there is no strong socialist movement (Stave, 1976), but analyses have suggested that the Democrat party for example, is generally more favourably disposed towards welfare spending (Ripley *et al.*, 1973). Thus the model should be expanded to

$$E = f(N, R, M, D)$$

where D is dispositions towards public welfare spending.

Tests of this model, in the form presented here, are relatively few, but there has been a great body of research aimed at parts of it. The remainder of this chapter summarizes its findings, within the context of the present argument.

Spending in the American States

The original political hypothesis on state expenditure levels, like so many others in American political science, was presented in Key's (1949) classic study of the South, in which he suggested that the one-party states, especially those with no stable intra-party factions, had conservative policies aimed at benefiting upper socio-economic status groups only. His idea was taken up by Lockard (1959), who compared the three modified one-party Republican states (Maine, New Hampshire, and Vermont) with the three competitive states (Connecticut, Massachusetts, and Rhode Island) in New England. He found that in the former group (the one-party states) taxation was much more regressive—taking relatively little from the rich and from business—and that spending on welfare programmes was relatively low (Table 5.4. New Hampshire is above the national average on spending but below that for the two-party states, except for AFDC). Lockard also indicated how the vote-buying is worked by the Republican party in Connecticut and Rhode Island. In both, the party is dominated by small-town and rural members, but seats are needed from suburban areas to obtain a legislative majority, so that although the small-town/rural legislators are against the high levels of public expenditure shown in Table 5.4 (Lockard, 1959, p. 333), 'so long as there remains the hope of victory, the small-town Republicans can often be persuaded not to act so as to embarrass the rest of the party' and thereby lose the suburban vote.

Table 5.4

State politics and vote-buying in New England

	Con- necticut	Two- Party Massa- chusetts	Rhode Island	New Hampshire	One- Party Maine	Vermont
			State			
Taxation Revenue						
% from Business	23·8	28·5	25·0	7·9	12·5	16·2
% Death/Gift Duties	5·4	4·4	3·3	4·5	3·4	1·9
Welfare Spending (100 = U.S. average per recipient)						
Aid to Blind	194	201	134	109	62	59
Aid to Disabled	259	237	152	147	64	66
Old Age Assistance	217	189	122	121	69	65
Aid to Families with Dependent Children	209	189	147	180	70	66
Per Capita Income (100 = U.S. average)	135	114	106	94	86	83

Source: Lockard (1959, pp. 329, 332). Copyright © 1959 by Princeton University Press and reprinted with their permission.

Statistical analyses: environment versus political system

Both Key and Lockard presented only qualitative evaluations of the vote-buying model, but their work has been followed by a large number of quantitative analyses. The first of these was by Dawson and Robinson (1963), who used four sets of independent variables to account for variations in levels of spending by states (Dawson and Robinson, 1965).

(1) Environment: they hypothesized that the more 'developed' states were, with higher levels of urbanization, industrialization, and residents who were either foreign-born, or the children of foreign-born, then the more liberal public spending would be.
(2) Needs: the greater the needs, the greater the spending.
(3) Resources: the higher the *per capita* incomes, the more that could be taxed and spent.
(4) Political dispositions: the more marginal the state, and the more motivated the voters (the higher the level of turn-out), the greater the welfare effort.

Rank correlations were used to test the hypotheses for each variable separately. The results (Table 5.5) confirm the hypotheses for environment, resources, and dispositions for three of the dependent variables, but there are two unexpected sets of results: first, correlations with total spending are low,

Table 5.5

Welfare spending in the American States, 1961: rank correlations

Independent variables	Dependent variable			
	Average payment per recipient	% payment from local tax	Per capita local tax	Per capita total spending
Environment				
Per cent urban	0·62	0·68	0·52	0·19
Per cent industrial	0·39	0·51	0·33	0·05
Per cent foreign	0·75	0·79	0·60	0·19
Needs				
Infant mortaility rate	−0·63	−0·56	−0·28	−0·17
Children without both parents (%)	−0·60	−0·53	−0·44	−0·03
Children not finishing high school (%)	−0·60	−0·43	−0·54	−0·03
Resources				
Per capita income	0·75	0·83	0·55	0·034
Political dispositions				
Inter-party competition	0·60	0·75	0·57	0·06
Turn-out (%)	0·53	0·55	0·39	0·08

Source: from Dawson and Robinson (1965, pp. 400–6). Copyright © 1965 by Little, Brown and Company, Inc.

indicating that federal grants to a considerable extent rectify the low levels of local revenue-raising for welfare spending; and secondly, the results for needs indicate that the greater the demand for spending, the less that is spent.

The independent variables in this analysis are themselves closely interrelated, and so Dawson (1967) expanded the work by using partial rank-order correlations. From these, he concluded that the environmental variables made the major contribution to a prediction of welfare spending levels, and that (Dawson, 1967, p. 237) 'the level of inter-party competition is not the crucial factor, intervening between socio-economic factors and policy outputs, that our original hypothesis and theory suggested'. Further analysis confirmed this (Dawson and Gray, 1971); because marginal states are the more developed states, there is no independent vote-buying effect or, as Dye (1966, p. 144) concluded from a very large investigation of 54 different policies, 'There is no empirical evidence to support the contention that party competition has any liberalizing effect on welfare policies', so that (p. 341)

Economic growth rather than party competiton will be the most significant factor in improvements in state education, welfare, highways, and tax programs. Negroes ... will find that economic development will define what the can provide in the way of public services as it has defined it for white policy makers.

Cho and Frederickson (1973a), too, concluded that the environmental variables accounted for variations in spending better than did those for political dispositions, although the latter group were relatively more important for programmes with a large local content, which were more 'person-oriented' (for example, welfare payments rather than highways expenditure), and which were politically more controversial.

The work of Sharkansky, spread over a decade, has been more broadly based and analytically sophisticated than any discussed so far. His position is that although general statements can be made on the basis of quantitative analyses, each state government's policies reflect the interaction of a unique set of historical and contemporary influences. Thus Oklahoma, despite being a very safe Democrat State, paid an average of $24.50 to welfare recipients in 1968 compared to a national average of $20.55 and only $6.95 in neighbouring Texas; this resulted from Oklahoma's experience of the depression, and its imposition then of a 2 per cent sales tax to finance welfare programmes (Sharkansky, 1972, p. 42). Similarly, Alabama has for long been very generous in payments to the old, as has Louisiana in its provision of a free education system, but many states are very constrained in what taxation they can raise, and how they can spend it, by their constitutions (Sharkansky, 1969, p. 88).

In his quantitative analyses, Sharkansky used many more variables than, for example, Dye, arguing that the latter's findings on the primacy of economic development variables were based on fairly weak correlations (Sharkansky and Hofferbert, 1971, p. 30). Initial investigations produced results similar to Dye's, however (Sharkansky, 1968), but later work showed that political dispositions were important independent variables (Sharkansky, 1969), particularly with regard to spending on welfare and education, but not on highways and natural resources because (Sharkansky and Hofferbert, 1971, p. 340) the latter policies.

produce conflict, but few of the issues seem to array taxpayers into the economic haves against recipients of the services and the have-nots ... Highways, parks and conservation programs are financed by earmarked taxes, licenses and user fees: thus, recipients pay for most of the benefits received.

The fiscal effort needed for different types of spending varies considerably, too, according to the federal grant formula (Tresch, 1975), so that some poor states are unable to raise sufficient to pay large sums to their many potential aid recipients. Indeed (Sharkansky, 1972, p. 120), 'The natural course of action for Mississippi and other low income states is to offer the low payments, receive the top Federal dollars, and provoke welfare recipients to move elsewhere', because in 1969 the federal grant for welfare programmes was 31/37 of the first $37 paid but only 50–65 per cent of the next $38 and nothing thereafter. The fiscal effort is not possible where resources are poor, irrespective of needs, leading to calls for a federal takeover of all welfare payments (Albin and Stein, 1971).

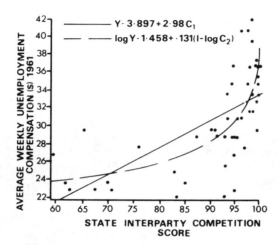

FIG. 5.4   The relationship between state government marginality and the level of unemployment benefits. Source: Wright (1975, p. 802).

On methods and interpretations

There are clearly considerable variations between researchers in the weight which they imply for the different independent variables. In part this reflects their methods (Munns, 1975), as suggested in Fig. 5.4 from Wright's (1975) work: the straight-line relationship between marginality (IPC) and level of unemployment benefits in 1961 accounts for only 40 per cent of the variance in the latter, whereas the curvilinear relationship accounts for 55 per cent. According to the latter finding, there is little difference in benefit levels between states all of which are highly non-competitive, but in the competitive states, slight variations in marginality produce major changes in the policy response.

One of the most detailed methodological critiques was provided by Fenton and Chamberlayne (1969), who paid particular attention to the opposite findings regarding the role of dispositions reported by Dye (1966) and by Fenton (1966). Some of their discussion focused on statistical errors by Dye, and they showed that, in fact, he was almost certain not to obtain substantial influences for dispositions variables because of the partial correlation procedures adopted. Fenton's tabulations, on the other hand (Table 5.6), showed that *both* the greater the resources in a state the larger the benefits (along rows) *and* the greater the competition (up columns) the larger the benefit: similar findings have been reported in a reworking (Johnston, 1978d) of Wohlenberg's (1976a, 1976b, 1976c) findings regarding the AFDC programme.

Table 5.6
Resources, dispositions, and welfare benefits

| Competitiveness of Political System | Per Capita *Income in State* | | |
	High	Medium	Low
Per capita expenditure (total less federal grant) 1959 ($)			
High	14.24	11.66	8.13
Medium	10.01	9.01	9.32
Low		6.71	6.67
Per recipient expenditure, AFDC programme ($)			
High	40.01	33.02	41.22
Medium	33.56	35.75	29.97
Low		17.24	16.92
Per capita expenditure on education ($)			
High	251.23	222.93	230.53
Medium	232.09	215.20	183.52
Low		195.07	130.16

Source: Fenton (1966, p. 38)

Competition is not independent of either environment or resources, however, as Table 5.6 shows, which is one reason why many of the partial correlation results have been very poor (Johnston, 1978b). The effects of the variables can only be interpreted in the light of theory in such cases (Rakoff and Schaefer, 1970) and, as Sharkansky (1971a, p. 724) points out,

Despite the prominence of the economics–policy relationship ... its proponents have failed to specify how the level of economic development may affect public policies. Two contradictory models of economic–policy linkages appear in the literature: one that sees policy-makers responding directly to the resources available in a jurisdiction, and another that sees policy-makers offering the most generous services where resources are poorest.

But why do either, unless the voters demand it and the governing party needs their votes? Industrialization and urbanization reflect development of a class system, attract ethnic groups with certain political values, and encourage the growth of mass organizations to represent the various political views. Thus competition is a function of industrialization and urbanization. If it were a direct, linear consequence, then it would have no independent effect (Cnudde and McCrone, 1969), but competition is often muted by electoral abuses (Chapter 8) and its effect on policies affected by nuances of political organization. Thus urbanization/industrialization creates the environment for a competitive political system, which might then influence the spending levels.

The ability/disposition of parties to react to a competitive political situation has been proposed as an extra independent variable by Fenton (1966). He identifies two types of two-party competitive states, those which he called issue-oriented, in which welfare-spending was an important policy focus, and those called job-oriented, in which (Fenton, 1966, pp. 66–7) politicians participate

out of a desire for jobs, contracts, or other personal gains rather than because of a concern for public policy ... programs that reallocate goods and opportunities are minimized, for the low-income voter seldom casts his ballot in terms of economic self-interest—thereby enabling the politician to largely ignore his needs.

Comparison of states in the two groups (Table 5.7) showed that indeed the governments of the issue-oriented spent more on welfare.

Table 5.7

Type of state government and welfare spending

State	Two-party com-petition score*	Per cent income in state tax	Per cent income on welfare	Per cent income on education
Job-oriented				
Ohio	77	6·9	0·55	15·7
Indiana	83	8·0	0·34	16·9
Illinois	89	6·7	0·45	15·4
Issue-Oriented				
Minnesota		10·3	0·76	20·6
Wisconsin	73	9·3	0·62	18·2
Michigan	80	8·7	0·60	18·9

*100 = most competitive. No score for Minnesota because it has a non-partisan legislature
Source: Fenton (1966, p. 76)

In similar vein, Carmines (1974) suggested that the degree of professionalization of the state legislature could strongly influence the policy response (professionalism was measured by such variables as the payments to the legislators, the size of their staffs, and the volume of work done: Grumm, 1971). His analyses showed that among the 'professional' legislatures there was a strong correlation between competition and spending, but the same was not the case in the more 'amateur' states. Full-time politicians, in other words, are more likely to react to voter demands in the manner postulated here.

To try and get closer to an identification of the true causal relationships, recent workers have replaced partial correlation methods by path analysis, which separates out independent effects within causal chains (Duncan, 1966;

Johnston, 1978a), but still cannot solve the theoretical problem of causal primacy in joint effects. Thus Tompkins (1975), for example, concluded that whereas industrialization and income create conditions of need and resources, it requires relatively high competition levels for the resources to be brought to bear on the needs, although foreign-born residents are better able to articulate their demands and get them met. Asher and van Meter (1974) suggested that legislative professionalism was perhaps more important than competition, however, and Dye (1975) still remains unconvinced of the role of competition. The debate will undoubtedly continue, therefore, since, in Dye's (1975, p. 293) words 'The object is to explain public policy, and not to assert the primacy of politics or economics in determining policy outcomes.'

Patterns of change

As well as the proscribed limitations on taxation and spending, one of the major constraints on local government policy-makers in the United States is what Sharkansky (1970b) terms incrementalism. Most state and local legislatures are relatively weak—their members are only part-time, have small personal support staffs, have little administrative experience, etc. Consequently, some of the most powerful individuals in the governing process are the permanent administrators, who are generally fairly conservative and not particularly innovative in policy developments. One result of their power is that, as Davis *et al.* (1966) showed, the main determinant of the size and structure of this year's budget is the size and structure of last year's budget (Rose, 1976a).

Table 5.8

Innovativeness and competitiveness of state politics

Type of state	Education	Mean rank for states on Welfare	Civil rights	All policies
One-party Democrat	27·4	34·2	48·0	35·0
Modified one-party Democrat	23·6	30·3	41·0	29·9
Two-party competitive	23·5	18·9	17·9	20·2
Modified one-party Republican	27·9	22·0	31·9	26·8

Source: data from Gray (1973)

Within this general trend, state legislators are free to attempt innovations, as Walker (1969), Gray (1973), and others have shown. If the general vote-buying model outlined here is correct, then it should apply to innovativeness; the more marginal a government's electoral position the more it should attempt to buy security through new policies. To test this, Gray's data can be used. She rank ordered the 48 conterminous states according to when they introduced certain legislation (rank of 1 = the first to introduce) in the fields of education, welfare, and civil rights. The mean ranks for each class of state, according to Ranney (Fig. 3.1), are given in Table 5.8, and clearly indicate the greater innovativeness of the competitive states, especially in the welfare and civil rights fields.

Detailed studies of changing patterns of expenditure have illustrated the strength of the incremental conservatism (Albin and Stein, 1971). Within this, Gray (1976, p. 240) hypothesized that 'to the degree that party leaders feel threatened by competition, they will mobilize voters and offer policy benefits to attract "have-nots"'. According to this competitive threat theory, policy expenditure this year should be related both to policy expenditure last year and to marginality and turn-out at the last election. Although there was some evidence to support this proposition, however, the correlations were mostly weak and the signs not always as predicted.

Other studies of changing expenditures have produced slightly more encouraging results relative to the competitive threat theory. Cho and Frederickson (1973a) indicated that political variables became more important as determinants of spending between 1962 and 1967–9 and were clearly more closely associated with the patterns of change than were economic variables. Asher and van Meter (1974) tested three models.

(1) AFDC spending at t_2 = f (all variables at t_1)
(2) AFDC spending at t_2 = f (change in all variables $t_1 - t_2$)
(3) Change in AFDC spending $t_1 - t_2$ = f (change in all variables $t_1 - t_2$)

Over all, the first produced the highest correlations and confirmed the incrementalism theory, but the third, which focused entirely on change, showed that the greater the increase in electoral competitiveness, the greater the change in spending.

State spending and the redistribution of income

The suggestion from the models and the tests of them reported here is that the more competitive states have more progressive tax systems and more liberal welfare policies. As a result, those states should display more redistribution of income towards the low-income groups, producing a geography of income redistribution. To test whether this was so, Fry and Winters (1970) calculated for each state the percentage of state taxes paid by each income group and the percentage of state expenditures which it received: the ratio of the two (receipts/taxes) provided an index of redistribution.

For households earning less than \$4000 per annum, the redistribution ratio ranged from 3·32 (Massachusetts) to 1·62 (Virginia). Correlations with economic and political variables led to a conclusion which was the opposite of that proposed (Fry and Winters, 1970, p. 521): 'Our data lead us to reject the venerable Key hypothesis that an increased level of inter-party competition will increase the level of redistribution in the states.' The less competitive states were redistributing more, it seemed, although Sullivan (1972) criticized the finding on the basis of variable selection.

A more telling critique of Fry and Winters's work was produced by Booms and Halldorson (1973), who produced an alternative set of redistribution indices, ranging from 6·00 in Massachusetts to 1·54 in South Dakota. These were positively correlated to electoral competition, and the means for states in the Ranney classification confirm this (Table 5.9). Clearly there are difficult problems of measurement in this area, and as yet there is no definitive evidence for or against the general theory.

Table 5.9
State politics and income redistribution

| | Mean redistribution ratio according to | |
Type of state	Fry and Winters	Booms and Halldorson
One-party Democrat	2·07	2·08
Modified one-party Democrat	1·99	2·38
Two-party competitive	2·23	3·70
Modified one-party Republican	2·00	2·22

Source: data from Fry and Winters (1970) and Booms and Halldorson (1973)

Spending within states

States are major political units and are used for much data reporting, so it is not surprising that much analysis has been at that level. Many decisions are made by local governments, but often within the cues, guidelines, and constraints outlined by their superior authorities (Sharkansky, 1970b). Nevertheless, there are considerable variations within states in the operation of policies. Sharkansky and Hofferbert (1971, p. 346), for example, computed inter-county coefficients of variation for each of 36 states on five welfare programmes, producing the following over-all mean variations (in percentages).

Aid to the Aged	15·4	Aid to the Blind	28·8
Aid to the Disabled	17·2	AFDC	14·8
General Assistance	51·7		

Greatest variability was for General Assistance, for which there are no federal grants and guidelines, and in some states no state guidelines either. No clear relationships between county patterns of spending and either political or economic variables were discovered (Sharkansky 1971a, 1971b). Instead, the main determinant of variations seemed to be the decisions of particular administrators (Sharkansky and Hofferbert, 1971, p. 349):

The equality of payments can be skewed by the peculiar actions of a few county welfare boards, whose work is less public than that of state officials. It may be easy for personal norms, political bargains, or numerous other factors to enter the decision process in individual counties.

The validity of this conclusion is illustrated by detailed studies in Massachusetts (Derthick, 1968, 1970). Some of the differences there in operation of welfare payments reflected community size and type (Table 5.10) with rural areas least generous and the cities most, especially with General Assistance. The relative liberality of the cities was very much a function of policies in Boston alone, however, where decision-making was decentralized to local, liberal officials. As Derthick (1968, p. 256) showed in a comparison of two towns of similar size, where the local administrators must apply the rules rigidly, according to directives from their chiefs, liberality of payments is rare.

Table 5.10

Welfare policy operation in Massachusetts

| | Rural | Type of community | | | City |
		Urban upper middle class	Urban middle class	Urban lower middle class	
Number of places	232	34	33	23	29
Average number AFDC recipients	7·7	24·7	37·9	46·9	
AFDC payments per month ($)	40.16	40.93	40.53	41.56	43.99
Medical payments per month ($)	6.28	6.79	7.18	6.87	5.79
Non-medical payments per month ($)	0.29	0.36	0.29	0.31	0.69
General Assistance payments per month ($)	21.01	24.79	25.79	36.97	38.75

Source: Derthick (1968, p. 262 and 1970, p. 82)

Derthick's findings are that, with the exception of General Assistance, the externally written rules for the federal grant programmes allow little scope for local political influence on welfare spending levels within the state programme. General Assistance is clearly political, since it is locally controlled, but variations in AFDC spending reflect the particular orientations of certain officials. This was shown also by Greenstone and Peterson (1968), who illustrated the greater success of the cities dominated by machine-politics—and thus highly centralized power—at obtaining Community Action Program funds. Democracy or benefits?!

Summary: and policy impacts

No concise summary of the work reviewed here is possible. Nevertheless, the vote-buying model does appear to be a relevant one, particularly with regard to welfare payments for the relatively poor who live where their votes are important. Dispositions are of importance, too, usually those of a conservative nature (measured by Tresch, 1975, for example, as percentage voting for Goldwater in 1964) but also those related to racial discrimination and the different political ethos of various immigrant groups. Such conclusions are drawn from studies which differ considerably in their methodologies and technical procedures, some of which have been questioned by others; the likelihood of a single, unqualified conclusion is remote, therefore, and the scope for future research great.

One of the problems with all of the research discussed here is that, because of the nature of available data, measurement of the policies has almost always been in dollar terms. Some studies have used their data with care—as with Wohlenberg's (1976b) investigation of the extent to which AFDC payments lift families out of the poverty bracket—but in general it is assumed that more spending is a 'good thing'. And yet the Coleman (1966) report on education, for example, showed little relationship between educational provision and educational attainment. Consequently, Sharkansky (1970b, p. 106) has developed the concept of what he terms the 'spending-service cliché', which 'assumes a relationship between spending levels and service levels, and promises service improvements by officials who increase spending. We evaluate this premise by comparing levels of government spending with levels of public service. The assumed linkage is frequently absent.'

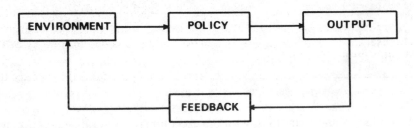

Fig. 5.5   Sharkansky's policy-impact model.

To support the final assertion, Sharkansky (1970c) studied the relationship between educational spending and output in Georgia, using a simple feedback model (Fig. 5.5) reminiscent of Easton's (Fig. 2.2). In this:

(1) Environment represented the demand for education;
(2) Policy represented various elements of spending on education;
(3) Output represented educational success (graduation rates, etc.).

The correlations between the sets of variables were all low, indicating that policy had very little impact on the output of the educational process, in terms of the variables studied: higher teacher salaries and smaller classes did not produce better overt educational success rates.

Does such a lack of correlation matter? In part it depends on the policy. Welfare recipients are likely to be impressed by larger payments, for example. For educational and other services, politicians can use spending as the lowest common denominator, boasting to the right audiences about how much they have invested in this service or, like Carter in Georgia, indicating how much unnecessary expenditure they have saved. In other words, if the electorate accepts the 'spending–service cliché' then the politician uses it.

Local authority spending in Britain

Within the context of the model

$$E = f (N, M, R, D)$$

D is more likely to be of importance in Britain than in the United States because of the more ideological orientation of the two main political parties in the former. Therefore, in this case, the adversary model should be more relevant than the vote-buying model, although large values of M could lead Conservative-ruled councils to increase spending in order to attract support from the 'have-nots'; Labour councils, on the other hand, may hold spending down in such situations in order to win votes from the 'haves'. In British local government elections, however, it is very unclear to what extent voters change their preferences from one party to another: most, it would seem, prefer to abstain if for some reason they wish not to vote for the party that they usually support, in which case the vote-buying model would seem to be largely irrelevant. Elections are won and lost by ensuring that your traditional supporters vote (see Taylor and Johnston, 1979, Chapter 6), not by policy initiatives aimed at the 'other side'.

Relatively little research has been reported which concerns the topic of this chapter, and much of what has been done refers only to the county boroughs of the pre-1974 reorganization. The largest volume of work has been conducted by Bleddyn Davies and his associates, but although his book (Davies, 1968) included one variable for political dispositons (percentage voting Labour), this was virtually ignored in the analysis. The main theme is that territorial justice involves a perfect match of services to needs, and a major conclusion is that the size of a local authority influences considerably the extent to which its council can meet needs within its territory; the greater the potential economies of scale, the better the local government is able to meet the needs of a wide range of minority groups.

The major work which uses all of the variables in the model, except M, is Boaden's (1971) investigation of variations during the 1960s among the 82 county boroughs in their spending on five areas—education, housing, personal social services, police and fire services, and libraries—and in their rate demands (fiscal effort). Indices of needs, resources (rateable value, rate levied, rate deficiency grant, etc.) and dispositions (Labour dominance, voter turn-out, administrative professionalism, etc.) were defined for each depen-dent variable, and relationships sought through the use of simple and partial correlations.

All three sets of independent variables proved to have significant associa-tions with spending levels with, not surprisingly, needs providing the most consistent set of relationships. In particular, Boaden (1971, p. 111) suggested that it was the concrete, visible needs—as in education—which produced the best relationships: 'Social problems in their more personal manifestations are much less easy to grasp and involve a great deal of subjective assessment.' Regarding dispositions, he found that in general Labour councils tended to spend more, especially on the biggest service areas and those which were more likely to benefit their supporters. The public impact, through voter turn-out, produced only weak spending relationships, as expected, and with regard to resources, as in America the poorest authorities tended to spend the most and to make the greatest fiscal effort (see also Oliver and Stanyer, 1969). Without the rate support grant, there would, it seems, be no redistribution from relatively rich to relatively poor, and even with it, according to Taylor (1971, pp. 346–7), speaking of education,

It is true that government grants narrow the gap between wealthy and poor authorities. But they do not produce equality of wealth, or less equality in relation to need . . . Many local authorities in the north are solvent only because they have few new schools (and therefore low debt charges), below-average numbers of children at school over the age of fifteen, and relatively few students at universities. If expenditure in these categories approached the national average . . . the demand on the rates would be beyond the capacity of the ratepayers to pay.

Thus needs are greatest, resources least, and dispositions to spend most favourable all in the same areas. There are many categories of need, however; the smaller on average an authority's schools, for example, the more expensive they are to run (Dawson, 1976).

Turning to Boaden's detailed findings regarding the dispositions component, Table 5.11 lists all of the zero-order correlations for percentage Labour, plus the main first- and second-order partial correlations holding constant various indices of needs and resources. Only with police and library services, and probably fire services too, all of which mostly benefit the middle class, do Labour councils spend relatively little, *ceteris paribus*. For all of the others, even when holding constant needs and resources, the mandated adversary model would appear to be valid.

Detailed investigations of local authority expenditure on housing and on roads have been reported by two economists, who used a model not very dissimilar from that of Boaden. Two theoretical constructs were derived. The first—Social Marginal Efficiency of Investment (SMEI)—is analogous to needs; the second—Social Marginal Cost of Funds (SMCF)—is comparable to resources. A set of variables was chosen to represent each, plus a third set

Table 5.11

Labour strength and local spending

Dependent variable	Zero-order correlations with % Labour	Partial correlations Variables held constant	
Per capita spending on education	0·52	Age 5–14: SES IV/V	0·31
		Age 5–14: rate support grant (R.S.G.)	0·25
		SES IV/V: R.S.G.	0·35
Percentage local housing built by Council	0·67	SES IV/V: crowding	0·38
		SES IV/V: R.S.G.	0·38
		Crowding: R.S.G.	0·54
Rate subsidy to housing account	0·47	SES IV/V: % council housing	0·40
		SES IV/V: R.S.G.	0·28
		% council housing: R.S.G.	0·48
Per capita spending on health services	0·33	SES IV/V: amenities in homes	0·14
		SES IV/V: R.S.G.	0·21
		R.S.G.: amenities in homes	0·15
Per capita spending on children's services	0·31	Size: amenities in homes	0·16
		Turn-out: amenities in homes	0·13
		Size: turn-out	0·30
Size of rate levied	0·44	SES I/II: R.S.G.	0·31
		SES I/II: rateable value	0·31
		R.S.G.: rateable value	0·31
Per capita spending on welfare services	0·01		
Per capita spending on fire services	0·24	Size: SES IV/V	−0·16
		R.S.G: SES IV/V	−0·19
		Size: R.S.G.	0·15
Per capita spending on police services	−0·23	Size: SES I/II	−0·15
		Size: density	−0·33
		Size: R.S.G.	−0·28
		Density: R.S.G.	−0·30
Per capita spending on library services	−0·06		

Source: various tables in Boaden (1971)

relating to local attitudes (dispositions). For the study of housing expenditure (Nicholson and Topham, 1971). SMEI was indexed by measures of housing conditions, SMCF by the authority's financial situation, and attitudes by percentage Labour on the council. The SMEI variables dominated the multiple regressions, suggesting that the volume of house-building is a reaction to poor local housing conditions; in addition, the SMCF variables suggested the operation of incrementalism—once a big spender on housing always a big spender—whereas local attitudes were of no significance (perhaps because of collinearity in that housing needs are generally greatest in authorities with Labour councils).

For their study of expenditure on roads, Nicholson and Topham (1975) used such variables as congestion and peak-hour traffic flows to represent SMEI. Again, these dominated the multiple regression results, though incrementalism was clearly a relevant factor also. On local attitudes, they concluded with regard to both studies (Nicholson and Topham, 1975, p. 22), in apparent disappointment, that 'the political balance variable does not reveal itself to be significant in either area'.

Nicholson and Topham, like Boaden, studied only the county boroughs in these two papers; the majority of these authorities are Labour-controlled (the mean percentage of council seats held by Labour was 60: Nicholson, Topham, and Watt, 1975), however, so it may be that they do not provide a good environment in which to study the effect of the adversary model, with insufficient marginal and safe Conservative C.B.s. Comparison of small and large county boroughs (Nicholson and Topham, 1972) did produce a stronger correlation with dispositions in the former category, but extension of the housing study to all types of authorities, although producing better fits to the model (i.e. more predictable decision-making) in the larger, urban authorities than in the rural areas, produced no further results of relevance to the adversary model (Nicholson, Topham, and Watt, 1975).

Table 5.12

Party control of local authorities, 1949–1967

| | County boroughs | | Counties | |
Number of election wins	Labour	Conservative	Labour	Conservative
6–7	23	11	12	10
1–5	44	39	17	19
0	16	32	30	30

Source: Ashford (1975, p. 291) by permission of the publisher, Sage Publications, Inc.

A study of both county boroughs and the counties over the period 1949–67 has been reported in several papers by Ashford. Election results for the counties, in particular, suggest a better setting for study of the adversary model (Table 5.12), especially since he was also able to study the degree of politicization of a council (the extent to which its seats are held by members of the main national parties). Perhaps not surprisingly, given the spatial division of labour, Ashford (1975) found that the borough councils spent more per resident than the county councils. Amongst the boroughs, politicization was highest where resources were least, suggesting greater political competition for the votes of the poor: amongst the counties, on the other hand, the richest were the most politicized, but the poorest were the biggest spenders per resident, suggesting enlightened altruism aided by the Rate Support Grant (counties get more from this source than do county boroughs: Ashford, 1974).

Ashford also looked in detail at changes over time. According to the adversary model, the greatest variations in spending should be in local governments which change hands. He found (Ashford, 1975, pp. 302–7) that

there appears to be less correspondence between spending levels over time where, first, no one party has dominated the borough or county throughout the period, and where, second, some degree of interparty activity has occurred such that neither party has been excluded throughout that period ... boroughs with more changes in party influence do make more changes in per capita spending in relation to each other

which leads to the conclusion (p. 309) that 'Despite the many constraints toward uniformity in over-all policy in British local government, party politics may yet produce differences that make party choices at the local level of more than marginal concern'. This investigation of the effect of party change in government on incrementalism is of value since, as Newton (1976a) notes, comparison of counties and county boroughs is needed because of the strong Labour hegemony over the latter. Most of the county boroughs are highly politicized (Ashford *et al.*, 1975), are relatively poor and so have Labour governments, and study of the relevance of the adversary model is impeded by this fact.

Ashford studied variations in total spending only, which may have clouded some of the differences predicted by the adversary model and picked out by Boaden's sectoral analysis (Table 5.11). Thus, according to Newton (1976a)

It is true that Labour and Conservative cities do not differ in many respects, but these tend to be the less significant services such as parks, libraries, sewerage, refuse, police, and fire, although their similarities on housing are more notable. On the other hand, there is a fair weight of evidence to show that the more costly and highly politicised services such as education, housing and personal services are influenced by political control, the Labour cities generally spending more.

This reflects the almost complete concentration on the adversary model in the British literature, and only Alt (1971) has looked at the relevance of the vote-buying alternative. Using measures of both M and D, he found among the county boroughs during the 1958–68 period that:

(1) Labour councils raise higher rates, with no correlation with M (indexed by the usual inter-party competition measure);
(2) both Labour councils and more marginal councils spend more *per capita* on education;
(3) Labour councils spend less than Conservative councils on the police service, and there is no relationship with M;
(4) both Labour councils and more marginal councils spend more *per capita* on housing; and
(5) Labour councils spend more on children and on health services, with a positive relationship between M and spending on children.

According to these findings, both models are relevant to different sectors of the local budget, posing difficult analytical problems in teasing out the extent and nature of the political influence on spending.

Despite the greater importance of partisan politics in Britain than in the United States, it cannot be stated with certainty as yet that the adversary model is more relevant than the vote-buying to the study of variations in local government spending, therefore. Indeed, some commentators are not convinced about the value of either. Writing of Western Europe as a whole, for example, Fried (1976, p. 24) claimed that 'A direct, independent, and strong impact on urban policy making owing to leftist party control is quite exceptional', although he modified this conclusion somewhat in his later work (Fried, 1971, 1974, 1976).

One problem with all of the studies reviewed here may be that their aggregate, correlation-based methodology is too coarse to capture the political influences, particularly within large authorities for which the crucial question is not 'how much spending?' but 'where?' Further, relationships may not be as simple as often hypothesized. The Labour party generally rules in the poorer authorities, for example, and so may find it necessary to cut a programme, especially if it does not particularly benefit the party's supporters. Whereas Labour is generally the party of more public spending, Conservative is more oriented to the *status quo*, which is probably easier to achieve, but the latter party may be a big spender (Newton and Sharpe, undated, p. 19): 'Where relatively high levels of expenditure are seen as being essential to maintaining the overall prosperity of the town—in a seaside resort or tourist centre, for example—anti-socialist parties, as parties broadly speaking of local capital holders, may be very enthusiastic big spenders.' The complexity is very great, therefore; the results obtained so far and discussed here are perhaps very encouraging with regard to the models outlined, that are undoubtedly too simple to capture the full detail of political decision-making.

Conclusions

In a substantial review essay, Fried (1975) showed that out of thirteen separate studies conducted in different countries, nine produced results in which the variables discussed here—needs, resources, dispositions, and political competition—accounted for more than half of the variation in aspects of urban policy and local government spending. Regarding the role of political variables (D and M) he concluded (p. 337) that 'almost any political variable ... *can* at some time be regularly related to urban policy outputs ... but political variables have relatively less direct and independent impact than socioeconomic variables' from which he argued that perhaps 'The implication of these findings is that most forms of political activity are either futile, or marginal ... The socioeconomic constraints are such ... that it makes little difference for urban policy who controls urban local government, what their values are, how many people turn out to vote.' But then he decided that maybe it was the form of analysis and type of variable used which led to such a conclusion, and that the political role should not be so readily dismissed.

Only an overly optimistic researcher would expect a simple answer to any question posed in the social sciences, and this is certainly so in the field discussed here. Given the great variety and complexity of socioeconomic environments within which the political process works, the many variations within the political sphere, and the almost infinite range of public and private attitudes to the actions of governments, it is perhaps surprising that any simple model receives more than the slightest confirmation. But there is evidence that governments do react to perceived needs, in particular those of their supporters, and that they do tend to be more perceptive to such demands in relatively competitive electoral situations; in all cases, the constraint of available resources is strong, but not overpowering. Thus both the adversary and vote-buying models outlined here are relevant to the study of spatial variations in public spending; what one gets is in part a function of which jurisdiction one lives in.

6 The Spatial Pattern of a Government's Spending

In the Commonwealth elections of 1961 ... the government suffered a heavy loss of voters in ... Queensland electorates; subsequently, ... specific purpose grants to the government of Queensland, per head of the State's population, almost doubled, while similar grants per capita to the other States rose only by about 40 per cent (May, 1972, p. 251).

We know nothing about political principles abstractly considered. If a man will but promise to make us roads no matter how ... then we shall consider him worthy of support—he is a good man and ought to be elected (Quaife, 1969, p. 54: quote from the *Kilmore Examiner*, 10 October 1856).

The Railway Construction Bill, 1890 ... accommodated '80 or 85 members' interested on behalf of their constituencies ... The amended Bill ... showed a continuing bias in favour of the Government supporters with forty-four lines compared with eleven for the Opposition and thirteen shared ... the constituencies demanded more railways (Rimmer, 1975, pp. 209–11).

THESE three Australian examples indicate the operation of two political geographical processes. The first is that individual governments distribute their political money, in a spatial sense, in order to buy votes, which is a continuation of the theme of the previous chapter; the second is that candidates are elected as constituency representatives in order to get political money for the area. Both processes are focused on in the present chapter.

Governments make spending decisions as reactions to competing pressures. In many cases, the geographical implications are indirect; a house-building policy benefits the brickworks towns, for example, whereas cuts in naval expenditure harm the dockyard ports. Perceived needs are brought to a government's attention by interested groups, either directly or through their elected representatives. Discrimination between these for the limited contents of the public purse is based on many criteria; the one highlighted here concerns the electoral implications of spending.

The contents of this chapter very largely represent a geographical extension to the Downs model. Some of the evidence used to assess the validity of the proposals is based on substantial research—virtually none of it by geographers—whereas other parts are sketchy and tentative. The end result is a body of circumstantial evidence providing further building-blocks for the political–geographic foundations to human geography.

Some simple models

Rational politicians and political parties, according to the previous chapter, create policies to meet the perceived needs of the electors whose votes matter.

The geographical component to this general hypothesis is added, for the purposes of the present chapter, because of the way in which plurality elections operate. Parties face not a single distribution of voters along an ideological continuum but a series of such distributions—one per constituency—which may or may not be on identical continua (generally it is assumed here that they are). How do parties operate in such situations?

The geography of Downs

To win an election fought on pluralities, a party must win in a majority of the constituencies. To do this, it is unlikely that it can create separate policies for each; instead, its package of policies must be such as to win it sufficient pluralities (Robertson, 1976: the American party system is to some extent a contradiction of this, since there is, for example, a lot of difference between the Northern Urban and Southern Rural wings of the Democrat Party).

Fig. 6.1 illustrates the difference between an over-all vote-winning strategy

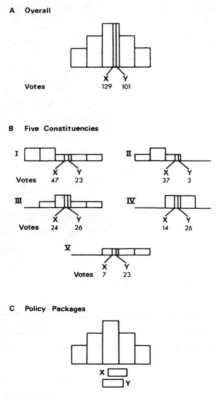

FIG. 6.1   The Downs model applied: A to an over-all voter distribution; B to five constituencies within that over-all distribution; and C to the policy packages X and Y would need to win at least three constituencies.

and a plurality strategy. The over-all distribution of voter attitudes in the territory is near-normal, so that with the policy positions indicated in Fig. 6.1A, party X would be the winner. In the five constituencies (Fig. 6.1B) comprising that over-all distribution, however, if X were to occupy the same position it would win only two and Y, with a minority of the votes, would win the election. No party produces policies for one point on the continuum, of course, but rather a package covering a certain contiguous area of it. Party X, therefore, would create a package skewed to the right of its position in Fig. 6.1 (Fig. 6.1C), because: (1) as it lies to the left of Y, all the voters to the left of its policies will support it which means that constituencies I and II are safe and the marginal utility of extra votes from them is nil (Coleman, 1968); (2) constituencies III and IV, in which the voter distributions are skewed to the right, are potentially very valuable in electoral terms and should be the focus of X's campaigning. Y, on the other hand, will ignore its safe seat—V—and focus on holding III and IV against X; I and II will be considered relatively hopeless unless a major shift in voter attitudes is possible (perhaps typical of British by-elections but not general elections; the effects of abstentions and third parties are ignored here).

The voter distributions produced by the constituency division are crucial to this model. As suggested in Chapter 4, with a normal distribution of voters the distribution of constituencies in terms of percentage support for one party is usually normal also, so that each party has some safe seats (one more than another if the distribution is skewed). With regard to winning constituencies, these safe seats are not particularly relevant, and each party is likely to develop a policy package which (Glassberg, 1973): (1) gives some 'political money' to its safe seats, as rewards for the 'party faithful' and bribes for them to stay so; (2) allocates very little 'political money' to the opposition's safe seats; and (3) distributes most 'political money' to the marginal seats, where votes won help to ensure over-all victory whereas votes lost make it less likely. If this strategy cannot win the election, then either a permanent majority–minority situation emerges, as seems to be the case in Ulster, with little vote-buying necessary and little inter-party electoral competition, or new partisan cleavages emerge which offer the possibility of a new 'coalition', a party with a core of safe seats and a winnable periphery if it can buy sufficient votes in the marginals.

There are two components to this type of electioneering: the promises and the allocation of rewards. All parties participate in the former; only the winner can operate the latter. Extending the Downs model in this way thus involves the axiom that for any one party seats can be divided into safe, hopeless, and marginal, within each of which classes there is a scale of, for example, degree of marginality. From this, it can be deduced that: (1) at an election, both (or all) parties make most promises to the voters in the marginal constituencies; and (2) when in power, a party will direct some 'political money' to its safe seats, a lot to the marginal seats (to those which it holds, as a reward and a sweetener for next time; to those which it lost, in the search for a larger victory next time); and (3) very little to its hopeless seats. These hypotheses are tested later in the chapter.

The elected representative

Elections are fought and governments formed, according to the discussion so far, by political parties. But in plurality systems, parties are represented by individual candidates, who can play a variety of roles once elected (Newton, 1976b). They may, for example, act as mandated delegates, taking instructions on how to vote from their constituents, or they may act as trustees, making what they consider to be the right decisions with reference back (Eulau *et al.*, 1959); similarly, they may be expected to follow their party's directive at all times, or they may have less fettered freedom to act as they see fit. Their electors may prefer them to act as local representatives, pushing parochial points of view and acting as a kind of ombudsman for their constituents, or they may be expected to operate in the interests of the wider electorate at large, perhaps specializing in one particular policy area. The combinations of these various roles are many: a representative may be expected to act as a local delegate on some issues, for example, but be free to vote as he thinks fit on others, irrespective of local lobbying.

The relative importance of these roles varies from country to country. In Australia, New Zealand, and the United Kingdom, for example, parliament is the sovereign body and the largest party (usually) forms the government: to protect the government party discipline must be tight, and in their legislative roles members must follow the party directive, while still being able to act for their constituents on other matters, perhaps in the formulation of government policy. Members of opposition parties are less constrained, except on vital votes, some of which may offer the chance of bringing down the government, and they are freer to act in their constituents' interests.

The division of powers between the three institutions of the United States' government—the Executive (headed by an elected President), the Congress, and the Judiciary—means that Congressional members (Senators and Representatives) are not subject to the same amount of party discipline as their counterparts just discussed. Most are elected on party labels, since access to the most powerful positions on Capitol Hill is gained through the majority party, but the roles of local representative and errand-boy, subject to lobbying pressure groups, forever seeking to further constituents' goals (in pursuit of their own, which is re-election, every two years for a Representative), are the crucial ones. Such actions may be aimed at their State as a whole, at their District within it for Representatives, or even their own home area (Tatalovich, 1975) since, according to Article I of the Constitution, all Representatives and Senators must live in the States which elect them.

Acting on the axiom that part of the power of a representative depends on his ability to get re-elected, so that obtaining 'political money' for their constituents is an important role for elected members, three general hypotheses can be suggested. The first is that members of the government party will generally be more effective at winning rewards for their constituents, because of their greater access to the seats of 'real power'. Secondly, representatives from marginal constituencies should be more responsive to their constituents' needs than those from safe seats, using the arguments advanced in the previous chapter. Finally, more senior representatives, with longer parliamentary service, can probably more successfully operate the system to their constituents' advantage than can their junior colleagues. These three are far from mutually independent, and will be tested using various data after the next section on how parties distribute political money.

Campaigning and canvassing

The removal of corrupt electoral practices (O'Leary, 1962) means that the direct buying of votes is no longer possible in the countries considered here, although illegal electoral practices are far from unusual in some (Bernstein and Woodward, 1974). But prior to an election, parties and candidates are allowed to spend certain sums on prescribed campaigning, via the media and other ways of distributing relevant information, as well as through the holding of meetings of various kinds. Parties invariably do not have as much campaign money as they would like, however, and so must decide where to spend what they can get, or what they are legally allowed to get.

Very large sums are spent on electioneering for major national offices in the United States (the classic study is Heard, 1960: see also Berry, 1974). In the contests for Congressional seats where incumbents are standing again they usually spend more on their defence than do their challengers; elsewhere, the minority party in the House, with more to gain, tends to spend most in the fight (Crain and Tollison, 1976). The implications of such activity are that campaign expenditure wins votes, that campaigning is an effective form of advertising (Palda, 1973; Welch, 1974), and that canvassing efforts should therefore be directed towards the marginal seats or areas (Blydenburgh, 1976). Evidence apparently in support of this assertion has been provided by Welch (1976), whose equation for House of Representatives contests showed that

$$\log RP = 4\cdot47 + 0\cdot10 \log RE - 0\cdot11 \log DE$$
$$+ 0\cdot01 \log RI - 0\cdot07 \log DI \qquad R^2 = 0\cdot737$$

in which RP is Republican percentage of the vote; RE is Republican expenditure during the campaign; RI is the number of years the Republican Party has held the district; and DE and DI are the same as the last two variables, but for the Democrat Party. This suggests that, *ceteris paribus*: the more the

Republican Party spent campaigning, the more votes it got; the more the Democrat Party spent campaigning, the less votes the Republican Party got; and incumbency brings more votes to the party. Several separate analyses suggested that incumbency was probably the main predictor of electoral success, but that the relationships with spending were 'real'.

Table 6.1

Campaign expenditure and votes in Welsh constituencies: October 1974 General Election

Dependent	Independents and regression coefficients		R^2
Conservative vote %	Conservative spending	+0·027	
	Labour spending	−0·007	
	Liberal spending	−0·004	
	Plaid Cymru spending	−0·009	
	Conservative incumbent	+12·376	0·864
Labour vote %	Conservative spending	−0·019	
	Labour spending	+0·003	
	Liberal spending	−0·003	
	Plaid Cymru spending	−0·010	
	Labour incumbent	+13·252	0·867
Liberal vote %	Conservative spending	+0·008	
	Labour spending	−0·007	
	Liberal spending	+0·005	
	Plaid Cymru spending	−0·002	
	Liberal incumbent	+22·873	0·866
Plaid Cymru vote %	Conservative spending	−0·014	
	Labour spending	+0·011	
	Liberal spending	−0·001	
	Plaid Cymru spending	+0·019	
	Plaid Cymru incumbent	+19·405	0·854

In Britain, there is a legal maximum to each party's campaign expenditure per constituency, the size of which is determined by the number of voters in the constituency and whether it covers an urban or a rural area. The parties are usually unable to raise the maximum sums, however, and their decisions where to spend, and where to raise money, reflect similar assumptions about the vote-buying power of campaigning as those reported for the United States. For the 33 of the 36 Welsh constituencies contested by all four parties at the October 1974 general election, equations show that, with two minor exceptions, the more a party spent, the more votes it got (holding all other variables constant), and the more its opponents spent, the less votes it got (Table 6.1)—the exceptions are that Liberal candidates apparently benefitted from Conservative spending and Plaid Cymru candidates from Labour spending. Incumbency was clearly a strong influence on success.

The inference to be drawn from these analyses of campaign expenditures is that money spent brings in votes. A better test of the effectiveness of such actions is provided by investigating whether changes in spending produce changes in total votes. If they do not, then it may just be that parties tend to spend more where they perform best, and political scientists in Britain believe that although campaigning may be good psychologically, for both candidates and party workers, electorally it is probably ineffective (Kavanagh, 1970; Rose, 1976b). But in a brief note, A. H. Taylor (1972) suggested that spending had a significant effect on changes in support for parties between 1966 and 1970.

Two steps are involved in testing for campaign effectiveness. At the first, it is necessary to inquire (as did Barnett, undated) whether parties allocate their moneys rationally according to electoral marginality. For Wales, this is calculated using the February 1974 general election results to predict spending in the following October. The dependent variable is the percentage of the allowable maximum spent by the party in each constituency; the independent variables are incumbency and either (1) if the party won in February, the distance between it (as a percentage of the poll) and that coming second, or (2) if the party lost in February, the distance between it and the winner. The results (Table 6.2) show that the more marginal the constituency for a party, the more it spent in the campaign; Conservative and Liberal spent more defending seats that they held, but Labour and Plaid Cymru were more concerned to attack those previously lost. The smaller the party, in addition, the steeper the regression slope, indicating that weak parties (in terms of finance) focus particularly on the marginals (Johnston, 1977a), but the correlations are not high.

Table 6.2

The allocation of campaign expenditure in Wales: October 1974 General Election

| Dependent variable: percentage of allowable expenditure for | Regression coefficients for independent variables | | R^2 |
	Percentage distance in February	Incumbent	
Conservative	−0·811	11·985	0·732
Labour	−0·611	−1·893	0·452
Liberal	−0·979	32·709	0·549
Plaid Cymru	−1·480	−3·353	0·643

Given a general tendency for British parties to direct campaign funds towards marginal seats, the second step in the analysis inquires into the pay-offs from their spending. First there is little evidence (Table 6.3A) that the parties readjusted their spending after the February result, using the dependent variable—Percentage Spent in October/Percentage Spent in February. A vote change variable—Votes in October/Votes in February—was then defined and the four spending change variables were used to predict vote changes. The results (Table 6.3B) show their best fits for the two smaller Welsh parties: Liberal votes tended to go up where that party spent relatively more and where the three others spent relatively less. Campaigning brought some pay-offs, but the psychological theory may be as strong as that based on the efficacy of advertising.

Table 6.3

Changing campaign and voters in Wales: general election, October 1974

A. Changes in spending and the February result

Party	Changes in spending		Regression coefficient for		R^2
	Mean	S.D.	Percentage distance in February	Incumbency	
Conservative	1·15	0·28	0·002	0·036	0·01
Labour	1·03	0·14	−0·003	0·118	0·16
Liberal	1·07	0·65	−0·017	−0·277	0·17
Plaid Cymru	0·99	0·42	−0·006	−0·112	0·04

B. Changes in spending and changes in votes

Party	Changes in votes		Regression coefficient—changes in spending				R^2
	Mean	S.D.	Conservative	Labour	Liberal	Plaid Cymru	
Conservative	0·90	0·12	−0·074	−0·174	0·055	0·010	0·12
Labour	1·06	0·05	−0·012	−0·076	0·017	−0·023	0·09
Liberal	0·83	0·38	−0·292	−0·602	0·348	−0·086	0·35
Plaid Cymru	1·07	0·25	−0·027	0·406	−0·054	0·238	0·23

Why should campaign expenditure win votes? There are two objectives to an election campaign. The first, and most important, is to win voter support; increasingly this is handled by the party leadership via the mass media. The second is to identify one's supporters and ensure that they vote, and this is the function of the local candidate and his organization. There is plenty of evidence on the value of the latter activity—canvassing (Taylor and Johnston, 1979, Chapter 6)—and the spending data used here index its intensity. But although people may cast a vote because of campaigner exhortation, how they vote will be a function of policies, for which the geography of campaign spending is but an introductory surrogate.

Pragmatic politics: the geography of allocations

The basic hypothesis being tested here is that governments create policies and |

distribute money for electoral gain; not all policies and money, of course, but enough to win the needed votes. Unfortunately, insufficient data are available for testing this fully, especially in Britain for which information on the geographical breakdown of central government spending is provided for eleven regions only (King, 1973). American data are much better, as will be indicated here.

In a comparative study of London and New York, which tested the above hypothesis, Glassberg (1973) found few relationships of the sort postulated here, despite earlier findings in New York of 'dramatic correlations between the voting returns for 1969 and the allocation of public funds' (Tolchin and Tolchin, 1971, p. 29). Perhaps Glassberg's tests were not particularly relevant, however. In the London borough of Greenwich, for example, he found that whichever party was in power, most public housing was built in Labour wards, but unless the Labour party wished to dilute a Conservative ward, such building was unlikely to occur elsewhere than in a working-class, Labour area.

Evidence from other studies is in line with Glassberg's, however, and indicates that within local government areas the spatial pattern of allocations does not reflect the electoral process. Illustrative of this work is Lineberry's (1977) study of San Antonio, Texas, in which he related a variety of service provision measures to aspects of the ecological, including the power, structure of the city. He concluded that the distribution of these public services can be best described as 'unpatterned inequality' and that this inequality is not related to the socio-economic status of the areas, nor to the residential pattern of the elected élites of San Antonio; rather, the least provided-for areas are the lower density, new developments on the edge of the city. Instead, Lineberry suggests that the major decisions about public services are made by a city bureaucracy over which there is very little political control in terms of its allocational policies. Those who are dissatisfied with such policies may choose either to voice their concerns or to move from the city (Hirschmann, 1970). Since it is the affluent who are best able to exercise the latter option, and either move to suburbia or obtain the relevant services in the private market, and the relatively poor frequently feel that the first option is of no value, that city hall cannot be influenced by the voters, the result is the continued power of the bureaucracy—a 'flabby monopoly' in Lineberry's terms—and if there is any trend towards equality in service provision, it is a levelling downwards trend. If this power-of-the-bureaucracy hypothesis is valid, and Lineberry suggests that it is for big cities of the United States in particular, then the 'geography of Downs' model developed here would seem irrelevant to patterns of spending within local governments from which the 'exit' option is available, either because of the possibilities of moving or the availability, to some at least, of alternatives to local-government-provided services from within the private sector. Thus most of the discussion in this chapter is set at a larger spatial scale, where political control of bureaucratic decisions may be closer.

Changing the spatial scale, at national level vote-buying exercises are most obvious in Britain at by-elections, when parties focus all of their attention on a particular place. Thus in January 1966 the Labour Party had to defend a majority of only 1181 in Hull North, at a time when it had a parliamentary majority of only one: given the usual trend away from the government at such by-elections, the chances of defeat were great. For many years, Hull residents had wanted the Humber estuary to be bridged, and Labour pledged in 1966 to do this. According to Crossman (1975, p. 394), 'The Ministry of Transport has no feeling for urban development or for the needs of crucial by-elections', but the Minister, Mrs. Castle, agreed to build the bridge—not 'as last minute election bribe' according to Crossman (1975, p. 437)—and Labour held the seat. The Humberside area showed its gratitude to Labour again with above-average swings at the 1966 general election (Taylor and Johnston, 1979). And then, in 1977, another vital by-election for Labour was held in Grimsby on 28 April: on 14 April, Grimsby was one of three areas raised to Development Area status to counter unemployment there (*The Times*, 15 April, 1977): Labour won the by-election. (The other areas elevated in 1977 were Hull and Shotton, where large factory closures were in the offing. Five areas had applications for similar status declined—Bridlington, Lancaster, Southport, Fleetwood and Skegness—and all but Lancaster were safe Conservative seats.)

The 1974 Labour government's policies towards Scotland also indicate its vote-buying. During the last decade, the Scottish National Party (SNP) percentage of the Scottish vote has risen from 4·7 per cent in 1966 to 30·5 per cent in October 1974, when it won 11 seats. To date, most successes have been outside the Scottish Lowlands and there has been no real threat to Labour strongholds in Glasgow and Edinburgh at general elections (later local government elections suggest otherwise). But Labour is the largest party in Scotland, and without 30–35 seats they could probably never win an over-all British parliamentary majority. As a consequence, in 1975 the government agreed to invest £150 m. in the ailing Chrysler Car Company, one of whose major plants is outside Glasgow, at Linwood in Renfrewshire, where higher unemployment could prove electorally embarrassing.

Welsh nationalism increased in the 1970s too, and Labour lost ground to Plaid Cymru (in the Merthyr Tydfil local elections, for example). The need to maintain Labour strength at Westminster in its Scottish and Welsh representation is great, and so devolutionists were courted by the Scottish and Welsh Bill (1975) promising locally elected assemblies to the two countries but not reducing Westminster representation. This was considered by many as blatant electoral politics, particularly as Scotland and Wales are already 'over-represented' there: in 1974 the average number of electors per constituency was England, 64 634; Scotland, 51 926; Wales, 55 798. (Ulster, with its own assembly—at present not operative—had an average of 86 824.)

In England, there was one Labour M.P. for every 38 000 Labour voters, and one Conservative M.P. for every 37 000 Conservative voters: in Scotland the respective figures were 24 000 and 37 000 and in Wales 29 000 and 46 000. For Labour to reduce Scottish and Welsh representation would be to write its own epitaph, particularly as the SNP and Plaid Cymru tend to support it on many non-devolution issues (or did, before the Scotland and Wales Bill was lost).

This analysis suggests that British governments survive by making pragmatic rather than ideological decisions on current issues, and that these may often be spatial in both design and impact. The Rate Support Grant (Chapter 3) is another example of this. The main determinant of its size is the needs element, and the formula allocating money to different items of need can be varied for political ends. Such manipulation has been charged recently, albeit by interested parties. According to the Association of County Councils (*The Times*, 3 February 1977): 'For the second year the Government had pursued a policy of taking money from the nonmetropolitan counties and giving more to the metropolitan authorities and to London', which formed the heartland of Labour's support; external evidence suggests, however, that if 'standard expenditure relative to need' is taken as the criterion, such rural–urban redistribution is needed (Moore and Rhodes, 1976).

Urban problems are immense in contemporary Britain, and their solution requires the input of very large sums of money. A government of any complexion would have to meet this need, therefore, but still there is evidence of the electoral influence. In late 1976, the Department of the Environment announced a run-down of plans for the continued development of New Towns and a consequent reallocation of money to inner-city rehabilitation. The latter areas provide some of Labour's safest seats (for example, Newcastle Central, where Labour polled 72 per cent in October 1974): but these are among the country's smallest (the Newcastle Central electorate was less than 40 per cent of the English average) and their populations have been declining. If the decline were not halted, therefore, safe seats could disappear (as had already occurred in Manchester: Busteed, 1975). Many of the New Towns, on the other hand, are in what are at best only marginal Labour seats. Political scientists have long argued the embourgeoisement thesis, that affluence produces a trend away from Labour (Crewe, 1973), and it may well be that the move to outer suburbia dilutes the Labour vote (Cox, 1968); the new policy could be an effective electoral counter, therefore.

Many other examples of pragmatism can be cited, as in transport policy. In Greater London, for example, Labour after 1973 adopted the anti-motorway lobby arguments against the building of ring roads, thereby winning G.L.C. seats in west London and stopping the planned developments. Nationally, also, the pattern of subsidies to uneconomic branch lines on British Rail is correlated with seat marginality. Finally, an example from New Zealand illustrates a clear geographical component. During the years 1969–72, the topic of regional development—largely the rest of the country versus the Auckland area (Johnston, 1974a)—become important. Labour made it a major plank in its 1972 election campaign, realizing that elections in New Zealand are very much won and lost in the provincial towns, which contain many of the marginal constituencies (Chapman, 1972; Johnston, 1978f): the party's election posters (Fig. 6.2) were scaled according to the audience, with the South Island being pitted against the North, and the provincial North Island against the two main cities. The opposing, incumbent National Party decided not to fight on this issue. It lost by a landslide, to which the regional development question probably contributed (Parry, 1973). The new Labour

FIG. 6.2   The geography of Labour Party campaigning on regional development in New Zealand at the 1972 general election: A, the poster used in the South Island; B, the poster used in the North Island outside Auckland and Wellington. Reproduced by permission of the New Zealand Labour Party.

government then instituted a regional development policy via a series of regional development councils, and electorally, according to Franklin (1975, p. 145), 'of the 16 marginal seats, four are located in metropolitan areas, and not subject therefore to regional development needs; nine are within the limits of proposed or established regional development councils; three are not, their marginality reflecting the influence of economic development or personalities'.

Policy and place

Most of the available evidence with which to assess the validity of the vote-buying model in the present context is quasi-anecdotal. Some policies can be studied in more detail, however, and two groups are discussed here; the first presents three clear examples of the vote-buying model, whereas the second is more relevant to the adversary model of the previous chapter.

According to a report in *The Times* (26 July 1976),

Mr. Mason, Secretary of State for Defence, has attacked the left wing of the Labour Party, which is seeking greater cuts in Britain's defence spending ...

Mr. Mason pointed out that left-wing MPs who had voted or protested publicly against the Government on defence had also approached him about the effect of defence cuts on employment in their constituencies.

Since the announcement of the Defence Review, he said he had been approached by 51 Labour MPs about the effects of the review and other defence cuts on job prospects in their constituencies ...

... He said the Defence Review would mean that by 1979 about 38,000 jobs in the Services and about 30,000 civilian posts (half of the latter overseas) would disappear. The 1975 expenditure review would cost another 10,000 civilian jobs in the United Kingdom. Sixty thousand job opportunities were likely to be lost in the defence industries in the next few years and a further 80,000 in ancilliary industries.

Consternation continued among Labour supporters, who at the Party Conference that year (*The Times*, 20 October 1976) claimed that

The defence cuts suggested by the national executive (NEC) in *Labour's Programme 1976* would mean the rape of the aircraft and shipbuilding industries ...

... without naval orders there would be no jobs for whole communities. The NEC wanted to scrap two anti-submarine carriers, one in Barrow and one on the Tyne, both centres of high unemployment ...

As for the aerospace industry. If the multi-role combat aircraft was killed half of Preston would be accounted for, three-quarters of Rolls-Royce Bristol would disappear, and 20,000 other jobs would go ...

The NEC plans for the aircraft industry would result in 100,000 new jobs being lost in the next few years.

The size of government defence spending means that the economy of many areas is dependent upon a continued build-up of arms. And so, despite its pacifist base, defence cuts are often anathema to the Labour Party, because of both their general effect on unemployment—also anathema to the party—and their local electoral impacts. Thus a government which won the two Preston constituencies by 4·5 and 9·5 per cent in October 1974 could find that the creation of widespread unemployment there alienated sufficient supporters to lead to a loss of the seats at the next election.

Change is continuous, however, and as priorities alter so some policies must be cut. According to the vote-buying model, cuts should avoid marginal constituencies whenever possible, the size of the margin being determined by the size of the cut. Thus as a result of a rapidly falling birth-rate and a consequent decline in the demand for teachers, the British government decided in 1976 to close a number of its colleges used for teacher-training (Johnston, 1978b). There were 125 parliamentary constituencies containing such colleges in England. Initially, the intention was to close colleges in 12, then 15, then 21; a final, leaked list suggested closures affecting 34 constituencies. All constituencies were classified according to the percentage of the votes which would have to change from Labour to Conservative or vice versa for the seat to be lost; the smaller the percentage, the greater the marginality. If anything, there were more marginal seats among the 125 than among all 516 English constituencies (Table 6.4), but the constituencies affected by the closures were clearly not the marginals.

Table 6.4

Electoral marginality and teacher-training college closures*

| | Percentage swing needed for seat to change hands | | | | | |
| | to Labour | | | to Conservative | | |
	<3	3–6	6–9	<3	3–6	6–9
England (N = 516)	3·1	5·4	8·9	3·3	5·6	7·4
125 constituencies with colleges	4·0	8·0	12·8	3·2	6·4	9·6
12 closures	0·0	0·0	8·3	0·0	0·0	0·0
15 closures	0·0	0·0	6·7	0·0	0·0	0·0
21 closures	0·0	0·0	4·8	0·0	0·0	4·8
34 closures	0·0	2·9	11·8	0·0	0·0	5·9
27 reorganizations	25·9	14·8	7·4	3·7	3·7	3·7

* Figures in the body of the table are percentages of the relevant numbers of seats

The circumstantial evidence of Table 6.4 is that the decisions on which colleges to close were clearly taken with electoral considerations in mind, although significance tests only partly support this interpretation (Johnston, 1978b). Though the quotations relating to the Defence Review suggest that such considerations do apply, with M.P.s and party agents lobbying the minister for those from marginal constituencies wishing to protect local jobs, it could be that the results shown here reflect the political realities by chance. The published criteria on which closures were based were: size of college; academic standards at college; quality of facilities at college; whether the college could easily be amalgamated with a neighbour; and the need for a regional distribution to provide in-service training facilities in all areas. The educationally and economically optimal list, produced by the application of these criteria, could well have also been the electorally optimal, suggesting the irrelevance of political implications in the final decision-taking. The latter interpretation is also suggested by the final row of Table 6.4. In 1977, a list of colleges which would lose their teacher-training functions but would not be closed was announced. These do not avoid the marginal seats, indeed one-quarter of the 27 are very marginal. Interestingly most would swing to Labour, so it could be that the issue of change without closure is politically less crucial, with respect to winning a seat, than to losing one.

Evidence from the American system also implies the use of political criteria in decisions on government spending. According to the model used here, Presidents should direct money to states which support them and to others which could easily be won. In 1970, the Department of Defense spent $57 653

m. and in 1972, $64 678 m.; where within the country did changes occur, and were these related to Presidential electoral politics? Among the fifty states, the changes varied from an increase of 43 per cent in Missouri to decreases of 32·7 and 19·5 per cent in North Dakota and Iowa respectively. In all, 9 states got less in 1972 than in 1970 and a further 15 received an increase of less than the national figure of 12·2 per cent.

Table 6.5

State electoral complexion and defense spending, 1970–1972

	Humphrey	State won in 1968 by Nixon	Wallace
All states	13 (26%)	32 (64)	5 (10)
Defense spending down	2 (22%)	6 (67)	1 (11)
Defense spending up 12·2%>	7 (47%)	7 (47)	1 (6)
Defense spending up 12·2%<	4 (15%)	19 (73)	3 (12)

Source: data from Barone, Ujifusa, and Matthews (1972, 1974)

Again, the circumstantial evidence favours the theme of this chapter (Table 6.5). President Nixon, it would seem, was able to direct Defense Department spending towards the states which he won, and also those which Wallace won, on the argument that as a Conservative Nixon could well inherit the Wallace states in 1972 if, as turned out to be the case, he had to fight a liberal Democrat. The states which supported Humphrey, on the other hand, got relatively small shares of the political money. There were states won by Humphrey and Wallace which did not record large gains, however, but these can be accounted for by other forces in American politics. As will be indicated below, Congressional committees are very strong as channellers of political money, and indeed all seven states not won by Nixon in the last row of Table 6.5 had a member on one of the relevant committees; of the six states won by Nixon with a drop in Defense appropriations, only one had a member on the relevant committee (a Republican Senator).

Offering benefits to voters in certain areas was a strategy employed in St. Louis in an attempt to get the necessary two-thirds majority at referenda on loan-raising for public works. Ten issues were put before the electorate in 1974, and the locational impact of each was stressed in the campaign to get them supported. In this 'strategy of locational logrolling' (Archer and Reynolds, 1976, p. 21) programmes were presented as likely to bring benefits to specific areas. The package of ten was put forward as a whole, with sufficient pluses for each area to provide a basis for support everywhere. Over all, the strategy failed to get the necessary votes, except on a bond to raise money for the fire department, but voter response was generally much better than at previous referenda.

Much voting on referenda follows self-interest, with lower-income residents most in favour of spending programmes since they contribute relatively little to their costs. Higher-income residents usually also vote for such spending, despite its cost to them, so the middle-income groups are the fiscally conservative (Wilson and Banfield, 1964). The locational log-rolling strategy was aimed at circumventing this conservatism. In part it did. Usually, many fewer vote in the referenda than in the concurrent Congressional elections, but the drop-out in voting rate was much less in those St. Louis areas offered benefits from the various bond issues.

Many policies cannot be spatially as specific as those just discussed, in which case policies reflecting the adversary model are more likely to be implemented. This is the case in the United States, where most of the non-Southern urban representatives are liberal Democrats in favour of civil rights and urban aid legislation (Lehne, 1972). To get urban aid bills passed, the northern Democrats need a majority over the combined forces of the southern (conservative) Democrats and the Republicans, for the latter groups tend to vote together against such acts (Caraley, 1976). Thus, whereas in the 87th Congress (1961–2) there were 263 Democrats, 104 were from the South and urban aid bills were lost, the 89th Congress (1965–6) had a majority of liberal-minded Representatives who voted in such programmes as Medicaid, Model Cities, and Rent Supplements.

Power to the people
Rather than the direct operation of a spatial policy, offering benefits to the residents of certain places, a government may conceive an indirect policy, offering benefits to a certain population group because many of them live in a particular place and so are electorally important there. Table 6.6 illustrates this with a simple, hypothetical example of five constituencies (A–E) contested by two parties (X, Y). In each constituency there is a 'hard core' of voters supporting either X or Y, but only in C and D does a party win a majority on these votes alone. Victory in A, B, and E requires both parties to seek the support of either the old or the coloured minority voters, who so far are electorally uncommitted. The various voter coalitions given in the table show that if a party could get the support of both groups it could win all three constituencies, but that the support of the old alone would be insufficient for victory. Because of where they live, therefore, the 69 coloured minority voters are much more significant to the parties than are the 42 old people.

This methodology has been applied in the United States by Spilerman and Dickens (1975). They applied the following formulae to see the effect of changing the Democrat vote.

$$\%D_2 = \%D_1 + \alpha(\%R_1)$$

$$\%D_2 = \%D_1 - \alpha(\%D_1)$$

where D_1, D_2, R_1, R_2 are Democrat and Republican votes at election 1 and

Table 6.6
Population distributions and electoral power

| | Constituency | | | | |
	A	B	C	D	E
A. Distribution of votes					
'Hard core'					
Party X	20	30	50	20	30
Party Y	24	35	10	50	30
Other groups					
Old	5	7	20	5	5
Coloured minority	10	15	12	20	12
Total	59	87	92	95	77
B. Coalitions*					
X +CM +O	35	52			47
X + O	25	37			35
X + CM	30	45			42
Y + CM + O	39	57			47
Y + O	29	42			35
Y + CM	34	50			42

*Winning coalitions are underlined

election 2 respectively and α is the magnitude of the change. Thus in 1960, in the 12 largest states the Democrat party won 55·9 per cent of the Electoral College votes (i.e. with $\%D_1$ for the votes cast); with $\alpha = 0.04$ to produce $\%D_2$—a swing of 4 per cent to the Democrats—it would win 66·5 per cent of the available Electoral College votes. A vote swing of 4 percentage points in the large states would produce an Electoral College swing of 10·6 percentage points, therefore, so that extra votes in the large states were worth 2·65 times their face value (this is the magnification of the swing). If there were a 4 per cent swing away from the Democrats, their Electoral College votes would be only 33·1 per cent, a magnification of 5·70 times.

Spilerman and Dickens averaged the magnification effects (positive and negative) to show the effects of vote swings, not only in different sorts of states, but also by different population groups. (For the latter, regression estimates of how groups voted were first obtained.) Their results (Table 6.7) show that capturing only a portion of the electorate invariably produces a magnification effect, but that the votes of the non-whites, the Catholics, and the poor are electorally the most valuable in terms of benefits in the Electoral College. (In other words, these groups tend to live in marginal states, and their votes are sufficient to swing those states.) To gain those electoral benefits, policies aimed at the relevant groups are a worthwhile political cost. (Similar results are reported by Yunker and Longley (1976), who show that rural and black voters are discriminated against by the Electoral College systems whereas urban voters are advantaged and relatively powerful. Between 1960 and 1970, the discrimination against blacks was reduced considerably, as a consequence of their migration to the northern cities.)

Table 6.7

The effects of vote swings on Electoral College results

| | Percentage swing | | | | |
	±4	±8	±12	±16	±20
A. States					
Large (12)	13·38	9·88	6·92	5·19	4·15
Medium (18)	4·95	5·88	6·73	9·31	8·96
Small (18)	7·16	8·33	8·29	6·96	6·95
B. Urban–rural					
Urban counties	13·27	12·71	11·54	9·74	8·49
Rural counties	11·61	9·98	6·65	4·53	7·25
C. Population groups					
Non-whites	18·69	24·57	17·12	19·74	21·97
Catholics	12·11	14·43	12·80	18·84	21·04
Whites, non-Catholics	6·40	7·51	9·23	11·17	8·67
Earning $3000>	18·92	10·92	12·78	16·08	13·78
Earning $3000–10 000	6·49	7·86	9·59	11·40	14·16
Earning $10 000<	7·88	9·62	9·00	13·50	12·83

Source: Spilerman and Dickens (1975, various tables) © 1975 by The University of Chicago.

To operate on these important groups, parties must put together coalitions of voters. Axelrod (1972) has looked at these coalitions for all Presidential elections between 1952 and 1968. The Republican party clearly puts together an overlapping coalition of white, Protestant suburbanites (Table 6.8), whereas the most interesting aspect of the Democrat coalition is the increased contribution of the black vote. (The Catholic vote was strongest in 1960, for Kennedy.) Axelrod calculated the contribution of a group to a coalition according to its size, its turn-out, and its loyalty. The increased contribution of blacks to the Democrat coalition reflected an increase of turn-out (from 23 to 51 per cent) plus very high loyalty (99 per cent in 1964). The important groups electorally are those which constantly support a party, and therefore are worthy of political rewards, plus those which could be won over by policy promises and actions. To Axelrod (1972, p. 19). 'if a group's response is sensitive to the magnitude of the efforts to appeal to it, then a party would do well to devote scarce resources to increase this appeal', especially if, as Spilerman and Dickens indicate, this group live where their votes are crucial.

The Catholic vote comes into the above category, According to Fenton (1960), Catholic socialization leads adherents to favour Catholic candidates and to follow the church's lead on voting. Fenton showed that this was so in a

Table 6.8

Electoral coalitions

Election	1952	1956	1960	1964	1968
A. Democrat					
Percentage contribution to coalition by					
Poor	28	19	16	15	12
Black	7	5	7	12	19
Union members	38	36	31	32	28
Southerners	20	23	27	21	24
Large metropolitan cities	21	19	19	15	14
B. Republican					
Percentage contribution to coalition by					
Non-poor	75	84	83	89	90
White	99	98	97	100	99
Non-union	79	78	84	87	81
Protestant	75	75	90	80	80
Northern	87	84	75	76	80
Suburban metropolitan areas	84	89	90	91	92

Source: Axelrod (1972, pp. 14 and 18)

variety of situations. For example, after the 1944 Supreme Court ruling against all-white primary elections, the Negro vote was courted by the parties, which involved obtaining their voter registration. In Louisiana, registration was handled by the elected county Sheriffs. In the Roman Catholic areas, these Sheriffs heeded the pro-civil rights views of their white constituents and registered on average 51 per cent of the Negroes; in the other counties it was not in the elected Sheriffs' interests to support civil rights, and only 23 per cent were registered.

'A voteless people is a hopeless people' was a catchphrase of the American civil rights movement: to what extent did winning the vote bring political power to the blacks? To answer this, Keech (1968) looked at local government in Durham, North Carolina—a city with a sizeable (30 per cent) black minority—and Tuskegee, Alabama, which has a Negro majority. In both places, as Axelrod suggested, power depends on turn-out and cohesion, and since cohesion was invariably high (all voting the same way) turn-out was crucial.

After 1945, the black vote in Durham was crucial for electoral success in 57 per cent of the mayoralty contests and 61 per cent of the ward contests. In 1964, for example, the victor for the mayoralty trailed by 279 votes in the white precincts but he won 89 per cent of all votes in the Negro precincts, where cohesion was clearly very great. On municipal referenda, too, the black vote was often crucial. The Durham Commission on Negro Affairs suggested to blacks how they should vote; it endorsed the winning position on 91 per cent of the occasions between 1947 and 1966, and in 54 per cent of these the black vote was crucial in getting the victory. In addition, the Negro vote has been important for the allocation of public goods (see also Levy, Meltszer, and Wildavsky, 1974), so that (Keech, 1968, pp. 78–9) 'Negro votes have had a demonstrable impact on who is elected to public office, on the distribution of fire stations and recreation facilities, and on the decision to have urban research'. In Tuskegee, the impact has been more local, for example on the paving of streets in black residential areas and on the frequency of garbage collection. Again, however, the importance of the black vote has been recognized by those having political money to disburse.

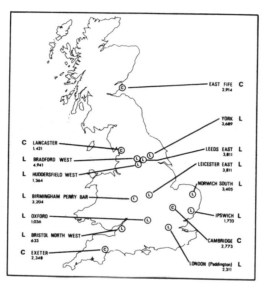

Fig. 6.3   Seats with small majorities which could be swung by the student vote in 1977. Source: *Sunday Times* (30 January 1977, p. 13).

Voter power in Britain

Under the title 'The short-haired student is back', *The Sunday Times* (30 January 1977) discussed a recruiting drive by the Conservative Party among Britain's 650 000 student voters. The party had identified a number of constituencies in which the student vote was probably crucial because of the small majorities (Fig. 6.3), and in each university and college was advising students whether to register as voters in their permanent home towns or in the towns where they attended courses.

With a government having a knife-edge electoral majority, almost any voter group is very relevant in the power game. Over the last two decades one group in Britain which has consistently been electorally important, for a variety of reasons, has been the immigrant population. Initial prominence came in the early 1960s with the legislative progress of the 1962 Commonwealth Immigrants' Bill, passed by the Conservative government as a measure to reduce substantially the number entering the country.

Since the mid-1960s, immigration has several times been brought to the forefront of British political controversy, usually either by the right-wing National Front or by Enoch Powell, sometime Conservative Cabinet Minister (Foot, 1969). In general terms, the Conservative Party has favoured the tighter controls, but Labour's liberality has not always been demonstrated in office. It is sometimes claimed that the immigrant vote favours Labour, however, perhaps by as much as 6 : 1, so that this could be crucial in certain marginal constituencies.

Of more importance than the votes of the immigrants are probably the votes of those they live among, who tend to react in one way of two ways (Foot, 1965, p. 235)—either 'decency, hospitality and solidarity' or 'resentment and xenophobia'. Often the latter condition has been catalysed by political action, as in the contest for Smethwick in the 1964 general election when the Labour incumbent was defeated by a notorious anti-immigrant campaign (Deakin, 1965). If candidates did not use the issue then often it was not crucial in a constituency, whatever the number of immigrants living there (Robertson, 1971), but in 1970 Powell's views seem to have won the immigrant vote for Labour (Steed, 1971) whereas 'indigenous' voters tended to prefer Conservative—as they showed in rejecting a coloured Labour candidate for a London seat held by the party. Thus between 1966 and 1970 the swing to Conservative was greater in the seats with above-average immigrant proportions than it was in the country as a whole (Taylor and Johnston, 1979).

Table 6.9

Voting groups, electoral marginality, and power

		Ratio of group to electoral margin*				
	2·0 <	1·5–2·00	1·25–1·49	1·00–1·24	0·75–0·99	0·75 >
Aged 18–20	21　(10)	4　(3)	3　(1)	2　(0)	12　(5)	474　(238)
Born Old Commonwealth	0　(0)	0　(0)	0　(0)	0　(0)	0　(0)	516　(257)
Born New Commonwealth	1　(0)	0　(0)	0　(0)	0　(0)	5　(0)	510　(257)
Owner-occupiers	452　(220)	28　(18)	12　(6)	12　(7)	5　(3)	6　(3)
Council tenants	486　(239)	17　(10)	6　(5)	2　(1)	3　(1)	2　(1)
Private renters	510　(255)	2　(0)	2　(1)	1　(1)	0　(0)	1　(0)
Car-owners	265　(117)	69　(34)	26　(13)	38　(25)	41　(20)	77　(48)
Families 2+ children	202　(92)	66　(35)	60　(31)	64　(33)	76　(35)	48　(31)
Working women who are married	125　(57)	41　(17)	35　(18)	61　(27)	81　(46)	173　(92)
Car commuters	192　(83)	88　(56)	43　(19)	61　(36)	65　(30)	67　(39)
Bus commuters	127　(67)	47　(22)	46　(20)	45　(21)	60　(29)	191　(98)
Train commuters	41　(16)	14　(6)	12　(3)	18　(6)	28　(10)	403　216
Self-employed	35　(16)	16　(8)	10　(4)	15　(4)	30　(15)	410　(210)
Lone parents	27　(15)	9　(3)	8　(2)	13　(6)	18　(8)	441　(223)
Students	12　(5)	6　(3)	4　(2)	6　(3)	11　(6)	477　(238)

* Figures in parentheses refer to seats held by Labour

The power of different groups in Britain to swing constituencies can be estimated roughly by comparing their size in each constituency relative to the vote difference there between the two main parties. If the result of dividing the former by the latter exceeds 1·0, then if all members of the group vote the same way they can influence the result. Table 6.9 shows the results of such calculations for the 516 English constituencies using 1971 Census data and the October 1974 election result. These suggest that New Commonwealth immigrants hold the balance of power in only a few seats and that policies directed at other groups—the young voters, for example, the large families, and the working wives—are more likely to produce electoral benefits. The most powerful groups shown are the various housing tenure categories, which perhaps explains why all governments are wary of putting up council rents and are unprepared to reduce the tax relief on mortgages.

Voting blocs and voting power

In electoral terms it is not a group's absolute size which is so significant as its voting strength relative to the balance of power. To measure this voting power (Brams, 1975), an index developed by Banzhaf (1968), Coleman (1972), and Rae (1972) is used to illustrate how a few votes in the right place are often worth much more than many votes somewhere else in the system.

Table 6.10
The measurement of voting power

Votes							
A	10	B	9	C	5	D	3

Possible coalitions	Votes*	Destroyers	Possible coalitions	Votes*	Destroyers
A	10		BC	14̲	B,C
B	9		BD	12	
C	5		CD	8	
D	3		ABC	24̲	
AB	19̲	A,B	ABD	22̲	A,B
AC	15̲	A,C	ACD	18̲	A,C
AD	13		BCD	17̲	B,C
			ABCD	27̲	

Member	A	B	C	D
Votes	10	9	5	3
Percentage of votes	37·04	33·33	18·52	11·11
Power to destroy	4	4	4	0
Percentage of power	33·33	33·33	33·33	0
Power/vote ratio	0·90	1·00	1·80	0·00

*Viable coalitions are underlined

The measurement procedure is outlined in Table 6.10 with a hypothetical example. There are four voting blocs (parties in a parliament) with the number of votes indicated. No one bloc has sufficient votes (14) to form a majority on its own, so a coalition is necessary. All the possible coalitions are indicated, of which there are eight. In these, a party is only powerful—i.e. can bargain for its policies—if its withdrawal would cause the fall of the coalition; parties A, B, and C could each cause the defeat of four coalitions, but party D could defeat none, and so has no power. A, B, and C thus have equal power to destroy, but as C has only half as many votes as A, it is relatively much stronger, as indicated by the final row in the table.

A clear example of a system for which this method is applicable is the American Electoral College, in which the 51 member-states have different numbers of votes. Banzhaf (1968) has applied the method, and shown that the power of a voter in the largest state (New York at the time) was 3·312 times that of a contemporary in the smallest (see Yunker and Longley, 1976, for a critique of these findings). He derived this conclusion as follows. Each voter has equal power to influence the result in his state, so that in a state with 50 votes this power is 0·02 of the total, whereas in one with 100 votes it is 0·01. The state with 50 voters has 4 Electoral College votes and can destroy 4 of the coalitions: that with 100 voters can destroy 17. The power of the voter in the first state is thus 0·02(4) = 0·08 whereas for the voter in the larger state it is 0·01(17) = 0·17, so that whereas the former has most power *in his state* the latter has most power *over the election*. Thus, because of the distribution of the Electoral College votes among the states, power lies in the largest states, a conclusion reached in a slightly different way by Brams and Davis (1973, 1974).

The European Economic Community is another weighted plurality system in which bodies such as the Council of Ministers comprise members with different voting strengths. Application of this method of analysis to that body (Johnston and Hunt, 1977) shows how the distribution of power among the nine varies with the size of the majority used. The European Assembly similarly has weighted voting blocs for countries, and again analysis suggests disparities between the allocations of votes and of power (Taylor and Johnston, 1978), with important implications for the issue of national sovereignty in the federal body (Johnston, 1977b).

Use of this method assumes that votes are equitably distributed according to an agreed criterion—'one man, one vote'—and inquires whether these votes carry equal weight—'one man, one vote: one vote, one value'. It also assumes that votes are cast as a bloc. Often they are not. Because the U.K. has 81 votes in the European Assembly does not mean that all 81 will be cast together. Nor is it valid to assume that all members of a group in a constituency will vote the same way in an election, which is the basis of the calculations in Table 6.9. But making this assumption does allow some evaluation of the importance of where a group is located within a constituency system (Johnston, 1977e) and so illustrates the general theme that a constituency system allocates power inequitably to the various groups of voters who live within it.

Patronage

The hypothesis has been advanced here that parties and candidates reward faithful voters and woo potential supporters with political money of various currencies. One possible reward is patronage. Many public positions are political appointments, especially in the United States, although there the Supreme Court has ruled that a change of government should not lead to a change of government employees (*The Times*, 28 June 1976). In one city alone (Gary, Indiana) the Democrats had 700 patronage positions to distribute to party workers and supporters (Rossi and Cutright, 1961)—excluding jobs in the police and fire departments plus school-crossing guards.

At higher levels, government leaders also have immense patronage power which they can use for rewarding and wooing voters. Thus analyses of American Cabinet appointments (Brunn, 1974, p. 91) suggest that a president may feel he owes posts to individuals from those states which ensured his election, particularly if he wishes to remain popular there; perhaps not surprisingly, therefore, both Kennedy in 1960 and Nixon in 1968 gave most appointments to political leaders from the large states where both Banzhaf and Brams and Davis indicated that the real voting strength is located.

The representative and the pork barrel

The implication of patronage at the federal level in the U.S.A. is not simply that a Cabinet appointment is a way of recognizing the electoral value of a state and saying thank you. The appointee is expected to bring tangible rewards to the state in the form of public money. This is widely known as pork-barrel politics, which are perhaps most fully developed in the United States because of its governmental structure. In a sense all representatives are seeking such rewards for their constituents; vote-buying is scraping the barrel for pork. (An early example of this is given by the clear geography of voting for the location of Canada's capital during the 1850s: Fig. 6.4: Knight, 1977.)

In the United States, the Department of Defense budget ($64 678 m. in 1972: Barone, Ujifusa, and Matthews, 1974) is a prime target for porkbarrelers, for so much military spending is locationally specific, whether on particular bases or on contracts for particular factories. Brunn (1975) has looked at the geography of contract spending by this Department during the Vietnam War, relating this to the districts represented by members of the powerful House Armed Services Committee, who decide all prime military contracts.

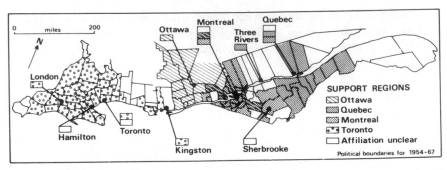

F<small>IG.</small> 6.4   Support regions in parliamentary votes, by ridings (constituencies), on the location of Canada's capital. Source: Knight (1977, p. 313).

Brunn found that over 25 per cent of the contracts awarded in 1968 went to the 40 districts represented on the committee, but that not all members were equally as effective in getting jobs for their constituents. Goss (1972), on the other hand, claimed that committee members obtained excessive military installation awards for their states, but not contracts for civil companies. Her data on average employment—military, civilian on military bases, and private

Table 6.11

Constituencies, jobs, and the House Armed Services Committee

	Type of district		Average jobs per congressional district	
			House (435)	*Members of Armed Services Committee (40)*
Region	South	Military	6740	14713
		Civilian	2890	6367
		Private	3761	2750
	North-east	Military	1300	1880
		Civilian	1348	2750
		Private	4425	5775
	Midwest	Military	1600	763
		Civilian	1105	1189
		Private	2570	1938
	West	Military	6780	23457
		Civilian	3840	10453
		Private	5620	6407
Party	Democrat	Military	4330	14274
		Civilian	2529	7294
		Private	3950	3562
	Republican	Military	3201	3164
		Civilian	1646	1622
		Private	3800	4457

Source: Goss (1972, pp. 223–4)

on military bases—show that Democrat representatives (members of the majority party) from the South and West on the House Armed Services Committee were most effective at getting jobs for local military installations, relative to other districts in those regions (Table 6.11). Thus the 64 Southern districts with a Democrat member averaged 10 025 military and 4209 civilian jobs, whereas those nine whose member was on the Armed Services Committee averaged 23 773 and 10 087 respectively.

The ability of individual members to get these benefits for their constituencies is very well illustrated by individual cases (from Barone, Ujifusa, and Matthews, 1974). The chairman of the House Armed Services Committee during 1965–70 was Mendel Rivers, the representative for South Carolina's First District, covering the Charleston metropolitan area. During his term, approximately one-third of all employees in that district were paid by the Department of Defense, and in 1970 $306 m. of the department's outlays went there—0·67 per cent of the national total to 0·22 per cent of the country's population. And not only the Armed Services Committee offers such large scrapings of pork. The largest payments of cotton subsidies go to farmers in the Sixteenth District of California, represented by the Chairman of the House Cotton Subcommittee, and to farmers in Mississippi's First District, which returns the Chairman of the House Subcommittee on Agricultural Appropriations.

Constituencies, representatives, and committees

The use of positions of power on committees is but one way in which American Representatives and Senators operate the pork-barrel system. Rundquist and Ferejohn (1976, p. 88) suggest three linked processes, as follows:

(1) members seek committee positions from which they can best serve the interests of their constituents (*the recruitment hypothesis*); so
(2) committees will over-represent constituencies with a major stake in their subject matter (*the over-representation hypothesis*); and
(3) the constituencies of committee members benefit disproportionately from the political money distributed by the committee (*the benefit hypothesis*).

The first major task for a Congressman is to get on to the committees from which he can best serve his constituents, therefore, since committee recommendations are usually adopted by the relevant full house (Fenno, 1966, 1973). Parties are known to stack committees with those having certain interests (Beth and Havard, 1961; Masters, 1961), especially in the Senate. In the House, legislative committees are treated similarly but members of the Appropriations committee and its many subcommittees, which handle all budgeting, are supposed to be neutral with regard to their task. (Thus the subcommittee on the Interior Department spends most of its money west of the Mississippi, but during the period 1947–65 81 of its 108 man-years of service were by Representatives from the east: Fenno, 1966, p. 141; Wallace, 1960, p. 31. The legislative committee on the Interior Department, on the other hand, is dominated by the Western states, and in 1974/7 of its 42 members were from California alone. The main work of the committees concerns public lands and water and power development schemes which mainly concern the dry interior lands where the Federal government holds most of its 761 m. acres. The ten westernmost states received 47 per cent of the Department of the Interior budget in 1972.)

Some state delegations (occasionally irrespective of party) believe that they have permanent rights to recruitment on certain committees. This in itself can bring immense pork-barrel power, particularly for the majority party. Until recently (Hinckley, 1976; *The Times*, 27 January 1977) seniority on a committee has been the major route to its chairmanship, so that states (1) with an interest in a certain committee, and (2) with safe seats allowing the seniority to be amassed, are most likely to obtain powerful representation: because of the second condition, the safe, Southern states are particularly powerful in Congress (Wolfinger and Heifetz, 1965). Fig. 6.5 shows the results with regard to all committee and subcommittee chairmanships in 1974. In the Senate, nearly 25 per cent of the committee chairmanships go to two Southern states—Arkansas and Mississippi, though because there are only 100 members the subcommittee chairmanships are widely spread, including one Republican (from Nebraska). In the House, Southern power is not as apparent, except for Texas, but nearly one-third of the 123 chairmanships are drawn from three of the largest states (California, Pennsylvania, and Texas) all of which have many 'safe' districts because of the geography of the vote and the gerrymander. There is then a clear geography of representational power, of which this is but one example, with major pork-barrel implications.

Rundquist and Ferejohn (1976) tested the full suite of recruitment, over-representation, and benefit hypotheses for two policy areas—military contracts and civil works programmes. Regarding the former they found: (1) a clustering of Democrats from interested states on the Armed Services Committee, but not the relevant Appropriations subcommittee; (2) no significant over-representation of states receiving large volumes of military contracts on either committee; and (3) no significant biased flow of benefits towards the representatives' states. This confirms the findings of Fenno and Goss, and suggests that the pork-barrel tradition is not as strong as hypothesized.

Other work by Ferejohn (1974) provides evidence very much in line with the benefits hypothesis, however. His focus was the budget of the Corps of Engineers, which is responsible for major public works on rivers and harbours. Its projects clearly can benefit particular states with large volumes

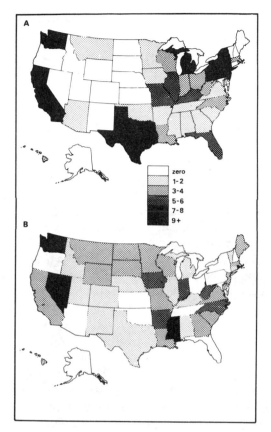

Fig. 6.5   Chairmanships of Congressional committees and subcommittees by states, 1974. A. House of Representatives; B. Senate.

of spending on such projects as flood control, and regressions of spending on new projects in 1967 produced the following results. Where NS is number of new project starts per state in 1967; N is a measure of needs (previous spending = incrementalism); M, DM, and RM are members, Democrat and Republican, of the relevant committees; S is senior member of a committee; FC is member of the Flood Control Subcommittee; RH is member of the Rivers and Harbors Subcommittee; and 56, 66, 67 refer to 1956, 1966, and 1967; then

$$NS_{67} = 0.032 + 0.787M_{66} + 0.504M_{56} + 0.017N \qquad R^2 = 0.62$$

$$NS_{67} = 0.181 + 1.21RM_{66} + 0.93DM_{66} + 0.019N \qquad R^2 = 0.60$$

$$NS_{67} = 0.208 + 0.91M_{66} + 0.025DM_{66} + 0.982SRM_{66} + 0.017N$$
$$R^2 = 0.59$$

$$06NNS_{67} = 0.164 + 0.282M_{66} + 0.302FC_{66} + 1.08RH_{66} + 0.020N$$
$$R^2 = 0.65$$

all of which indicate the power of committee members to get projects for their states (not necessarily their districts). Both the legislative committees, which approve schemes, and the appropriations committees, which provide the finance, were important in this process, so every member seemed to have a finger in the pork barrel. Thus, Ferejohn (1974, pp. 233–4) could conclude that: (1) members of the public works committees in both houses get more projects for their states than do non-members; (2) legislative committee members are less successful than appropriations subcommittee members; (3) committee leaders, from both parties, are most successful; and (4) Democrat members tend to get more than Republicans. Such results represent the operation of complex bargaining and coalition formation by members (Fenno, 1973; Ferejohn, 1974). Many get their prize project through, perhaps not at the first attempt, by in return agreeing to support that proposed by someone from another state. In particular, the chairman's support is invaluable.

The Congressional committees are only one element in the politics of spending in the United States, however. For grants-in-aid (p. 47) the main decisions are made by the state governments and it is those which choose to be most liberal (i.e. the competitive states) that get most of the grant money. Thus grants must be separated out from general expenditures. The latter tend to go to the states with the strongest Congressional delegations (i.e. the safe seats), and to those represented on the relevant committees; the former go to the needy and the competitive states. In both cases, the executive too may direct some spending towards the crucial states for Presidential electoral politics (Johnston, 1978e, 1978g, 1978h).

Log-rolling by representatives

Another way in which representatives can serve their constituents is by their voting in the House or Senate. In particular, members for marginal seats may be most attentive to their constituents' needs, meeting with them more frequently (Clarke, Price, and Krause, 1975) and acting as errand-boys (Chubb, 1963). In the House, they may vote with their party or, if they think it more in their constituents' interests, against it, and they may even try to get others to support them, by promising to reciprocate on other issues (this is known as log-rolling). Such activity is often associated with the so-called military–industrial complex. Large defence contractors are well organized and are likely to lobby their representatives not to vote for defence cuts and, indeed, even to be hawkish on security matters, thereby keeping their factories open and constituents in jobs (Cobb, 1976).

An example of the geography of voting with constituents' interests is provided by Smith and Hart (1955). A basic political issue dividing urban and rural interests, in many countries over several centuries, has been that of protection versus free trade, with the farming community in general supporting protectionist tariffs. There were nine votes in the House of Representatives during 1929–53 on this issue. The general pattern of voting, as illustrated by the 1945–53 roll-calls (Fig. 6.6), suggests a north–south division, but the detail far from conforms to the expected urban liberality and rural conservatism.

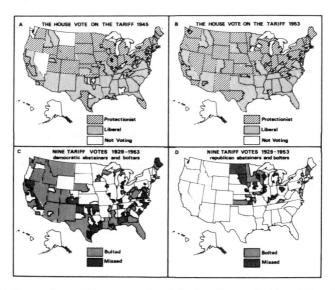

FIG. 6.6   Voting on the tariff by congressional districts. Source: Smith and Hart (1955).

The apparent lack of clarity in Figs. 6.6A and B reflects the party political base of the issue. The Republicans have always been strongly for protectionism and the Democrats for free trade, and only 1 in every 15 votes has been cast against the party line (out of 3724 cast); in addition there were 173 abstentions. The interesting geographical pattern is thus that of abstainers and 'bolters' (those who vote against party), the majority of whom were Democrats (Fig. 6.6C and D) because (Smith and Hart, 1955, p. 341) 'Democrats rather than Republicans are more likely to find their traditional tariff stand a political liability'. Farmers in the Democrat areas of the South and West produce the sorts of crops which require protection, and their representatives have recognized this. Republicans generally serve protectionist constituencies; most of their abstentions and bolts were in 1929 and were related to the lack of export subsidies rather than an attack on the tariff *per se*.

The voting records of representatives relative to the views of their constituents has been a source of much interest and debate among American political scientists. Deckard (1976, p. 480) has argued recently that the 'hoary hypothesis attributed to Key linking electoral marginality to party disloyalty in roll call voting can be rejected', although studies by Shannon (1968), Brady (1973), and others suggest otherwise. Fiorina (1974) has recently rationalized both sets of findings. He shows that representatives invariably vote with the majority view of their constituents, but that in marginal constituencies, of which there are relatively few (Chapter 8), these views are likely to be less radical than in safe seats; representatives can be both loyal to the majority of their constituents yet disloyal to the party they support.

In their congresssional voting, unless they wish to win a majority over for a particular issue, representatives can largely ignore the actions of others; their vote simply is their affirmation of what their constituents want, and log-rolling is unnecessary. This is because, for many, certain issues are irrelevant. A New York representative has no interest in irrigation projects: he may abstain, since his constituents will be unconcerned; he may vote in favour, to win support on some other issue: he will not fight it in case it loses him support on something that his constituents want (Cobb, 1976). Instead of being a series of overlapping coalitions, therefore, Congress is to a considerable extent a set of independent interest groups.

Log-rolling and the pork-barrel elsewhere

Outside the United States, party discipline is generally stronger, and it is parties which tend to pursue major sectional interests rather than individuals. Thus in referring to inner-city areas in Britain, Peter Walker said that (*The Times*, 11 February 1977)

The Labour Party has, over the decades, come to take those seats for granted. The Tory Party, because it looks on them as safe seats and not marginal to be won in elections, has not directed anything like the concentration it should to this desparate national problem.'

The pork-barrel operates at a larger scale in Britain. Individual M.P.s may act as local ombudsmen, especially if they represent marginal constituencies (Newton, 1976b), but only rarely does a case occur, as on the Dock Labour Bill, when an M.P. will vote against his own party—who are the government—saying (*The Times*, 12 November 1976) 'he had abstained because he did not see why workers in the four ports in his constituency should see their jobs reserved for dockers'. On the same Bill, 'Mr. Walden said he had acted according to his convictions in abstaining on a thoroughly bad Bill. He did not believe that it had any support from Labour voters in his constituency.'

Conclusions

The basic theme of this chapter has been that plurality electoral systems produce vote distributions by constituencies which mean that, in terms of party competition, votes from some people in some places are more important than others. From this it has been deduced that parties should concentrate their vote-buying activities in certain constituencies whilst at the same time individual representatives seek to promote the interests of their constituencies, as a means of securing re-election. Evidence to test these deductions is available from a variety of sources. In general it validates them, indicating that the allocation of political money, as part of the geography of social well-being, is spatially biased by the electoral geography of the relevant territory.

Part IV
Reorganizing the Systems

7 Local Government Reorganization

THE administrative map of most countries is a complex mosaic of overlapping jurisdictions. For each separate territorial unit, there are interest groups who can provide a rationale for its existence, and thus for the *status quo*. Opposing them will be groups who are disadvantaged by the current system, and who thus require change for their own ends. Local government reorganization is a political struggle between self-interested groups, therefore, which, as made clear in Chapter 5, has many implications for public policy. The focus in this chapter is on that struggle.

Some local governments are more readily reorganized than are others. At the highest levels, change is very unlikely. The states of the United States are virtual fixtures, since West Virginia seceded from Virginia in 1863 and the former territories west of the Mississippi attained statehood; the only recent changes have involved the incorporation of former territories as new states (Alaska and Hawaii). In Australia, too, there has been no change in the map of the states for several decades and attempts at new state formation have failed to win popular support. And within Britain, although the England/Wales boundary was shifted by the Local Government Commission in the 1970s, the three 'subsidiary kingdoms' of Wales, Scotland and Ulster remain virtually inviolate, whereas the possibility of establishing similar new units—one based on Cornwall, for example—is remote. The sovereignty of sub-national units is receiving powerful support in recent years, however, as in Quebec, and is a crucial issue in supra-national organizations such as the E.E.C. (Johnston, 1977b).

Local governments below the levels of states or provinces are very much the creatures of their 'administrative superiors' and can have their functions changed and their boundaries re-drawn, albeit often only after a detailed administrative procedure. The extent to which such change is imposed depends on both political will and the political balance-sheet. With the nationalization of politics, parties operating at the higher levels are dependent on the constituents at the lower levels, and must judge their actions accordingly. In this way, national political conflicts are often played out on the local stage.

Local government reorganization: some general themes
The case for local government reorganization usually begins on the twin axioms (rarely disputed) that urban areas are divided, particularly into central cities and suburban districts, and that adjacent rural and urban areas are

administered by independent authorities. From these, the argument then proceeds as follows.

(1) Planning and administration should deal with an entire functional area rather than dividing an interdependent whole into independent parts, which may or may not co-operate with each other. In particular, it is argued that town and country/hinterland are indubitably interdependent, and that entire urban areas should be treated as single units.

The interdependence of town and country argument stems from a tradition of research in sociology and geography that has concentrated for nearly fifty years on nodal regions focused on towns or central places (Herbert and Johnston, 1978). Administrative separation of the town from its hinterland ignored this basic interdependence, but such functional regions form ideal frameworks for local government systems based on communities of interest.

This argument gained strength with the growth of town and country planning legislation after 1945, especially with regard to the interactions of transport and land use. Today, the town/hinterland symbiosis is more usually known as the urban field or the daily urban system, based often on commuting distances (Berry and Kasarda, 1977; Hall, 1971; Hall et al., 1973; Drewett, Goddard, and Spence, 1976). All parts of these areas share the same problems of planning for transport and communications systems, and their current sprawl, especially where planning is relatively weak (Berry, 1976), adds to the arguments for unified administration of the entire functional unit.

(2) Local government fragmentation within urban areas creates inequalities in levels of well-being, through free-rider effects, spillovers, and maldistribution of resources relative to needs. As indicated in Chapter 3, the evidence on some of these operations is far from conclusive, but it does seem that suburbs are in general parasitic on central cities, that resources are often least where needs are greatest, and that attempts at equalization are far from successful.

(3) The complexity of the local government mosaic is beyond the grasp of the average citizen, who thus has to abdicate his democratic rights of control to the organized interest groups (Hawkins, 1976). This argument has particular force in American suburbia, with its chaotic assemblage of special districts. Single-authority control, it is claimed, would make service provision more accountable to the public. On the other hand, it is countered, special-purpose districts allow the electorate to express opinions on each issue, rather than giving a general mandate to a political party to run all aspects of local government, which would happen as a consequence of reorganization. The referenda and initiatives of the reform movement to some extent meet the latter claim.

(4) Bigger authorities are more efficient, because they enjoy economies of scale and can employ specialized staff. This is by far the major argument, stressing economic criteria over democratic (cf. Sharpe in Chapter 3). Again the evidence is not entirely on its side, but the case is strongly put. It is based on the general capitalist ethos that 'growth is good'; if this applies in the private sector it should hold in the public sector too. (There are arguments of scale diseconomies, of course: Schumacher, 1973.)

The 'bigger is better' case was accepted by Britain's Royal Commission on Local Government, which heard a (1968, p. 38) 'strong case that witnesses made for the provision of services by much larger units than most present authorities ... The movement of opinion in favour of large authorities is impressive', although one of its members claimed in a major memorandum of dissent that (Senior, 1969, p. 60) 'The relationship between "size" and "efficiency" obtruded itself upon us as an obvious starter. That some such relationship must exist appeared to be almost universally accepted as axiomatic.'

Both evidence submitted to it by interested groups and that produced by its own research staff was used by the Royal Commission. In the latter category, the inspectorate of schools reported that (Royal Commission on Local Government, 1969b, p. 231) 'factors other than size significantly affect the performance of local education authorities', whereas for children's services, too, it was concluded (p. 242) that 'factors other than size affect the efficiency of local children's authorities'. But much of the evidence came to the Commission from central government departments, which view local governments very much as administrative arms of centralized services. Thus, despite (Royal Commission on Local Government, 1969a, p. 58) an 'overriding impression ... that size cannot statistically be proved to have a very important effect on performance', the conclusion was (p. 42) that 'Proposals for a new structure of local government should start ... from the basis that most existing units are too small for the provision of main services'.

Senior (1969) treated these arguments scathingly, noting not only that correlations with spending tell nothing about quality of service (p. 61) but also that if strong correlations between size and efficiency had been established (p. 62) 'We should ... have found ourselves in something of a quandary ... for we should then have had to choose between groundlessly assuming that it would hold good in a radically reformed system, and unconvincingly proclaiming the irrelevance of our researches'. The bureaucracies which gave the evidence have a vested interest in size for their own power and status (Tullock, 1976). If effectiveness is to be judged solely on costs, perhaps their case is valid, but if it is measured (p. 64) 'from the standpoint of the people served—for the service to be community-based, accessible and promptly responsible to changing needs' then small units may be better. Concentration of services to a few major delivery points may be less costly to the bureaucracy, but less efficient for the consumers (Garner, 1975).

American evidence similarly indicates no direct relationship between unit size and financial efficiency. Hawkins and Dye (1970) found no evidence that the more fragmented metropolitan areas provided services less efficiently, and in a major study of police services Ostrom and Parks (1973, p. 382) found that 'every significant relationship runs counter to that predicted ... those who advocate consolidation as *the* answer for all size ranges are definitely *not* supported'. There was no apparent increase of economic efficiency with larger jurisdictions, and the public did not perceive the larger units as more efficient.

As in Sharpe's theoretical analysis of the functions of local government, therefore (see p. 27), most analysts and polemicists clearly see the main role for local authorities as the efficient provision of services. The lack of supporting evidence for their cause does not seem to have dulled their arguments. And yet, as Hill (1974, pp. 217–9) notes,

Effective local services, efficient administration and citizen involvement immediately bring conflict. Local government is a political process, not just a matter of administrative convenience. It is more profitable, therefore, to focus on the problem of democratic control as a criterion and a measure of reform and its efficiency

and (p. 157) this 'is an argument about power. Power is the crucial issue; who is to decide local policy and where control is to lie, are central.' In the remainder of this chapter, British and American examples of manipulation of the local government map to get and keep such power are outlined.

Local government reorganization in Britain's centralized democracy

British local government is in many senses an administrative arm of central government. Its politics are very much subservient to those at the national level. It is traditional for local government elections to be used by the electorate as an indicator of their feelings about the national government, and Stanyer's (1975) theory of local government is built on the strong correlation between election results at that level and opinion poll ratings of the national government's popularity.

Local government is important to national politicians, therefore, so it is not surprising that the morphology of the local administrative system is very much controlled by the national parliament. This system has been thoroughly revised since 1960 by two acts—the London Government Act, 1963 and the Local Government Act, 1973. Study of these two will illustrate the strength of the political lobby on the conflict over the drawing of new administrative maps.

Reorganization of London's government

The basic government of London until 1963 was created in the late nineteenth century when the London County Council area was carved out of Middlesex, Surrey, and Kent, and divided into 28 Metropolitan Boroughs. The 'Great

Wen' soon spread well beyond this county's boundaries into Essex, Hertfordshire, Kent, Middlesex, and Surrey, and a Commission was appointed in 1921 to consider the need for a larger, unified area: no recommendations for change were brought forward (Rhodes, 1970, p. 6). From then until 1960, the general attitude in central government seemed to be that a convincing case of overpowering need to change something that worked reasonably well would be required, for no government wanted to take on the vested interests of 125 or more separate local government areas unless this was necessary.

By the late 1950s there were two elements pointing to such a convincing case. Middlesex was by then almost completely urbanized and contained nine municipal boroughs which met the criterion (100 000 population) for county borough status. Should this be granted? Secondly, the growth of traffic problems suggested the need for an over-all transportation policy for Greater London (traffic was *the* planning problem of the late 1950s–early 1960s: Buchanan, 1965). Instead of meeting individual requests for C.B. status and making *ad hoc* arrangements for traffic planning, a Royal Commission was announced—somewhat surprisingly—in 1957 by Henry Brooke (minister responsible until 1962), who was a former leader of the Conservatives on the London County Council.

According to Smallwood (1965, p. 11), the terms of reference for the Royal Commission included the key phrase '*effective* and *convenient* local government'. Its function was to suggest a new administrative map in concert with the efficiency ethos of local government, yet at the same time not compromising too much the Conservative ideology of local democratic control. (Labour, according to Smallwood (1965, p. 129), sees local government as a 'medium for the provision of specific services, especially those that are responsive to the needs of a socialized state', which implies a map that gives as much control as possible to the party of socialism.)

In evidence to the commission, the existing local bodies not surprisingly favoured the *status quo* ('the counties took a look at themselves as they presently existed, and they very much liked what they saw'—Smallwood, 1965, p. 181). The only major request was for the equivalent of county borough status in parts of Middlesex. Central government departments, too, produced few arguments for change. Of the political parties, Labour very much favoured the *status quo*, for it had held power in the London County Council since 1934: Smallwood (1965, pp. 100–2) notes that their

partisan motivations boiled down to two ... The first involved the local and national prestige ... enjoyed by virtue of their control over the major offices of central London's government which ... has been of tremendous political and strategic importance ... the second is London's usefulness as a political laboratory in which the two major parties could bring their differing policies and philosophies to bear on such substantive issues as education and housing.

Thus, 'The London Labour Party was flatly opposed to any reform that would lead to the abolition of its local political prize, the L.C.C., and dilute its central area strength in a sea of Conservative suburban votes.' The Conservatives, on the other hand, wanted stronger, local boroughs, both to dilute the L.C.C. power and produce more local democracy, and they proposed a Greater London authority for certain functions—traffic, land use planning—only. The Liberals wanted electoral reform.

The strongest arguments for change, which were clearly very influential (Rhodes, 1970, pp. 80–1), came from the academics in the Greater London Group at the London School of Economics. They proposed, and the Royal Commission unanimously adopted in general, the following two-tier structure. There should be a Greater London County, divided into 52 boroughs, with populations ranging from 81 000 to 249 000. The County should have exclusive control over traffic planning, fire and ambulance services, and operation of the Town Development Act; the boroughs would handle personal health, welfare and children's services, libraries, housing, and environmental health; the County would provide over-all planning policies, which the boroughs would operate, and would maintain main roads, with the boroughs handling other roads; a similar division of planning and detailed administration would hold for education. The whole was based on a belief in 'strong but not too large boroughs' (Rhodes, 1970, p. 81).

Not unexpectedly, the existing counties were all against the planned changes, which would mean their demise. Within the L.C.C. area, the boroughs run by Conservative were in favour, those ruled by Labour were against (with two exceptions—Fulham and Hackney). In the other counties, most of the second-tier authorities favoured the proposals, for they involved something akin to county borough status, plus freedom from a Labour-controlled centre. Strongly against was the National Union of Teachers. From 1947 on the London County Council had been reorganizing its schools on comprehensive lines; the comprehensive movement had become very much an ideology for the union, which saw its ideal as likely to disappear with the anticipated Conservative takeover of the Greater London Council.

The White Paper based on the report accepted the case for fundamental change with a Greater London Council. The number of boroughs was to be smaller, however, and they were to be given complete control of education except in central London, where an Inner London Education Authority was to be created. The teachers continued to fight on this point, and eventually won an enlarged I.L.E.A. covering the whole of the former London County Council area. On the fringes of London, areas were removed (covering 4·5 per cent of the population), which was seen as a concession to the Conservative government's own supporters (Rhodes, 1970, p. 126).

The increased average borough size to handle the education function involved further amalgamations, reducing the number from 52 to 34. To handle these in a 'neutral' way, a panel of four town clerks (from Cheltenham, Oxford, Plymouth, and South Shields) was established who produced a final map of 32 boroughs involving (Rhodes, 1970, p. 153) 'marriages of administrative convenience ... they may form workable patterns for running education, welfare or public library services, but it would be hard to find any constant reasons for the particular amalgamations'; with political consequences such as (Smallwood, 1965, p. 256): 'The Conservative Borough of Hornsey ... was now about to be submerged by the Labour hordes of adjacent Tottenham.'

The Bill was fought in the House of Commons, where the Labour leader— Hugh Gaitskell—claimed that (*The Times*, 2 July 1962) 'it would not be unfair to describe this as a squalid attempt on the part of the Tory Party to snatch the banner of London for itself by altering the boundaries because they cannot get the votes', and he promised further reorganization when Labour won the next general election. (In fact this was not introduced, for the election was not until late 1964 and it was deemed too late to impose further major change.)

The Royal Commission's report had been based on concepts of functional efficiency and local democracy, but the debate on the resulting bill was clearly political, concerned with redrawing (or not) the boundaries on a map to the electoral advantage of one group over another. For Labour, the bill was a Tory plot, hatched by a minister with L.C.C. experience who was determined to break their hegemony there. But Brooke's motivations are far from clear, and although he undoubtedly was aware of the political consequences of his actions, Rhodes (1970, pp. 235–9) believes that in general he was following the lead for more efficient local government being given then by his civil servants. But in any case, the Conservatives had always favoured the strong, decentralized pattern of local government that he proposed (Young, 1976).

After establishment of the new system in 1964, the electoral consequences were much as predicted. The Greater London Council is not a Labour stronghold, so that whilst it won the Council at the first election by 64 to 36, and also won 20 of the 32 boroughs, four years later, when Labour were in power nationally, Conservative took control of Greater London. Labour regained control in 1972, and lost it again in 1976. The impact of this changing control has been varied, as has that of the entire structure: Rhodes (1972) suggests that those functions performed entirely at one tier have been satisfactory, but that this has not been the case with the important functions—planning and housing—which are shared between the G.L.C. and the boroughs.

Reorganizing the rest of England and Wales

Development of the extra-London local government system during the present century largely reflected the urbanization trend. More county boroughs were created, and most of those already existing were allowed to expand. The original 59 covered 297 000 acres; by 1927 the 79 then extant covered 622 000 (Royal Commission on Local Government, 1969b, p. 4). Seventy-three county districts disappeared, but 290 others were created. After a Royal Commission reported in 1926 there was some slowing down in the pace of change, but between 1927 and 1937 110 000 acres were added to the C.B.s in 179 separate extensions, and another 123 000 acres were annexed during the period 1937–58. All the time, governments tried to hold the present system together while they contemplated how best to introduce change (Self, 1957, p. 51).

Eventually, in 1958 a Local Government Boundary Commission was instituted to reorganize boundaries within the present system. It worked until 1966, paying particular attention to definition of the conurbations (used for the first time in the 1961 Census). Several major boundary changes were also suggested—such as that involving the demise of the smallest county, Rutland, which was a cause of much controversy (Freeman, 1968)—but most were shelved with the appointment of the Royal Commission in 1966.

The evidence and arguments used by the Royal Commission have already been discussed. From them, the majority agreed the following broad principles.

(1) There was a need for unitary authorities on the county borough model, handling all services unless they were so large that a second tier was necessary for certain of them (especially personal services).
(2) The range of populations should be 250 000–1 million.
(3) Present boundaries should be respected wherever possible.
(4) Local councils within the unitary authorities were needed to foster 'the pride and interest of local communities' (Royal Commission on Local Government, 1969a, p. 74) and 'to represent and express the identity of local communities' (p. 75).
(5) A set of provincial councils was needed to provide the broad framework for economic, land use, and investment planning.
(6) The town/country distinction should be removed.

Applying these, a new map for England and Wales was produced, comprising:
(1) Eight provinces;
(2) Fifty-eight unitary counties;
(3) Three metropolitan counties (SE. Lancashire/NE. Cheshire; Merseyside; W. Midlands) with a two-tier structure; and
(4) Local councils, comprising the pre-existing units, which had no statutory powers but were to act as communication channels.

There was some dissent. Two members wanted more authorities (63 not 58) because they felt that bigger was not necessarily better, and one wanted fewer (50) to ensure that all were big enough to provide an efficient education service. Major disagreement came from Senior (1969) who criticized the others for being too concerned with size and efficiency and for not overthrowing the constraints of existing boundaries. His alternative, two-tier system—based on communities of interest ('the facts of social geography': Senior, 1969, p. 3)—comprised 35 regions and 148 districts.

The majority report was adopted in large measure for the 1970 legislation (Wilson, 1974), although the constitutional implications of provinces led to that issue being delayed pending a Royal Commission on the Constitution. Two further metropolitan regions were added—W. Yorkshire and SW. Hampshire—and some functions were reallocated between tiers. But in June 1970, before the legislation was passed, the Labour government lost a general election. The Conservatives introduced a new bill in 1971, which was passed in 1973. The new system came into operation in 1974 (1975 in Scotland).

The system eventually enacted removed the town/country distinction but reintroduced a two tier organization. Six metropolitan counties were included—the original three plus W. Yorkshire, S. Yorkshire, and Tyne and Wear. In these six, the metropolitan counties handle transport, strategic planning, police, fire, ambulance, and environmental health services; the metropolitan districts are responsible for education, libraries, housing, detailed planning, and personal services. In the non-metropolitan counties, all major functions except planning, housing, and environmental health go to the upper tier. One consequence is that whereas before 1974 there were 141 planning authorities in England and Wales there are now 401, with important consequences for the planning profession (Brand, 1974, p. 81).

The differences between the 1970 and 1971 systems reflect the ideologies of the Labour and Conservative parties, and also their political environments. Labour had some commitment to reform since the 1940s, when a conference concluded that (Brand, 1974, p. 137) 'larger units of local government are required for efficiency and economy, planning and administration, and for equitable distribution of cost'. Local government was to be a major vehicle for socialism, and for the technological reforms of the 1960s. The Conservatives were not so committed to reform, however, and their main view was that 'local government should be local' (Brand, 1974, p. 147).

Both parties foresaw electoral difficulties springing from reorganization. Labour would probably lose by integration of town and suburb, let alone town and country, and yet the 1970 proposals received little Labour opposition. This was because Labour fortunes were at such a low ebb, Brand suggests, that by then the party had little left to lose in local government. As a consequence, Cabinet and the party were willing to follow Crossman's lead, as the minister responsible and the only one with local government experience. As such, Wilson led them into what could at best be a much more finely balanced set of electoral swings and roundabouts, at worst wholesale slaughter.

For the Conservatives, town–country integration clearly threatened rural bastions of power, which probably accounts for their retention of the two-tier system with considerable local autonomy in some major services. The six metropolitan counties, on the other hand, gerrymandered Labour support into a few areas only, particularly in Yorkshire and Tyne and Wear. This came through in the 1977 landslide to the Tories.

The debate on local government reorganization was never as politically partisan as that on Greater London. Nevertheless, the final map bears the imprint of political design, and in general it has worked to Conservative advantage.

American local government reorganization

In Britain, the current local government map reflects elements of both the Labour Party belief in 'big is efficient' and the Conservative ethos of local democracy. In the United States, much of the local government pattern reflects the continued strength of privatism, especially among the more affluent, and the inability of a 'bigger is better' movement to succeed in suburbia. As described here, the changing map perhaps reflects what in Britain would be the demands of the Labour Party by city supporters fighting the vested interests of small-community Conservative voters.

Annexation and city growth

The twentieth century has seen a massive urbanization of the American countryside. In administrative terms, this expansion of the built-up area has taken two forms; the incorporation of county areas for municipal government and the annexation of areas to existing municipalities, usually large cities.

Annexation is part of the 'bigger is better' philosophy. By the mid-nineteenth century arguments were being advanced that the management of small units was inefficient but (Jackson, 1972, p. 449)

In many cases the cry for efficiency was a mask for the desire to exploit and to control: it might be termed the local or downtown brand of urban imperialism. Often the large merchants and businessmen of the central business district sought to eliminate neighborhood governments that in their view inhibited progress.

They were backed by land developers and speculators, for whom city councils were more likely to provide the services which guaranteed their profits. And so annexation proceeded apace with, for example, Philadelphia expanding from 2 to 129 square miles in 1854 and Chicago adding 133 square miles in 1888.

In most states it is the legislature which exercises power over annexation. In a few, the issue is determined by the state courts, and annexation may be forced on communities by judicial fiat (Jackson, 1972, pp. 451–2; Eyre, 1969). Missouri and Texas allow annexation by cities without any permission from outside or from those affected (Blair, 1964), but in most cases decisions on city boundaries are taken by the legislature. Referenda may be taken to indicate the views of those likely to be affected, but legislators have not been obliged to respect these statements of opinion. Thus annexation cases have been political issues.

As the nineteenth century proceeded, so opposition to annexation grew.

Warner (1968) points out that until the 1870s Bostonians moving to the suburbs maintained the desire for a Boston address, and so did not oppose annexation. But in 1873 Brookline residents voted against a Boston takeover, their motives being that (Warner, 1968, p. 165) 'to join Boston was to assume all the burdens and conflicts of a modern industrial metropolis. To remain apart was to escape, at least for a time.' Suburban autonomy was preferred to being 'the tail end of the 35th Ward', as one Oak Park, Chicago, protester put it. And the rural-dominated state legislatures took note of these views, for they wanted suburban support in their fight against big-city domination.

According to Jackson (1972, p. 454), annexation was halted, especially in the north-east, by a combination of three factors: growing ethnic and racial separation; unworkable annexation laws; and improved suburban services. Previously, annexation had been necessary to obtain certain services. Los Angeles grew from 85 to 440 square miles between 1910 and 1930 because of its monopoly—via Spanish water laws—over the waters of the Los Angeles river; suburbs could not buy water from the city and so places like Hollywood had to agree to annexation (Bish, 1971, p. 82). Only when the river was fully used, in 1927, was the city's growth halted. More recently, such monopolies have been challenged. In 1955 the Milwaukee City Council voted not to sell water to a neighbouring suburb—Wauwatosa—because this might encourage industry to move to the suburbs and thereby damage the city's tax base (Gladfelter, 1971). After unsuccessfully applying again in 1956, Wauwatosa appealed to the state Public Service Commission, which could require authorities to provide services. Wauwatosa's case was that Milwaukee already provided water to six suburban municipalities, and so its refusal was discriminatory; Milwaukee lost, and water supply was no longer a bargaining tool for annexation.

Suburban constraints to central-city expansion are now severe in many parts of the country but annexation still continues. Of the country's 212 metropolitan areas, the central cities in over 150 achieved some annexation during the 1950s, which involved the homes of six million people (Dye, 1969, p. 304), and another 3·8 million people were added to central cities in this way during the 1960s (Zimmer, 1976). Annexation is now the main cause of central-city population growth (Berry and Kasarda, 1977), as shown by Table 7.1 which refers to the twenty fastest-growing and twenty fastest-declining cities of the 1960s. A map of these forty cities (Fig. 7.1) shows that most of those still able to grow through active annexation are in the South and West of the United States. Annexation is least in the older-established cities where (Dye, 1969, p. 365) 'Over time, persons and organizations adjust themselves to circumstances as they find them. The longer these adjustments have been in existence, the greater the discomfort, expense, and fear of unanticipated consequences associated with change.' Annexation is most likely still to occur where cities and suburbs do not differ markedly in socio-economic status.

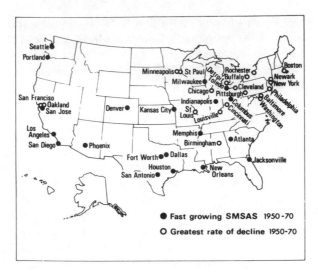

FIG. 7.1   The fastest-growing and the fastest-declining metropolitan areas, 1950–70 (after Jackson, 1972).

Such metropoli are concentrated in the South and West, where cities are of relatively recent development and prior transport technology has not led to a prior suburban decamping and barricading by the middle class (Schnore, 1965).

Table 7.1

Central-city growth/decline and annexation in the United States

| | Square miles annexed by | |
	20 growing cities	20 declining cities
1850–1870	NA	305
1870–1890	229	338
1890–1910	332	444
1910–1930	646	280
1930–1950	408	33
1950–1970	2752	50
Total	4631	1685

Source: Jackson (1972, p. 453)

De-annexation and apartheid: a special case with general implications

A clear example of the manipulation of local government boundaries for political ends was provided by the small town of Tuskegee, Alabama, in the 1950s. The aim was to produce an all-white town, in exactly the same style as the goal of white South African apartheid policy. In the end, the aim failed, the apartheid being overruled by the Supreme Court in the 1960 *Gomillion* v.

Lightfoot decision, which was the first to state that political actions were justiciable when they involved the Fifteenth Amendment to the Constitution.

Tuskegee had a population of some 6700 in the mid 1950s, of which blacks comprised about 80 per cent. Most of the blacks were not registered as voters, but when in 1954 a black candidate ran for the local school board the white minority began to fear a takeover, particularly by the well-educated blacks employed at the Tuskegee Institute. And so they decided (Taper, 1962, p. 14) 'to run the Negro voters out of town or, rather—since unlike Birmingham or Montgomery, this is a peaceable spot, whose citizens believe in law and order and disapprove of physical violence—to run their residences out of town'. In 1957, the state legislature passed Alabama Act 140 which redrew the town boundaries in such a way to put all but a handful of blacks outside Tuskegee, in Macon County, while keeping every white household inside.

The blacks countered this apartheid with a boycott of Tuskegee businesses, and by the legal action which reached the Supreme Court in 1960. Their case was that Alabama Act 140 was discriminatory; the defence was that a discriminatory motive could not be proved, and that town boundaries were a state prerogative alone. The defence lost, with the court ruling that the blacks had been denied their former municipal rights. The old boundaries were reinstated; the registration of black voters was speeded up; and while Tuskegee sank back into oblivion the Supreme Court began to hear many more cases of political discrimination (see next chapter).

City–county consolidation: the voter speaks

Many American metropolitan areas occupy but a single county, and so to many it has seemed a sensible proposal that city and county should consolidate, thereby providing a unitary metropolitan government. Such plans arouse suburban opposition, however, for residents there fear being swamped in the decision-making, higher taxes, integrated schools, and so on.

Most proposals for city–county consolidation have required voter approval, and most have been defeated. (Exceptions come mainly from Virginia, where different rules apply and relatively small communities have been involved: Eyre, 1969.) Of 28 such referenda held between 1948 and 1971 only nine were passed (Marando and Whiteley, 1972); eight were proposed in 1972, and seven failed (Zimmer, 1976). In the voting, county (suburban) residents tend to turn out in much larger proportions than their city counterparts; invariably they seem to be against the proposals, and their larger turn-out usually counterbalances their smaller numbers to defeat the consolidation. Defeat, according to Marando and Whiteley (1972), is usually because:

(1) The demand for consolidation is not a grass-roots movement but comes from civic leaders: as a consequence there is no public perception of a problem to be solved.

(2) The supposed benefits are long-term and abstract, and most voters are satisfied with current service provision (Hawley and Zimmer, 1961, 1970).
(3) Campaigns for the proposals in the mass media have not been well staged.

In other places, central-city residents have as much to lose as suburban. This applies where blacks have gained control of the mayoralty, for example, for they may be in the majority in the city but would be in a minority in the county (Bryce and Martin, 1976).

Table 7.2
Fringe resident attitudes to proposals for improved services

| | | Percentage ranking proposal | | |
Proposal	First	Second	Third	Fourth
Expansion of township services	54	17	14	11
Incorporation	8	28	39	15
Expansion of county functions	17	42	23	11
Merger with central city	18	6	13	53

Source: Hawley and Zimmer (1961, p. 170). Copyright © 1961 by the Free Press, a corporation. Reprinted with permission of Macmillan Publishing Co., Inc.

Suburban resistance to consolidation has been demonstrated many times and in many ways. Hawley and Zimmer (1961), for example, asked suburban fringe residents of Flint, Michigan to rank order four solutions to their perceived 'problems': merger with the central city was clearly the most unpopular (Table 7.2). Similarly, Zimmer (1976) reported that both suburban residents and suburban school officials were against consolidation, the latter especially for they had their bureaucratic positions to protect. On all services, suburban officials were most opposed to consolidation. They perceived the need for change, and recognized (Zimmer, 1976, p. 199)

the deficiencies of local government, but they did not believe that the remedy must be so extreme as governmental consolidation ... special districts ... provide a mechanism for providing services without loss of local autonomy and without threat to official positions and do not endanger local control of land use and zoning.

The relative anonymity of special districts makes them ideal vehicles for interest group protection. They are easy to create and difficult to dissolve, and the taxpayer may not be fully aware of their existence. In San Mateo County (San Francisco Bay Area), for example, taxes for some 75 special districts are collected by the county in a lump sum so the taxpayer, unless motivated to discover, does not know who he is paying. Elections, too, are often far from well-known, and in the Bay Area (Scott and Corzine, 1971, p. 203), 'Fire protection districts ... hold their elections on the first Tuesday in April; sanitary districts, biennially, on the second Tuesday in September in even-numbered years; county water districts biennially, on the fourth Tuesday in March every second year after the district's formation ...' Continued suburban defence of this autonomy is certain, particularly with regard to school districts, given the spectre of integration which is a perceived threat to so many white families.

City-county consolidation referenda have been passed in some places, of course. Notable among these is metropolitan Miami (Dade County) which approved a consolidation charter by 1784 votes out of 82 064 cast (a 26 per cent turn-out). Central city businessmen gave the proposal most support and they were supported by the local press (Sofen, 1971). Nashville voters also supported a consolidation charter (Grant, 1965), reacting positively to predictions of a more efficient and cheaper government organization despite opposition predictions of the end of grass-roots democracy and rapidly increasing taxes. Many of the former predictions seem to have come true, but few other voters have followed Nashville's lead.

Alternatives to annexation and city-county consolidation

There has developed, therefore, both a voter distrust of annexation and city–council consolidation and a feeling that change is needed to get more efficient local government. This has led to the search for alternatives, most of which involve partial consolidation, often on the vested-interest groups' terms.

Consolidation has been an aim of the federal grants-in-aid and general revenue-sharing programmes. The number of school districts was halved between 1962 and 1972, for example (Table 3.1), although most of the change was in rural areas and involved very small districts; in metropolitan areas the decline was only from 6604 to 5275 (Zimmer, 1976), and again most of the losses involved very small districts, in the suburban fringe. In such consolidation, the choice of which districts to amalgamate is constrained by location, and as neighbouring districts are usually similar in character, consolidation will probably only rewrite existing differences at a slightly larger scale. If there is a variety of choices, since complete consolidation into one district is ruled out, that which maintains separateness and homogeneity of character is likely to be chosen.

In a slightly different situation, the choice of which districts to consolidate to maintain existing divisions is illustrated by Jenkins and Shepherd (1972). The City of Detroit operated 21 high-school board areas for 277 000 students, 37 per cent of whom were black. In 1969, the Michigan state legislature required school decision-making to be decentralized, and so a smaller number of school boards, each catering for 25 000–50 000 students, were to be produced as amalgams of the existing districts. There were 7330 ways in which such a procedure could be carried out, to produce 7, 8, or 9 boards. For each, Jenkins and Shepherd (1972) measured four indices of racial integration in those board areas: (1) the percentage of black students in areas with a majority of black voters, and thus under black control; (2) the percentage of white children similarly under white control; (3) the homogeneity for both races, which gives each race control over its own children's schooling; and (4) the integration of areas—the difference between the city's racial composition and that of each school board area. A 7-board scheme was decided. Of the 3154 possible divisions, 1662 would have given a 4 : 3 split of white : black control, but that chosen gave a 5 : 2 split. Clearly the decision favoured the white community, producing, as Fig. 7.2 shows, both a poorly integrated system and one with relatively little black control over the schooling of that community's children.

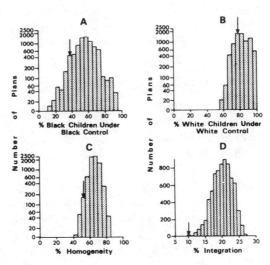

FIG. 7.2   Histograms showing the possible solutions to the problem of defining school-board areas in Detroit. The arrows indicate the values for the chosen solution. Source: Jenkins and Shepherd (1972, p. 101).

This example illustrates the ability of the most powerful group in a situation to manipulate a local consolidation scheme for its own ends. The Detroit solution gave less control to blacks than a random allocation might, and more control to whites. Similar application of this practice in all consolidations will merely rewrite the pattern of inequalities between local government areas, and in no way remove them, whether the issue be racial control of schools or financial control of fire services.

Often complete consolidation of adjacent local government areas is opposed, but co-operation occurs, usually again between adjacent communities which are similar in their characteristics (Dye et al., 1963). Thus in 1960 there were 756 co-operative agreements among the 456 local governments of the Philadelphia metropolitan area. Co-operating and non-co-operating adjacent units were compared on their social rank, the market value of their properties, and their conservatism (Republican percentage), to see whether co-operation involved similar places. With school districts, co-operation was most frequent in the semi-rural fringe, but there were no statistically significant differences between the co-operating and non-co-operating pairs (Table 7.3), largely because of a general over-all similarity; in the urban areas, the smaller number of agreements involved similar neighbours (although not on the market value of property, because of the influence of industrial premises in some areas). With sewerage agreements, high and low value areas did not co-operate: with police radio networks, the issue of co-operation did not involve political conflict, and so there were no significant differences.

Table 7.3

Differences between co-operating and non-co-operating municipalities: Philadelphia, 1960

	N	Social rank	Market value of property	Republican percentage
A. Schools				
Urban				
Co-operating	26	10·4*	1131	9·0*
Non-co-operating	172	16·9	1467	11·5
Rural-urban				
Co-operating	13	8·6*	1685	7·1*
Non-co-operating	29	14·1	1437	10·2
Semi-rural				
Co-operating	162	7·3	957	8·0
Non-co-operating	132	7·8	994	8·8
B. Sewer Agreements				
All				
Co-operating	113	15·9	1223*	10·5
Non-co-operating	63	15·3	1829	11·4
C. Police radio agreements				
All				
Co-operating	80	14·2	1645	11·3
Non-co-operating	114	17·1	1304	11·5

*A significant difference between the mean pair differences at the 0·1 level
Source: Dye *et al.* (1963, p. 150)

In some metropolitan areas, rather than co-operate in joint services, local governments prefer to purchase them, often from the central city: Los Angeles, for example, has 1500 agreements for the sale of between 4 and 45 services to each of the 76 municipalities in its suburban fringe (Dye, 1969). As Dye points out, such agreements allow the purchase of services by small municipalities at much lower costs than they could provide themselves, because of the benefits of scale economies so gained. In Los Angeles County, this has been realized in the suburban areas and has led to the incorporation of 'single interest' cities (Cion, 1971), operating the Lakewood Plan. Small agricultural and industrial communities did not want to be annexed, but if they incorporated as municipalities they would have to provide a wide range of services, at considerable expense to the local taxpayer. And so they became contract cities, which involved 'defensive incorporations' (Bish, 1971). They buy all of their services from Los Angeles, from special districts, or from private contractors. They act as demand articulators, with no control over supply so that (Cion, 1971, p. 229)

the cities' drive for independence paradoxically results in a gross restriction of their freedom of action in all fields save one. While left with the ability to control their own landuse patterns, Lakewood Plan communities are unable to set independent policy in other areas. This is the price they pay for the ability to retain their particular character in the face of rapid growth of the metropolitan area.

As shown earlier, this independence to zone for land use is crucial to the dairy (p. 37) and industrial (p. 36) cities of the district, as well as some exclusive residential areas ('Hidden Hills is literally a walled city; its residents can close the gates and refuse to let anyone in': Cion, 1971, p. 230). To retain one crucial freedom, the residents are willing to forgo many others.

Conclusions

In Britain's highly centralized government system, therefore, where national political parties and issues are relevant at the local level, changing the country's administrative map is very much a national political issue. In the United States, on the other hand, the tradition of privatism continues and local government is an issue to be fought out between local interest groups. The result is a consistent pattern of sub-national administration in Britain, imposed from above, and a much more variable one in America, reflecting the different strengths of local interest groups as they fight to reorganize the administrative map to their own ends.

8 Manipulation and Reorganization of Electoral Systems

Several feedback loops are included in the model of electoral systems (Fig. 2.7), whereby political actors, particularly parties in power, manipulate or reorganize the system to their own ends. Three of these feedback loops are investigated here. First there is the manipulation of the system to produce electoral bias. Four types of electoral bias were identified in Chapter 4, associated with constituency-size variations, differential majority sizes, abstentions, and minority parties. Only the first two of these can be engineered, by the practices of electoral malapportionment and gerrymandering; both are extensively reviewed. Such engineering usually involves manipulation of constituency boundaries, but it can also be achieved by changing population distributions, a technique also treated here. Finally, and most fundamentally, the electoral law itself can be changed, with spatial components and/or consequences.

Electoral engineering I: malapportionment

Chapter 4 illustrated how the relationship between the percentage of votes and the percentage of the seats won by a party can be influenced substantially by variations in constituency size. Given the desire of political parties to obtain electoral biases in their favour, it is not surprising that there have been many attempts at this via malapportionment, the deliberate creation of constituencies of different sizes so as to benefit one party electorally.

No 'ideal' malapportionment can be prescribed, but the sort of end aimed at by electoral engineers is illustrated in Figure 8.1. Twenty-five 'building-

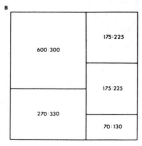

FIG. 8.1   Hypothetical example of malapportionment showing: A, the distribution of votes for parties X (the first figure) and Y in 25 areas; and B, a set of five constituencies designed to maximize seat-winning for Y.

blocks' are to be amalgamated into five constituencies (Fig. 8.1A). The first party (X) gets 1290 votes (51·6 per cent of the total), but because nearly half of its votes are concentrated into the big, north-western constituency (Fig. 8.1B—it has 46·5 per cent of X's votes and 36 per cent of all votes), X wins that constituency only, and Y, with less than half of the votes, wins 80 per cent of the seats. Deliberate malapportionment therefore involves creating larger-than-average constituencies in the areas where your opponent has an electoral majority, and smaller-than-average constituencies where you win, thus maximizing your opponent's excess and wasted votes.

Australia: constitutionally malapportioned

Malapportionment in favour of rural-based parties has been practised constitutionally in all three ex-British Dominions in the southern hemisphere. It was abolished in New Zealand in the 1940s but is still prevalent in both South Africa and Australia. In all three, the franchise was initially based on property ownership, thereby giving rural landowners a controlling interest over the allocation of political power. Extension of the franchise to eventual universal adult suffrage (only for whites in South Africa) threatened this rural hegemony, and to counter it the rural interests, while still controlling the relevant parliaments, enacted malapportioned constituency systems. In South Africa, in 1910 a variation of up to 10 per cent in constituency size (population) around the average was allowed (Fair and Browett, 1979), and this was used to favour rural areas; later amendments to the Electoral Act extended this allowed variation, first to 15 and then to 30 per cent (Heard, 1974). As a consequence, the urban-based parties amass many more excess votes than do their rural adversaries and the latter have maintained their parliamentary superiority.

In Australia, the allowable size variation around the national average population for a House of Representatives constituency is 20 per cent, and this is almost always used by the Electoral Commissioners to favour the sparsely populated rural areas (Rydon, 1968). The rationale behind this was defended in 1973–4 when the urban-based Australian Labor Party government attempted to introduce a new law requiring constituencies of equal populations. May (1974, 1975) has evaluated the pros and cons, as presented in the Parliamentary debates. Labor based its arguments on the concepts of 'one man, one vote' and 'equality of representation'. The opposition, which of course believed that any change would favour Labor, argued that:

(1) There are two main classes in Australia—rural and urban—and to protect the interests of the former, who are a minority, they must be given electoral advantages;

(2) The rural areas provide 60 per cent of Australia's exports and this major contribution to the country's economic health needs to be recognized electorally;

(3) Equal-sized electorates would put six-thirteenths of Australian political power in the two metropoli of Sydney and Melbourne, which would impair balanced development; and

(4) Rural electorates are large in area, and so it is harder for residents there to exercise their constitutional rights of contacting their M.P. and for the M.P. to meet his constituents and identify their problems, so that equality of representation requires inequality of constituency populations.

The last point makes accessibility a primary influence on the nature of representation. May points out that there may be other such influences—wealthier people could be better able to contact their representatives, for example—which requires reflection in a weighting system, but it is accessibility *qua* population density which is recognized at present. (In Queensland, state electorates tend to get smaller with increasing distance from the capital, Brisbane: McDonald, 1976.) Because of the history of the franchise, therefore, it is the special pleading of the rural interests which has been recognized, and which the non-Labor parties fought to protect. In the federal House of Representatives, the major beneficiary of this is the Country Party.

Table 8.1

Zonal quotas in the Australian states

	Seats	Quota	Permitted deviation (%)
New South Wales (96 seats; 1970 redistribution)			
Central	63	28 377	15
Country	33	19 823	15
Victoria (73 seats; 1965 redistribution)			
Port Phillip	44	25 000	20
Provincial Centres	8	22 250	20
Country	21	18 200	20
Queensland (82 seats; 1971 redistribution)			
South East	47	12 657	20
Provincial cities	13	12 603	allocated to cities
Far North/West	7	7641	none specified
Country	15	9976	20
South Australia (47 seats; 1969 redistribution)			
Metropolitan	28	15 055	10
Country	19	9647	15
Western Australia (51 seats; 1966 redistribution)			
Metropolitan	23	11 523	10
North-western	4	specific areas	none specified
Agricultural/mining/pastoral	24	5822	10

Source: Blewett (1972, p. 296)

In the states—excluding Tasmania which does not use single-member constituencies—malapportionment is enacted via zoning systems. Each is divided into from two to four zones. A zonal quota is then established (an average population size per constituency), and the seats allocated, with little malapportionment within zones. Table 8.1 shows that the variations in quotas very much favour the rural areas and the parties based there. The ability to influence the quotas—the number of seats allocated to each zone—allows parties to manipulate the degree of malapportionment. In New South Wales, for example, Labor were in power in the late 1950s and early 1960s, and in the 1959, 1962, and 1965 elections won two, five, and two seats respectively *more* than their percentage of the vote suggested. After Labor lost in 1965, however, the new Liberal–Country coalition has several times altered the allocation of seats to the two zones, and in 1968, 1971, and 1973 Labor won 4, 3, and 3 seats *less* than its percentage of the votes apparently entitled it to.

There is little call for intra-zone malapportionment because the main electoral contest—between Labor and the Liberal and Country parties—is muted in all but the metropolitan zones by Labor's weak electoral performance in rural areas. The zones can cause conflict between Liberal and Country, however, since the number of seats won by each strongly influences its relative power in the ensuing coalition government. In Queensland at the 1969 state election votes and seats won were as follows (Kelly, 1971, p. 41):

	Rural zones		Urban zones	
	Votes	Seats	Votes	Seats
Labor	132 839	9	165 730	11
Country	165 146	26		
Liberal			143 561	17

The County Party won only 15 per cent more votes than its urban partner, but 53 per cent more seats, thereby making it the dominant party in the coalition. This situation was first introduced with the redistribution in 1949; it has been termed a quota gerrymander, which is when 'discriminating quotas for regional groupings of electorates favour one particular party' (Kelly, 1971, p. 41).

The quota gerrymander has been termed the 'Playmander' in South Australia after the Liberal–Country League Premier, Sir Thomas Playford, who benefited from it for two decades (the Liberal–Country League is a joint party formed out of the two separate groups which fight federal elections in the State). Single-member constituencies were introduced for the State Legislative Assembly in 1936, with the rural areas getting 26 of the 39 seats in a 2 : 1 rural : urban ratio which was written into the 1856 constitution. (In 1856, Adelaide's population was about one-third of the state total; in 1936 it was over half, and by 1966, it was nearly two-thirds.) Table 8.2 shows the extent of the 'Playmander'. Of the nine elections fought under the 1936 scheme (which was varied slightly in 1955) the Liberal–Country League (LCL) won a majority of the votes in only two, but it won eight of the nine contests thanks to the malapportionment indicated by the difference between its median and over-all vote percentages. (In 1968 there was a tie in seats 19 : 19 between LCL and Labor but the independent holding the final seat supported LCL.)

Table 8.2

Representation of the Liberal–Country League:
South Australian Legislative Assembly

Election	Total seats	LCL seats	LCL seats Cube Law	LCL% vote Total	Median	Over-representation
1944	39	23	15	46·2	53·7	7·5
1947	39	26	18	48·9	55·1	6·2
1950	39	27	21	51·6	61·3	9·7
1953	39	25	16	47·1	56·1	9·0
1956	39	24	20	50·4	57·4	7·0
1959	39	22	19	49·5	60·1	10·6
1962	39	20	14	45·1	53·1	8·0
1965	39	18	15	45·6	47·5	1·9
1968	39	19	15	46·1	50·3	4·2
1970	47	20	18	44·6	44·8	0·2

Source: Jaensch (1970, p. 99)

Throughout the Playford era (he retired in 1966) Labor was unable to obtain any electoral reform, even after its 1965 victory, because of opposition in the upper house. Playford had introduced a new, malapportioned, system after the 1962 election, but this was defeated by a Labor non-voting ruse (Blewett and Jaensch, 1971). Eventually, the LCL government felt obliged to introduce a much less malapportioned, 47-seat assembly in 1968, which Labor supported and won in 1970.

Malapportionment: American style

Rural forces in the United States have worked hard to maintain their initial hold over political power, also, long after the findings of the 1920 Census that more than half of all Americans lived in urban areas. Success was achieved by malapportionment in three separate legislatures—the federal House of Representatives, the state Legislative Assemblies, and the state Senates—with the greatest 'electoral abuses' in the third of these.

The extent of malapportionment is often measured in the U.S.A. as the percentage of the population who can elect a legislative majority (i.e. in a 100-seat house, this would be the populations of the 51 smallest constituencies). The minimal majorities for all state legislatures in 1962 and 1968 are shown in Table 8.3; the averages for 1962 were 31 per cent for the state Senates (as few as

Table 8.3

Minimal majorities in the state legislatures

| | Minimum percentage of population that could elect a majority | | | |
| | Senate | | House | |
	1962	*1968*	*1962*	*1968*
Alabama	25	48	26	48
Alaska	35	51	49	48
Arizona	13	52	NA	51
Arkansas	44	49	33	48
California	11	49	45	49
Colorado	30	50	32	54
Connecticut	33	48	12	44
Delaware	22	53	19	49
Florida	12	51	12	50
Georgia	23	48	22	43
Hawaii	23	50	48	43
Idaho	17	47	33	47
Illinois	29	50	40	49
Indiana	40	49	35	49
Iowa	35	45	27	45
Kansas	27	49	19	49
Kentucky	42	47	34	45
Louisiana	33	48	34	47
Maine	47	51	40	43
Maryland	14	47	25	48
Massachusetts	45	50	45	46
Michigan	29	53	44	51
Minnesota	40	48	35	47
Mississippi	35	49	29	48
Missouri	48	52	20	49
Montana	16	47	37	48
Nebraska	37	49	—	—
Nevada	8	50	35	48
New Hampshire	45	52	44	46
New Jersey	19	50	47	50
New Mexico	14	46	27	46
New York	41	49	33	49
North Carolina	37	49	27	48
North Dakota	32	47	40	47
Ohio	41	50	30	47
Oklahoma	25	49	30	49
Oregon	48	47	48	48
Pennsylvania	33	50	38	47
Rhode Island	18	50	47	49
South Carolina	23	48	46	46
South Dakota	38	47	39	47
Tennessee	27	49	29	47
Texas	30	49	39	47
Utah	21	48	33	48
Vermont	47	49	12	49
Virginia	38	48	37	47
Washington	34	48	35	47
West Virginia	47	47	40	46
Wisconsin	45	48	40	45
Wyoming	27	47	36	46

Source: Dye (1971, p. 120). Copyright © 1963 by Wayne State University Press, and reproduced with their permission.

8 per cent of Nevada's population could elect a majority of the senators there) and 34 per cent for the state Houses (Legislative Assemblies). Extremes of the anti-urban extent of this malapportionment occurred in Connecticut, where the urban areas contained 23 per cent of the state population but only 8 of the 279 L.A. districts, and in Los Angeles, where 40 per cent of California's population returned just one of the 40 state Senators (Jewell, 1962, pp. 17–18).

An example of the rigidity of many of the state constitutions producing such malapportionment is provided by Florida's Senate. Until the mid-1960s the rules for allocating the seats were (Price, 1962, p. 85):

(1) There should be population equality between districts;
(2) No county should be divided between two or more districts;
(3) No county should return more than one Senator; and
(4) Multicounty districts must be contiguous.

Because of rules 3 and 4 Dade County returned only one Senator for 495 000 residents, one-fifth of the state's population. Similarly in New York, the rural-based, Republican-dominated legislature malapportioned in its own favour so that L.A. districts were structured as follows:

	Average number of residents per district	
	Republican-held	Democrat-held
All districts	398 000	424 000
New York City	384 000	421 000
Manhattan	382 000	439 000
Brooklyn	351 000	444 000
Up State	406 000	445 000

As a consequence, the state was dubbed 'Constitutionally Republican' by Tyler and Wells (1962).

Such malapportionment is possible because district boundaries are drawn in most states by the party in power (including those boundaries for the federal Congressional Districts). Taylor and Gudgin (1976a) have illustrated the extent of this power (Fig. 8.2), showing how in all cases bar one the party with the power to redraw boundaries received a larger percentage share of seats than votes at congressional elections. In this way, rural hegemony was maintained for more than 40 years after the urban areas become dominant in the settlement pattern.

America's reapportionment revolution

Attempts to change the malapportioned legislatures were made in some states, using the initiative and referenda procedures, but the concerned minorities were never able to win sufficient support for their stance. Only in the 1960s was the abuse successfully challenged, in the courts, by the use of the equal protection amendments to the Constitution. A series of Supreme Court

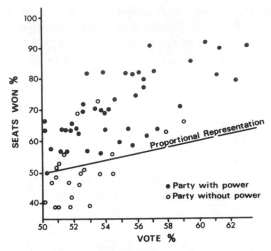

FIG. 8.2   The relationship between seats and votes in American states at Congressional elections 1946–64, differentiating states according to whether their governments had the power to redraw constituency boundaries. Source: Taylor and Gudgin (1976a, p. 15).

judgements made population equality the supreme criterion for judging the acceptability of districting schemes. 'One man, one vote' became the guideline, producing an optimism that this would be a solution to many of the country's pressing political problems (Dixon, 1971, p. 7).

State legislatures were unlikely to enact bills which would reduce, if not remove, the power of those currently in them, and for many years citizens apparently had no redress against their intransigence. The Supreme Court first looked at the issue in 1932 (Dixon, 1968, provides the best general history), with the referral of two cases relating to gubernatorial vetoes of new districts. The appellants claimed that the new schemes overrode the criteria of compactness, contiguity, and size laid down for Congressional Districts in the 1911 Federal Reapportionment Act, but the Court ruled that the act had expired and so it was unable to comment on the districting schemes. Again, in 1946 in the *Colegrove* v. *Green* case, which referred to severe malapportionment in Illinois, the Supreme Court ruled, by a majority of four to three, that (Jewell, 1962, p. 35)

the area of apportionment was one that the courts had traditionally, and properly, refused to enter because of its 'peculiar political nature'. 'It is hostile to a democratic system to involve the judiciary in the politics of the people'. The issue must be left to Congress and the state legislatures.

The 'reapportionment revolution' which replaced this traditional view is usually dated from the Supreme Court's 1962 decision on *Baker* v. *Carr*, which concerned population disparities between state districts in Tennessee (a range of from 2340 to 42 298 in the L.A., 25 190 to 131 971 in the Senate). A majority of the court ruled that the issue of population equality between constituencies was not political. They did not define what would be considered as acceptable equal treatment, however, merely noting that 'some systems of apportionment might constitute abridgement of the equal protection clause' (Jewell, 1962, p. 38).

The *Baker* v. *Carr* judgement began what became known as the 'reapportionment revolution', which was charted by a series of further Supreme Court decisions, of which the following were salient:

(1) *Grey* v. *Sanders*, 1963, which concerned Georgia's 'Electoral College'-type system of weighted plurality constituencies for electing its state Senate. There was a 99 to 1 weighting disparity, which the Court said should be reduced to a maximum of 5 to 1.

(2) *Wesberry* v. *Sanders*, 1963. Another Georgia case (Sanders was the governor), this was concerned with Atlanta's under-representation; the city's Congressional District was the second largest in the country, with a population of 823 680 compared to only 272 154 in the state's smallest district. The Court ruled that apportionment should be more equitable for the forthcoming 1964 elections, and similar decisions were made later for Alabama, New York, Maryland, Virginia, Delaware, Colorado, Michigan, Washington, Oklahoma, Illinois, Idaho, Connecticut, Florida, Ohio, and Iowa.

(3) *Reynolds* v. *Sims*, 1964, an Alabama case in which for the first time the Court defined equality of apportionment, covering three unsettled issues.

(i) 'the equal protection clause of the Fourteenth Amendment requires both houses of a bicameral legislature to be elected from districts of substantially equal population' (Dixon, 1968, p. 263); before this statement, it was thought that state Senates were exempt.

(ii) A 2 : 1 vote in a Colorado referendum to accept a districting scheme outside the equal-representation guidelines was ruled irrelevant to the need for equality of apportionment.

(iii) 'How equal is substantial equality?' was indicated by the degree of latitude allowed by the Court in particular cases. The 'most equal' was the Colorado L.A., with a minimal majority of 45·1 per cent, but the only stated guideline, from the Chief Justice, was that (Dixon, 1968, pp. 435–40) 'the Equal Protection Clause requires that a State make an honest and good faith effort to construct districts, in both houses of its legislature, *as nearly of equal population as is practicable*'. The Colorado case suggested that a ratio of 1·67 between the populations of the largest and smallest districts was acceptable.

In line with these rulings, 29 states redistricted for the 1966 elections, including 12 which had already redistricted for 1962 following the reallocation of

Congressional seats in 1960 (the latter are reallocated every decade after announcement of the Census figures): a further 17 redistricted for the 1968 elections. The consequences are shown in Table 8.3: in 1968 the minimal majorities were 47·5 for the Legislative Assemblies and 48·9 for the Senates, both very near to the 'ideal' of 50·0 with 'one man, one vote'. Much greater equality among Congressional Districts was produced as well (Bushman and Stanley, 1971).

In 1969, two further cases heralded even tighter constraints on the variations between districts. Maximum deviations of 3·1 per cent from the average population in Missouri, and 6·6 per cent for New York were disallowed by 5:4 majority decisions in the judgements on *Kirkpatrick* v. *Preisler* and *Wells* v. *Rockefeller* respectively, despite a belief that the 1960 Census figures on which they were based contained an error of at least ten per cent (Dixon, 1971). All mitigating arguments favouring the deviations— community of interest, political compromise, use of existing administrative boundaries to prevent gerrymanders, avoidance of large non-voting populations, recognition of forthcoming population shifts, and compactness—were overruled. New York was then redistricted with only a 0·12 per cent deviation from the average, but (Dixon, 1971, p. 45)

The new plan was not to Mr. Wells's liking for alleged gerrymander reasons. Accordingly, he returned to the federal district court in 1970 to plead that ... it at least should restore the very plan which he had successfully contested the year before. The court refused, and the Supreme Court affirmed.

In some states, the political parties in the legislature could not agree on a new set of districts. The Washington legislature was stalemated, for example, and so a judge gave a geographer, Morrill, one month to: (1) define 49 districts, each to elect one state Senator and two state Representatives; (2) define 7 Congressional Districts; (3) for the 49 state districts, allow a maximum deviation of one per cent around the quota population of 68 495; (4) maintain, as far as possible, the integrity of all boundaries of areas for which census data are available; (5) make districts as compact as possible; (6) avoid boundaries which cross natural barriers, such as rivers; (7) reflect district community of interest as far as possible; and (8) change the political complexion as little as possible. Items (3) to (8) are in order of priority. Despite the availability of computer algorithms, Morrill had to work by hand to remain within the constraints: later application of the algorithms produced more compact districts, but had little potential political effect (Morrill, 1976).

The very tight population constraints introduced in the late 1960s produced arguments such as Dixon's (1971, p. 11) that the Supreme Court 'has not been content only to lop off extreme population malapportionment. It has come close to subordinating all aspects of political representation to one overriding element—absolute equality of population in all legislative districts.' Perhaps recognizing this, the Court has recently relaxed its rules somewhat (Knight,

1976). In a Virginia case—*Mahan* v. *Howell*, 1973—it permitted a 16 per cent deviation around the average, in order to allow a district scheme designed to ensure minority representation. In *White* v. *Weiser*, 1973, it allowed a redistricting scheme designed to prevent competition between incumbents, and a 1977 decision allowed New York redistricting designed to protect black and Puerto Rican representation (*Sunday Times*, 4 March 1977). Under these new rules, deviations of 7·9 per cent (*Gaffney* v. *Cummings*, 1973) and 9·9 per cent (*White* v. *Register*, 1973) were allowed, but one of 20 per cent (*Chapman et al.* v. *Meier*, 1975) was not, indicating that in future margins of 10–15 per cent will be acceptable if there are strong political or other arguments for them.

Malapportionment, reapportionment, and policy

In terms of policy, it is reasonable to deduce that where states are malapportioned in favour of the rural areas: (1) the more malapportioned the state, the less it would spend, *ceteris paribus*, on welfare programmes; and (2) there would be an urban-to-rural redistribution of money via the exchequer. Price (1962) illustrates the latter with an example from Florida of 22 rural senators holding key committee positions, known as the porkchoppers (lickers of the pork-barrel!): their districts paid 14 per cent of the taxes but received 22 per cent of the payments. They distributed income from the greyhound-racing tax, for example, equally to each county: Dade County thus received about 20c. per resident annually, whereas Glades County received $61.07 per resident, enough to pay 43 per cent of the total education budget.

The hypothesized illiberality of malapportioned states has been investigated in regression studies such as those discussed in Chapter 5 (pp. 87–96). Most have produced insignificant results (e.g. Dye, 1966), in part because of collinearity problems. A review of five such studies criticized both their logic and their method, however (Bickel, 1971): the most positive finding was that, holding constant needs and levels of party competition, the more malapportioned states spent less *per capita* on education and public welfare programmes but not on cash assistance (Pulsipher and Weatherby, 1968).

If malapportionment did result in rural conservatism and illiberality in policy, reapportionment should have brought major changes. Cho and Frederickson (1973b) used survey data to show that post-reapportionment legislators were more responsive to public views on two (fire-arms control and civil rights) of six issues, as did Cantrall and Nagel (1973) in their study of civil rights legislation. Regarding expenditure, Hanson and Crew (1973) compared 15 states which had reapportioned against 33 which had not for their spending during 1965–68 on five items. They found 101 significant changes in the increase of spending over time, with a 52 per cent success rate in the 15 reapportioned states (Virginia apparently responded on all five items, and four other states on four items) and 38 per cent in the non-reapportioned states. The main changes in the former were greater spending on highways and hospitals, where the more liberal policy is more apparent to all than are increased welfare payments to individuals.

Hanson and Crew concluded that while reapportionment may be a sufficient condition for policy changes, it is not a necessary one. Why has reapportionment had such little impact, even over a few years? In Georgia (Hawkins, 1971) and California (Sokolow, 1973), urban representation in the state Houses was increased as much as threefold, but the new urban coalitions were unable to obtain legislative power, which was retained by the remaining senior legislators from the rural constituencies (Hawkins and Whelcher, 1968). Further, the newly elected representatives were often divided among themselves (Sokolow, 1973), so that challenges to the established order were not immediate. Indeed, as Table 8.4 indicates for the House of Representatives, the rural areas are now opposed by relatively equal central-city and suburban factions and alliance between rural and suburban groups can lead to a conservative coalition, which could dominate with the growth of suburbia in the rest of the century (Phillips, 1969). Only on certain issues, such as education spending, are rural and suburban views likely to deviate markedly, so that in the future there may be 'a Congress slightly more favourable to urban, social-service measures' (Lehne, 1972, p. 96) but in general 'gently but profoundly Conservative' (Lehne, 1975, p. 149).

Finally, it should be noted that, during all of the reapportionment revolution (Dye, 1971, p. 29), 'The basic reality, often overlooked, is that generically all districting is gerrymandering ... Gerrymandering opportunities may actually be increased.' Review of this allied electoral abuse is taken up later.

Table 8.4

Representation in the House of Representatives, by type of district

Year	Rural	Metropolitan areas				Within metropolises		
		100 000–499 999	500 000–999 999	1 000 000–4 999 999	5 000 000+	Central	Suburban	Mixed
1950	198	98	30	54	55	109	76	52
1960	168	76	33	82	76	103	112	52
1970	136	78	37	109	75	96	145	58
Predicted								
1980	97	67	29	117	125	77	202	59
1990	73	58	32	127	145	66	240	56
2000	63	40	44	116	172	58	259	55

Source: Lehne (1975, pp. 90–1)

Removing America's Electoral College
Although the *Wesberry* v. *Sanders* case ruled that Georgia's weighted

constituencies were unconstitutional, the weighted constituencies of the Electoral College used to elect the President remain, despite numerous attempts at their replacement. (In 1948 the Senate voted for this, but the House did not; in 1969, the reverse occurred; in 1977, President Carter proposed it—*The Times*, 23 March 1977.) The College is attacked on a variety of grounds (Longley and Braun, 1972), most prominent of which are the distortion of the voting percentages by the weighted pluralities, which can lead to victories by candidates with a minority of the votes, and the key role of but a few large, marginal states. The number of minority winners is uncertain, because of the uncertain circumstances in two cases; the only clear example was when Harrison beat Cleveland in 1888 (Best, 1975). There have been many contests settled by narrow victories in a few states, however, with large states such as New York often holding the key to the election (Pierce, 1968).

In addition to a single, national, direct election, a variety of other district-based systems have been proposed. Although usually not likely to produce as biased a distortion as the Electoral College, all would give greater weight to the votes of some groups and some places than others (Spilerman and Dickens, 1975; Yunker and Longley, 1976; Banzhaf, 1968). In 1970, for example, a Californian's voting power relative to that of a District of Columbia resident would be 3·127 under the Electoral College plan; under a district plan, an Alaskan's voting power would be 4·442 times that of a Californian (Yunker and Longley, 1976).

Changing the system involves a constitutional amendment, which must pass both houses of Congress by a two-thirds majority and be ratified by three-quarters of the state legislatures. It is not easily obtained, therefore, especially since there are strong arguments from some for retaining the Electoral College. The small states want to retain their perceived power, and the College ensures that candidates fight a wide and not a sectional campaign. According to Best (1975, p. 158),

It is in the national interest that the winning party and candidate be at least acceptable to all groups. No major party can afford to take an extreme stand on any issue, because it must build majorities and distribute its strength in a large number of separate geographical units.

Clearly, the problem is whether the President is elected by the nation or by a federation. (The same problem arises with party nominating conventions and their election: see Lengle and Shafer, 1976.)

Temporal malapportionment

As well as spatial malapportionment, the American electoral system has been criticized recently for its temporal malapportionment. In 1976, of the first 18 primary elections, none was held west of Texas and Nebraska, where almost one-fifth of the electoral votes are located. This operates against the chances of a western candidate for a party nomination. Regarding 1976, for instance

(Beniger, 1977, p. 237), 'Consider how different Reagan's chances might have been, for example, if five of the first nine primaries had been held in the West, rather than—as they happened to be—in New England and the Middle Atlantic states.' There is still a strong regional element in American politics, and the local candidate who can win a few early primaries develops a momentum against which those not helped by the sequencing of these elections find it hard to fight.

Electoral Engineering II: Gerrymandering

Differential majorities lead to electoral bias, as illustrated in Chapter 4. When such differential majorities are deliberately created by a party to produce an electoral bias for its own ends, this is known as gerrymandering, after Governor Elbridge Gerry of Massachusetts, who in 1812 signed what is generally recognized as the first redistribution bill to produce such bias deliberately. One of the districts created had the shape of a salamander, so as to capture a series of areas supporting his party into a single district, hence the name. According to Musgrave (1977) the noun gerrymander should be separately identified from the verb to gerrymander: the former relates to a result; the second to an intent—the result can occur without an intent, since 'every district line drawn—intentionally or unintentionally—has a political effect different from another equally possible one' (O'Rourke, 1972, p. 38).

Gerrymandering by a party for its own ends is usually termed partisan gerrymandering; according to Orr (1969) it can be undertaken in five different ways.

(1) Creating stacked districts, of unusual shapes, which seeks out relatively isolated pockets of the party's support and amalgamates them to produce a seat in which the party has a majority, as in the original gerrymander.

(2) Creating packed districts, by concentrating the opposition party's votes into a few very safe seats, creating a large number of excess votes for them.

(3) Creating cracked districts, by diluting the opposition voting strengths as a minority in a large number of seats, producing many wasted votes for them. This method is more risky than the packed districts method since the gerrymanderer can be too ambitious and create many marginal districts which, with a sufficient swing, the opposition could win.

(4) Creating racial gerrymanders, depriving certain population groups of representation by one of the first three methods. (This is in effect a special case of the more general practice of gerrymandering.)

(5) Operating a silent gerrymander, which involves not changing boundaries for many years, thereby creating malapportionment if the population distribution changes.

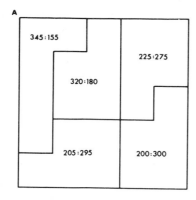
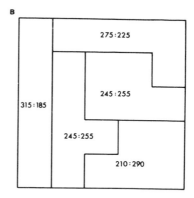

FIG. 8.3   Two gerrymanders of the electoral areas shown in Fig. 8.1, both in favour of party Y (whose votes are shown second in each constituency): A, using packed districts; B, using cracked districts.

Although the results of the first of these are the most obvious, the second and third are the most usual. Employing the set of areas in Fig. 8.1A, Fig 8.3 shows two possible gerrymanders for party Y (which has only 48·4 per cent of the votes), the first (A) using two packed districts and giving it a 3 : 2 victory, the second (B) using two cracked districts to give it a 3 : 2 victory. In the latter, a small swing to X would give it a 3 : 2 victory, whereas a much larger swing would be needed in the former, indicating the generally greater efficacy of packed districts.

Partisan and bipartisan gerrymandering in the United States

Gerrymandering has traditionally been operated in the United States, alongside malapportionment, because of the power given to incumbent State parties to redistrict. Operation of the various processes is well illustrated by recent experience in North Carolina where (Orr, 1969, p. 43) 'After each new redistricting, the elongated eastern districts remained essentially unchanged while assuming a smaller proportionate share of the population, thereby reflecting a multi-featured gerrymander that was "stacked", "cracked" and "silent"'. After the 1960 Census, North Carolina's Congressional representation was reduced from twelve to eleven. The state was safely Democrat, and at the previous election had returned eleven Democrats to Washington. In redistricting, the State government created eleven districts, one each for the Democrat incumbents. Jonas, the incumbent Republican, was put in the clearly gerrymandered 8th District (Fig. 8.4A); other districts were given odd shapes to ensure that no two Democrat incumbents lived in the same one. Despite—or, more likely, because of—the gerrymander, Jonas won the 8th and the Republican also carried the adjacent 9th.

After the *Wesberry* v. *Sanders* Supreme Court ruling, the North Carolina

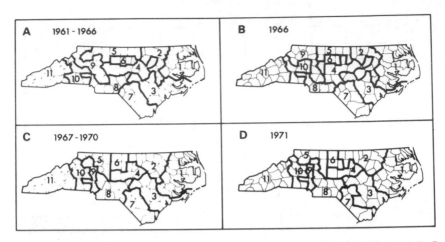

Fig. 8.4   Congressional districts in North Carolina since 1961. A, 1961–6; B, 1966–7; C, 1968–71; D, 1971– . Source: A, B, C, Orr (1969); D, Scammon (1974).

Democrats redistricted the state using a 10 per cent deviation around the average population. Stacked Republican districts were created—'the Apostle Paul couldn't be elected on the Democrat ticket' in the 9th (Orr, 1969, p. 48), but although these were used for the 1966 election (Fig. 8.4B) the Court ordered a further redistricting for 1968 (Fig. 8.4C). To meet the equal-population constraint (the maximum deviation produced was 2·31 per cent), two Democrat incumbents living in the same district were pitted against each other. A further redistricting in 1971 (Fig. 8.4D) served to protect the Democrat hegemony: it won by 7 : 4 with 52·4 per cent of the votes cast in the ten contested districts in 1972, and by 9:2 with 58 per cent in the eight contested districts in 1974.

Greater detail of gerrymandering by cracked and packed districts is illustrated for Iowa in Fig. 8.5. Between 1958 and 1962 the state's Congressional representation was reduced by one, and in the subsequent redistricting (Jewell, 1962, p. 15) the Republican legislature changed district boundaries so as to nullify the representational impact of the central Iowan population which returned a Democrat previously. As elsewhere in the Midwest, the main Democrat strength was in the towns, and in 1960 it won districts 5 (Des Moines—10 per cent of the state population) and 6 (Fort Dodge) (Fig. 8.5A). After the redistricting, the counties containing Des Moines and Fort Dodge were packed into a new district 5, won by the Democrats in 1972, while the remaining Democrat strength in the centre of the state was 'cracked' among the other districts (Fig. 8.5B) all of which produced Republican victories in 1972.

Morrill's (1973, 1976) work on Washington illustrates how both parties attempt to gerrymander for their own ends. In Table 8.5, seats in the rival

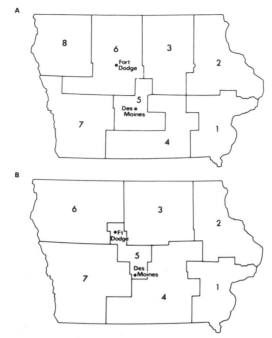

FIG. 8.5   The gerrymander of Iowa, showing Congressional Districts in (A) 1960 and (B) 1962.

Table 8.5
Redistricting and representation: Washington

	1970 election	Party plans		Court plan	1972 election
		Democrat	*Republican*		
STATE SENATE					
Democrat					
Safe	8	5	9	8	8
Fairly safe	13	20	10	12	13
Marginal	5	{6	{6	{10	7
Marginal	5				3
Fairly safe	11	10	18	12	11
Safe	7	8	6	7	7
Republican					
STATE HOUSE					
Democrat					
Safe	15	10	17	16	16
Fairly safe	28	40	21	25	27
Marginal	8	{12	{12	{19	14
Marginal	12				3
Fairly safe	25	20	36	24	24
Safe	14	16	12	14	14
Republican					

Source: Morrill (1973, p. 477)

plans presented by the two parties, Morrill's Court plan, and the 1972 result are classified into six categories. Comparison of the safe and fairly safe seats for each party in its own plans illustrates how each would have pursued its aims. In the Senate, for example, the Democrats would have produced 25 seats for themselves and only 18 for the Republicans; the Republicans would have given the Democrats 19 and themselves 24. Each party gave itself fewer safe seats and more fairly safe seats, indicating the use of the cracked district procedure to maximize wasted votes for the opposition, alongside some packing of opposition votes into safe seats.

In recent years, the tendency has been to use packed rather than cracked districts, creating safe seats for both parties. This may reflect a conservative strategy by a districting party in order not to risk the possible losses which can result from a cracked strategy; it may represent a bipartisan approach to districting, as is now officially practised in New Jersey, Pennsylvania, and Hawaii (Dixon, 1971); or it may, with Congressional districts, result from the political pressure of powerful incumbents from either party obtaining safe seats for themselves in order to get senior representatives from the state in Congress (Mayhew, 1971; Noragon, 1973). Non-partisan districting by computer, although feasible, is unpopular, because its neutrality cannot be politically controlled (Taylor and Johnston, 1979).

Partisan gerrymandering still exists after the reapportionment revolution, as with the Republicans in New York (Tyler and Wells, 1962, 1971), but most schemes appear to be bipartisan, aimed at protecting incumbents of both parties and reducing the number of marginal seats (as in the rival plans of Table 8.5 when compared with the Court plan). Noragon (1973, pp. 321–2) shows that before reapportionment 40 per cent of the House of Representatives' seats were marginal, whereas after reapportionment only 29 per cent were. Tufte's (1973) figures show a drastic reduction in marginal seats since 1948 (Fig. 8.6). The large number of safe seats protected the Republicans from a rout in 1974 after Watergate, preventing the Democrats from getting the two-thirds majority necessary to override the Presidential veto. (Not all commentators accept Tufte's argument that more safe seats reflects bipartisan gerrymandering, however; both Ferejohn (1977) and Fiorina (1977) suggest that safety results from successful incumbency.)

One problem with gerrymanders is that although the result is apparent, the intent is hard, if not impossible, to prove. The perfect gerrymander is hard to define (Musgrave, 1977), so it is perhaps not surprising that although the Supreme Court was eventually prepared to investigate malapportionment, it has not been prepared to look at charges of gerrymandering.

Partisan gerrymandering elsewhere
The period 1820–70 has been called the 'age of open gerrymandering' in French political history (Campbell, 1958, p. 22), and this tradition was

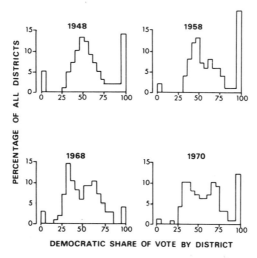

Fig. 8.6   The Democrat vote for House of Representatives districts, showing the development of a bipartisan, bimodal distribution from a normal (excluding the 100% Democrat districts of the South). Source: Tufte (1973, p. 533).

continued a century later by de Gaulle. Under the Third Republic, for example, urban areas were given separate representation wherever possible, so that in the Sarthe Department the town of Le Mans had one seat—usually won by the Communist Party—and the rural area was divided into four further seats, usually won by parties of the centre/right. In 1958 mixed urban/rural seats were created: Le Mans was divided between three of Sarthe's five constituencies, 'cracking' the Communist vote and winning all five for the centre/right (Criddle, 1975: in the cities, this gerrymandering was impossible, so the Communists were disadvantaged by malapportionment).

Gerrymandering is frequent in Ireland, too. In Ulster, there is considerable evidence of packing of Catholic voters, both in the wards of Londonderry and in the former Stormont constituencies of County Fermanagh (the latter designed by the Premier, Lord Craigavon, in 1929). In Fermanagh, the minority Unionist Party was able to win two of the three seats with a vote distribution as shown in Table 8.6. The Republic of Ireland uses the STV method with multi-member constituencies, which are defined by the Minister of Local Government (i.e. by the party in power). Over time, the average size of constituencies has decreased; this makes it virtually impossible for minority parties to gain representation, since with eight seats in a constituency 13 per cent of the votes will probably win one of them whereas with only four seats 25 per cent are needed. Most constituencies now return either three or four members. If party X wins 42 per cent of the votes, it will probably get one seat in a three-seat constituency (33 per cent) but two in a four-seat (50 per cent); if it wins 58 per cent, on the other hand, it will get two seats in both a three-seat (67 per cent) and a four-seat constituency (50 per cent). In terms of electoral biases, therefore, a governing party should aim to have three-seat constituencies where it is strong and likely to win two of the three, and four-seat constituencies where it is weak. This is what successive Irish governments have realized. In 1969, Fianna Fáil, whose main strength is in the western, rural areas, created six four-seat constituencies and one three-seat in Dublin and three-seat constituencies throughout the west of Ireland; four years later, the Fine Gael/Labour coalition divided Dublin into nine three-member constituencies (which gerrymandering was insufficient, because of the large swing to Fianna Fáil, to win the 1977 general election for the coalition).

Table 8.6

The gerrymander in County Fermanagh

| | Votes | |
Constituency	Unionist	Nationalist
Enniskillen	5706	4729
Lisnakea	5593	4129
South Fermanagh	2596	6680
Total	13 895	15 582

The Anglo-Saxon neutral gerrymander

In Britain and some other countries which use the Westminster parliamentary model the definition of constituency boundaries is not a political operation. Instead, the countries have neutral Parliamentary Boundary Commissions, who define the constituencies within constraints set by governments. Their neutrality is beyond doubt, and yet their effect in most areas is a gerrymander favouring the majority party.

The rules for the English Boundary Commission include the following three (Taylor and Gudgin, 1976a).

(1) Rule Four states that no constituency shall contain either parts of two counties or parts of two county or metropolitan boroughs, or parts of one county and another borough; in addition no county district (or ward in a borough) shall be split between two constituencies.

(2) Rule Five states that the populations of all constituencies should be as near to the national average (quota) as possible, and Rule Four can be overridden to meet this constraint.

(3) Rule Six states that both of the above rules may be disregarded if special geographical conditions—e.g. size, shape, accessibility—make a deviation desirable.

Local government areas are the basic building-blocks, therefore, and violation of their boundaries was rare in the 1954 redistribution (which covered general elections from 1955 to 1970).

Application of these rules to the amalgamation of wards in boroughs is likely to produce a packed gerrymander favouring the majority party, since British parties have a strong class basis to their support and social classes in the cities and towns are spatially segregated. Taylor and Gudgin (1976b) have demonstrated this for the boroughs of Sunderland and Newcastle upon Tyne. Sunderland comprises eighteen wards which had to be grouped into two constituencies. There are 87 different ways in which this can be done: 73 of them give both seats to Labour, which gets only 58 per cent of all the votes in the town (Fig. 8.7A). In Newcastle upon Tyne, 20 wards had to be grouped

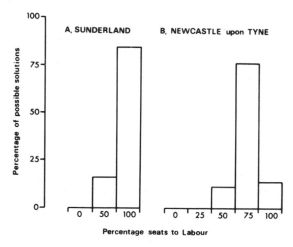

Fig. 8.7   Histograms of the possible constituency solutions for two boroughs: Source: after Taylor and Gudgin (1976b).

into four constituencies: of the 337 different possible solutions, 37 result in a 2 : 2 draw between the two parties, 256 in a 3 : 1 win for Labour, and 44 in a 4 : 0 win for Labour, which again gets about 58 per cent of the vote (Fig. 8.7B). In both towns, therefore, the frequency distribution of possible constituency arrangements produces a majority of solutions with an electoral bias in favour of the majority party. Not surprisingly, the neutral Boundary Commissioners chose the most likely result for each town—a 2 : 0 Labour victory in Sunderland and a 3 : 1 win in Newcastle. Thus (Taylor and Gudgin, 1975, p. 413) 'whereas partisan agencies may be accused of intentional gerrymandering, non-partisan agencies may be equally guilty of unintentional gerrymandering'.

Extrapolating their results to the country as a whole, Taylor and Gudgin note that the minor of the two main parties (Conservative and Labour) is likely to be discriminated against in each area by the unintentional gerrymander. Thus Labour will get more seats than votes in the borough constituencies, but less seats than votes in the counties; the Conservatives will get the reverse of that pattern. This is shown by the distributions of wasted and excess votes at the 1970 general election (Table 8.7), with Conservative wasting most votes in the boroughs and Labour in the counties. The implications of this greater spatial polarization of party representation than of votes are that governments are spatially biased in their constituency origins, with probable repercussions on the areas favoured by various policies.

Table 8.7
Wasted and excess votes: 1970 General Election, England

	Conservative	Labour
County constituencies		
Wasted	838 000	3 205 000
Excess	2 019 000	550 000
Borough constituencies		
Wasted	2 447 000	1 987 000
Excess	789 000	1 073 000

Influencing the neutral gerrymander

Although the British Boundary Commissions are politically neutral, the rules under which they operate are politically defined, and so biases can be introduced to their work. Such political influence was charged in 1948 when the Labour Government asked the commissioners to make an *ad hoc* report subdividing the eight seats with more than 80 000 voters each and adding an extra seat to each of the nine largest county boroughs (Butler, 1963, p. 127): the results of such action were almost certain to favour Labour.

The work of the commissions can be influenced in two ways:

(1) in the design of the building-blocks—the county boroughs and their wards: the counties and their urban and rural districts; and
(2) in the implementation of the commissioners' reports.

Both ways were used by the Labour Governments of 1964–70, and the former is being used during the mid-1970s.

Local government boundary adjustments are agreed to by a Minister. In 1964–6 this was the Minister of Housing and Local Government—Richard Crossman—whose decisions clearly reflected the national political influence of local changes. On entering office, he inherited proposals for considerable change in several areas, including his constituency town of Coventry (Crossman, 1975, pp. 64–5, 87–8, 621).

I soon discovered that as a Labour politician these are for me not merely decisions about the boundaries of *local authorities* but decisions which will influence the boundaries of *constituencies* . . . every time . . . I alter a county borough boundary I may affect the fate of the M.P. sitting for the borough . . . Come what may, no decision would be taken about a local government boundary without the parliamentary repercussions being fully considered and without my trying to shield the Labour position.

Crossman was under obvious pressure from incumbent Labour M.P.s not to put their seats at risk, and so his solution for Leicester was to (Crossman, 1975, p. 240)

put the maximum number of Labour voters inside the borough and the maximum number of Tory voters outside in the county . . . It has been an anxious job because I have to be sure that no one can accuse me of gerrymandering the boundary for party purposes.

Shades of Tuskegee's packed gerrymander!

Throughout his ministry, Crossman was determined to replace the Local Government Boundary Commission by a Royal Commission on Local Government, reflecting his own dissatisfaction with the system when an Oxford City Councillor. He was unsure of when to set up the Royal Commission, however. In 1965, he and the Prime Minister agreed to wait for the L.G.B.C.'s report on Lancashire: one month later (Crossman, 1975, p. 441) a local expert on Lancashire reported that the L.G.B.C.'s recommendations could lose Labour 20 seats there, and so in January 1966 the decision was made that the L.G.B.C. was to be dissolved and a Royal Commission set up.

The Royal Commission reported in 1969. At about the same time, the Parliamentary Boundary Commissioners presented a revised set of constituencies, as they were required to do fifteen years after the last changes. The Labour government was uneasy about the possible electoral impact of the revision, long before it was produced, and in January 1967 the Home Secretary and the Lord President of the Council agreed that (Crossman, 1976, p. 202)

the right line to take is to let them complete their recommendations and then say that it is absurd to implement all of them pending the local government reform. They should be asked to propose a list of twenty to thirty constituencies which have become grossly disproportionate and we should limit the changes to these urgent cases.

Crossman (1976, p. 318) makes it clear that one of his Cabinet arguments for the Royal Commission on Local Government was that it could be used to help avoid the electoral consequences of a 1970 redistribution of seats.

The Government believed that Labour would lose 12–20 seats under the new set of constituencies, although clearly there was disagreement over this.

There's no way of knowing whether the calculations were right or wrong. Somehow they became an accepted doctrine, with the result that the Government decided to defer carrying out the recommendation (Brown, 1972, p. 256).

The Conservatives ... believed, and their press with them, that the Commission's recommendations would work strongly to their advantage, to the extent of some twenty seats. I had the strongest reason to doubt this. The view of the Labour Party's then national organizer ... was that at most six or eight seats, on balance, would be at risk (Wilson, 1974, p. 854).

The decision not to implement the new constituencies had some logic since the Royal Commission's (Wilson, 1974, p. 853) 'recommendations to end the distinction between town and country destroyed the very basis of a great many parliamentary boundaries, including the distinction embodied in the Representation of the People Act between "borough" and "county" constituencies'. The Home Secretary—Callaghan—introduced legislation to delay implementation but this was defeated in the House of Lords. Under threat of a High Court order, he felt bound to introduce the new constituencies in an Act before the House of Commons, but avoided the problem by the simple expedient of ensuring that his party's majority voted them out.

One commentator (Steed, 1969, p. 996) claims that in fact there were only about seven cases where the new parliamentary constituency boundaries crossed boundaries proposed for local governments by the Royal Commission, so that Wilson's argument was a false one. Nevertheless, as agreed by Jenkins and Crossman, the 1970 election was fought in the 1955 constituencies, with some minor changes (taking eleven seats from Greater London and subdividing nine of the largest constituencies) which Steed (1969, p. 997) claimed produced a net loss of three or four seats from the Conservatives to Labour. 'The Home Secretary denies, of course, that party political considerations have affected his decision. If so, he has done a remarkably good job for his party by chance.' Charges of a gerrymander were widespread, although as Brown (1972, p. 256) ruefully notes, 'as in the end we lost sixty seats, it was not a very successful gerrymander'. He had cause to be regretful. Non-implementation of the changes made his seat at Belper a Tory gain; after the subsequent redistribution, it reverted to Labour.

After the local government reorganization was eventually introduced in 1972, taking effect in 1974, a new set of building-blocks was provided for the Parliamentary Commissioners. The English Local Government Boundary Commission then set to work providing new units within the boroughs: new sets of wards were to be defined, with the intent that they should be of equal population size and reflecting communities of interest. The relevant local government submits its plans to the Commission, after these have been published so that alternatives can be proposed (by opposing political parties, for example), and the Commission makes its decision based only on its criteria. Like reapportionment in the U.S.A., this is an invitation to gerrymander, both for local government and, eventually, for Parliamentary constituencies. Thus a new system of 29 wards was proposed for Sheffield in

1976 by the Labour-controlled Metropolitan District Council. The Conservatives charged that the boundaries had been so drawn that they would never win more than 18 of the 87 seats in the Council Chamber (*Sheffield Morning Telegraph*, 31 July 1976): four wards, it was claimed, were being changed from marginal to safe Labour.

Continuing the trend of naming an electoral abuse after its perpetrator, *The Guardian* (30 December 1976) has invented the *Crossmander*. This involves the use of political influence, for partisan ends, in the delimitation of local government and parliamentary constituency boundaries. It is intentional gerrymandering within a system which is ostensibly neutral.

Changing the population distribution

Instead of altering the boundaries of electoral areas to obtain partisan benefits, the same end can be achieved by changing the population composition of constituencies. This can only be done with difficulty, since large-scale movements cannot be engineered in a short period. It is the basis of the South African Bantustan policy, however, in which the white government is creating puppet black states (whose boundaries are as carefully drawn— around Durban for example— as were those of Tuskegee) to ensure that no blacks are residents of the white homelands.

Population distributions change 'naturally', in recent years as a consequence of two trends; the rural-to-urban shift of population and the suburban sprawl within urban areas. Thus any system of constituencies defined on population equality criteria soon becomes obsolete. The urban-to-suburban movement has been the major trend within Britain. Within the large urban areas, the central-city seats are characteristically Labour-held and the suburban ones Conservative, so that in 1966 and 1970 the former were characterized by population decline and the latter by growth (Rowley, 1970, 1975). Eventually this will be to Labour's disadvantage, because of both moves to eliminate the remaining central-city seats that are too small and the tendency for Conservatism among former Labour voters who move to the suburbs (Cox, 1968). As Brown noted (1972, p. 257) with regard to the 1970 revision of boundaries,

Belper, with an electorate of 87,100, was one of the constituencies due for revision. The electorate had increased by over 10,000 since 1966, mainly from the growth of middle-class housing estates, so that most of the new electors could be expected to vote Tory. Since my majority in 1966 was 4,274, an influx of 10,000 new voters, mainly Tory, obviously imperilled the seat.

Altering population distributions, at a variety of spatial scales, is a topic of considerable interest to planners and to social scientists (Johnston, 1976c). At the neighbourhood level, for example, social integration via spatial integration is often proposed to replace social and spatial segregation, with the attendant conflict (for a review see Sarkissian, 1976). As the neighbourhood is a major social context within which voting decisions are made (Taylor and Johnston, 1979, Chapter 5) such spatial engineering could have important political consequences; it would also, of course, remove the possibility of any form of gerrymandering. Its feasibility is very much in doubt, however.

Changing the electoral law

A major way of altering the outcome of a contest is to change the rules. As illustrated in Chapter 4, there is a great variety of rules available for electoral contests; all produce some kinds of bias, but some are more prone to bias, and to manipulation to produce that bias, than are others. Thus under any system there is always likely to be a move towards change (electoral 'reform') both from losers attempting to get a more favourable situation and from winners aiming to protect their possession of power.

Plurality or preferential: Australia and Ireland

The use of preferential voting systems, rather than the traditional British plurality method, dates back in Australia to the nineteenth century. Queensland experimented in 1892 and Tasmania in 1896. The debate was between those who wanted proportional representation to achieve minority representation in a plural society, and those who saw P.R. as producing a fragmentation of parties and weak governments. Preferential systems were introduced in most states during the first decade of this century, but the federal House of Representatives was elected by the plurality system.

The change to a preferential system for the federal House, in 1918, was not the result of philosophical debate, but a pragmatic political decision that the Alternative Vote (AV) was the best way of defeating the onset of socialism. In 1916, the Labor Party split over conscription, and in the general election the Federal National Party (FNP), which included Labor dissidents, won by 53 to 22. Within the FNP, however, the Liberal faction felt insecure. In 1918, it fought a by-election at Flinders (South Australia) against both Labor and a farmers' candidate, who eventually was persuaded to withdraw in order to avoid splitting the anti-Labor vote: later in the year, three anti-Labor candidates split the vote between them at Swan (Western Australia) and the Labor candidate won with only 34·36 per cent of the vote. Another by-election was due at Corangamite (Victoria); before it was held the FNP government introduced the AV system, which allowed its contesting factions to ensure that their preferences defeated Labor (Graham, 1962). The system has been used ever since. It benefits the Country (rural) and Liberal (urban middle class) coalition against Labor (urban working class) so that although Labor in Australia has won proportionally more votes since 1945 than its British and New Zealand counterparts, it has won many fewer elections (Taylor and Gudgin, 1977). Manipulation of the system has benefited the manipulators.

Proportional representation—the STV method (p. 55)—was introduced to Ireland in 1918 by Lloyd George's government as a way of blunting the electoral success of the Sinn Fein (republican) party (O'Leary, 1961, p. 6). It was a policy of divide and rule with regard to Irish politics. The Proportional Representation Society (now the Electoral Reform Society) was responsible for much of the pressure leading to the adoption of STV, and this was maintained in 1922 with the establishment of the Irish Free State. (Democratic theory of the time was very much pro Proportional Representation: Headlam-Morley, 1929.)

From 1923 to 1935 no party won a majority in the Irish Dáil. The feeling developed that STV was anti-democratic, producing post-election, back-room, inter-party deals which excluded the electorate (O'Leary, 1961, p. 26). In 1938, de Valera, the Fianna Fáil leader, spoke against STV for this reason. The opposition, Fine Gael, defended it, including the use of such arguments that any other system (O'Leary, 1961, p. 36) 'breeds muzzled, sullen, discontented minorities, predisposed to doctrines of violence'. De Valera backed down, and the issue remained quiescent until 1958, when the Fianna Fáil government produced a bill replacing STV by the AV system. Fine Gael and the small Labour Party opposed the bill, which passed the Dáil but not the Senate (where the six senators representing the country's universities contributed to its defeat). And so the proposed change went to a referendum on the same day as Fianna Fáil's leader, de Valera, stood for the Presidency. De Valera won, but his party (always the country's largest) did not get its electoral change because (O'Leary, 1975, p. 167) 'fear of the *Fianna Fáil* plurality being converted into a near-permanent majority enhanced the opposition of *Fine Gael* and Labour', although the vote against was narrow (486 989 to 453 322). Fianna Fáil tried again in 1968, but 60·8 per cent of the voters decided that (O'Leary, 1975, p. 170) 'Irish politics had been remarkably stable and permanent *Fianna Fáil* supremacy would be too high a price to pay for the alleged blessings of single-party government'.

P.R. or not? The vacillations of the French

The debates and politics regarding electoral systems in Australia and Ireland pale into insignificance beside the changes in France since 1789. Campbell (1958, p. 17) opens his definitive study of the topic with

Only once has an electoral system survived for as long as thirty consecutive years (1889–1919); twice a system has been used for about eighteen years (1831–1848 and 1852–1870); for the remaining 103 years no system has been used for as long as twelve years before being considerably changed or completely discarded. The electoral system has been treated as a weapon in the struggle between different political camps and between different social forces for the control of the State and society.

The current system has lasted since 1958.

Two main types of system have been used: the multi-member constituencies using the list system and the single-member constituencies using the double ballot variant of the AV, with the latter currently in favour. The double ballot allows the various conservative forces of the centre and right of the political spectrum to protect themselves, first against popular local candidates, and then against candidates of the left. For the multi-member constituencies, the arguments in favour stressed that they encouraged the dominance of national over sectional political parties, whereas those preferring the single-member system argued the benefits of close links between representative and constituents. Lists favour large, nationally organized parties, too.

Table 8.8
Seat allocation rules and electoral engineering

Party		A	B	C	D	E
Votes		35 279	26 744	62 780	4273	55 820
Seats	5	Total votes 184 896			Quota 36 979	
Highest average system						
Seats above quota		0	0	1	0	1
Average votes		35 279	26 744	31 390	4273	27 910
Seat to		1	0	0	0	0
Average votes		17 639	26 744	31 390	4273	27 910
Seat to		0	0	1	0	0
Average votes		17 639	26 744	20 926	4273	27 910
Seat to		0	0	0	0	1
Total seats		1	0	2	0	2
Largest remainder system						
Seats above quota		0	0	1	0	1
Votes less quota		35 279	26 744	25 801	4273	18 841
Remaining three seats to largest remainders		1	1	1	0	0
Total seats		1	1	2	0	1

Source: Campbell (1958, pp. 105–15).

France has a great diversity of political attitudes which is reflected in the multiplicity of parties. No electoral system is likely to produce a parliamentary majority for one party, therefore, but any grouping in power can use the electoral law to reduce the influence of the opposition. This can be illustrated by the electoral engineering introduced by the parties of the centre in 1951 to counter both the growing Communist vote and also the right-wing strength of de Gaulle's French People's Rally (RPF). The list system was manipulated for this. In Paris, where the Communist vote was large, the largest-remainder allocation system—which favours smaller parties—was used, whereas in the provinces the centre was strong and the Communists relatively weak and the highest-average allocation procedure, which favoured the former, was employed. Table 8.8 illustrates how these two systems differ for one constituency electing five members. Under the highest-average system, votes are divided by the number of seats the party would have if it won that currently being allocated. In this case party E benefits most, getting 40 per cent of the seats with 30·2 per cent of the votes. Under the largest remainder, the parties with most votes left after removal of those exceeding the quota receive the remaining seats. These are A, B, and C in the example, so E with 30·2 per cent of the votes gets only 20 per cent of the seats.

Use of this manipulation against the Communists was very successful in 1951, when they were probably deprived of 71 seats relative to the law of 1946 (they won 97); the R.P.F. was probably deprived of 26, winning 107. And so the left and, to a lesser extent, the right were discriminated against, with the parties of the centre getting 51 per cent of the votes but 62·5 per cent of the seats.

Similar anti-left manipulations are used in French local government elections. These are conducted with a list system plus a double ballot: the top two parties in the first ballot contest the second. A party which does not make the second ballot thus gets no representation at all; if parties are to amalgamate their lists, they must do this prior to the first ballot. This system was devised by the centre parties to counter the Socialist and Communist opposition (*The Times*, 19 March 1977); it rebounded against them in the 1977 elections when the Socialists and Communists formed a Union of the Left prior to the first ballot and won in many towns (*The Times*, 15 March 1977).

Voting for American city councils

Three types of electoral systems are used for American cities: wards; at large; and mixed (Kasperson, 1969). Wards allow representation of minorities which are spatially concentrated, whereas at-large systems allow majorities to carry the whole city (unless there are many votes for individuals rather than parties: Johnston, 1974b). Prior to 1949, Boston's city council was elected from wards, and various immigrant groups were represented: since then an at-large system has been used, with the 'Boston Irish' dominating the Council as a result.

An example of a mixed system is Durham, North Carolina, where half of the councillors are elected at-large and the other half by wards. The ward candidates must live in the area they hope to represent. They are voted for by the whole city, so a black candidate standing for a 100 per cent black ward must obtain majority support among the whites living elsewhere (Keech, 1968, p. 16). In mixed wards, of course, white candidates will have a great advantage over blacks, and so the system militates against minority representation, assuming that local white candidates can be found to stand; this mixed system, like the at-large one, is not conducive to black representation (Sloan, 1969).

Electoral 'reform' in Britain

Extension of the parliamentary franchise in Britain occurred in the late nineteenth century with the use of multi-member constituencies, from which election was based on pluralities. The present system of single-member pluralities was only introduced in the 1885 Reform Act when (Steed, 1975, p. 41) 'members appear to have been persuaded that equal-sized single member districts would avoid the injustices in the relationship of votes to seats that were beginning to be noted'. From then on, most parties seem to have been fully aware of the inequities of the adopted system: some were opposed to change, since they in general benefited from the inequities; others were for change, but their uncertainty as to what should be instituted meant that nothing was done.

The electoral system has almost been changed on two occasions. In 1917, a Speaker's Conference reported unanimously that the single-member plurality system should be replaced, but in the subsequent debate on the Representation of the People Act, 1918 (Butler, 1963, p. 39)

The House of Commons had resolved in favour of the alternative vote. The House of Lords, to kill the alternative vote, had insisted on proportional representation, and the Commons had very reluctantly yielded and agreed to a trial of it in a hundred constituencies; later even that had been abandoned owing to the vested interests of the members in the areas affected ... the survival of the existing system plainly expressed not so much an endorsement of its merits as a failure to agree upon the remedy for its faults.

In 1931, during the period when Labour was replacing Liberal as the second major party, a change was again nearly brought about. The Labour Government elected in 1929 relied on Liberal support. As part of their bargaining the Liberals had demanded P.R., but had accepted the alternative vote, and Labour, although wanting no change, was prepared to give this. A Speaker's Conference made two recommendations (Steed, 1975, p. 49): 'that the alternative vote should not be used (Conservative and Labour versus Liberal) and that any change in the electoral system should involve proportional representation (Conservative and Liberal versus Labour)'. Eventually, however, the government introduced a bill proposing to use the alternative vote, but it had not been enacted when the government fell in 1931. After that, normal politics were virtually suspended for some years; when they were revived, Labour and Conservative in turn both benefited from the manufactured majorities of single-member pluralities and Liberal was powerless to press its demands for change.

Despite the continued work of the Electoral Reform Society, the issue faded away until 1974. At the two general elections of that year the Liberals won 21·5 per cent and 20·32 per cent of the votes, but only 1·74 and 1·55 per cent of the seats. This bias incensed many observers. Polemics on electoral reform were issued (Rogaly, 1976; Mayhew, 1976); academics joined the debate (Finer, 1975); and the Hansard Society (1976) proposed adoption of the German mixed system in which party lists are used to allocate a second set of seats to correct the biases produced by a single-member plurality election.

The debate has remained alive, partly because the Liberals later gained the balance of power in the House of Commons (1977) and argued that they would support the government only if it agreed on electoral reform (*The Times*, 12 March 1977). Secondly, the devolution of some, if not all, power to Scotland and Wales was a major issue of the 1976–77 parliamentary session, and was seen by protagonists of electoral reform as an ideal opportunity to press their case. Finally, the system was being prepared for the 1979 direct elections to the European Parliament and the Labour Government was reluctantly pressed by the Liberal Party to propose a list system for multi-member constituencies, which could be seen as a trial for use of a similar system for Westminster elections. (Debate on how these elections were to be conducted was very lively in all nine countries: *The Times*, 25 February 1977.)

Any change in the electoral system would clearly disadvantage the Labour and Conservative parties, whose share of the vote has fallen considerably from 87·6 per cent in 1945 to 75·1 per cent in October 1974 but who still win 93·8 per cent of the seats. The actual consequences of changes are hard to predict, but it does seem (Berrington, 1975; Steed, 1974; Johnston, 1976b, 1977c) that the main losers would be the Conservatives and the main gainers the Liberals (see also Taylor and Johnston, 1979, Chapter 8). But in 1978 the likelihood of any change was remote, especially in comparison to 1918 and 1931.

Conclusions

All electoral systems produce biases and so are open to abuse by those who want the biases to favour them. No system is the best for everybody, and it is interesting that at the same time as influential British protagonists for electoral 'reform' were proposing the West German system, the two main West German parties were seriously considering a change from that system in order to remove the political influence of a minor party (Conradt, 1970). Thus although the system may not be changed in most places as frequently as it has been in France, if it is changed at all, there will always be parties and groups who see benefits for themselves from some form of 'reform'.

Operation of the electoral system can be taken out of political hands, and tasks such as the definition of constituencies given to neutral bodies or even to computers. But neutrality of intent does not necessarily produce a neutral effect; malapportionment may be outlawed, but gerrymanders are still feasible and electoral biases likely. And so those who write the rules for the neutral bodies or the computers will orient them to their own ends. Elections, it seems, are almost certain to generate electoral abuse, however sophisticated and covert.

**Part V
Finale**

9 Conclusions

THIS book has developed two main themes concerning spatial variations in levels of social well-being: that the amount which a government chooses to spend in an area (and what it spends it on) is partly a function of the election situation there; and that both the areas—notably their boundaries—and their electoral situation can be manipulated by political action. These themes have been pursued in the context of two main spatial systems—that used for local government and that used for elections. Evidence has been provided which supports the general argument, but no attempt has been made to assess the relative importance of the findings. (If electoral considerations are responsible, for example, for only a one or two per cent spatial variation in levels of social well-being, it may well be concluded that this is insignificant, both in substance to the recipients and as a valid topic for further research. Much of the evidence presented here, however, and especially that in Chapter 5, suggests more substantial variations.)

One of the problems of the sort of work reported here concerns validation criteria with regard to the substantiation of hypotheses. This is a general concern for human geography, and is not peculiar to the present book. What evidence is needed to support the general theses advanced here (and repeated in the first sentence of the previous paragraph)? Undoubtedly, many examples could be found which would not substantiate the arguments advanced here, to parallel those cases which conform to expectations. Only the latter have been presented, however, which could generate charges of bias, of an intent to substantiate the hypotheses without weighing the alternative evidence which might suggest otherwise. The defence for such an approach is that the political and electoral variables examined here are but a part, often a small part, of a complex set of operating processes. They have been isolated here in order to stress the case that such variables form an important component of geographical argument and explanation. That examples can be quoted which do not indicate the influence of political and electoral variables indicates that such variables are neither universal in their influence nor consistent in their importance: in some cases they might be overridden by the operation of other variables; in other cases, trade-offs may have been made whereby political–electoral advantage in one place has been forgone in order that other advantages may be obtained elsewhere. That evidence in line with the theses of the book is available in quite considerable volume is taken as sufficient to indicate that the arguments advanced here regarding the importance of a political–geographical viewpoint to the study of the geography of social well-being are valid and worthy of consideration.

What do the conclusions which have been produced here imply with regard to the systems models introduced in Chapter 2? The basic system, as portrayed by Easton (Fig. 2.2), sees the state reacting to the demands of its constituents, and thereby winning its support. This was modified in two ways. The first (Fig. 2.3) accepted that society is divided into a series of competing interest groups (classes in a Weberian sense) and suggested that governments are often more responsive to some than to others. Empirical evidence suggested that this is often so, that certain minority groups, especially minority groups in particular places, will have their demands ignored because their support is not crucial to the government. Only when support is needed will a government in power (or a party out of power) solicit it by meeting the voters' demands. Demands are not completely ignored, of course, since this could generate considerable minority group unrest (as in Ulster), but usually minorities will not have their demands met substantially unless either their support is needed to sustain a government in office or they are able through some device (such as a gerrymander, of which the South African apartheid scheme is the extreme example) to control the government despite their minority status. Often, the spatial components of the electoral system are manipulated so as to minimize the necessary support needed from certain groups, and thus the degree to which their demands need to be met.

The second way in which Easton's model was modified involved the recognition that much of the operation of welfare-state policy, involving decisions about type and level of implementation, is handled by subordinate local governments (Fig. 2.4). Each local government area comprises a sample of the total population, almost certainly a non-random sample which is biased towards certain interest groups, and the majority within its territory is able to determine, usually within nationally defined constraints, what and whose demands will be met. The creation of these local government areas is itself an arena of conflict between various interest groups; the evidence presented here, especially that from the United States, suggests that the protagonists are unequal in this conflict, and that the consequences often are harmful, not necessarily only to minorities but also to majorities, particularly the relatively poor and the politically weak.

The ways in which these two types of system operate were modelled in terms of the role of elections in the search for political power (Fig. 2.5). Both short-term (Fig. 2.6) and long-term (Fig. 2.7) aspects of this model were isolated. The short-term aspects emphasize both policy differences between local governments and variations between the constituent areas of a single government's territory in the implementation of policies: Part III of the book provides the evidence which illustrates these processes in operation. The long-term aspects are concerned with manipulations of the two systems for sectional gain, and Part IV of the book illustrates local government reform and electoral reform in operation.

One final point should be noted here about the findings presented in the book and their relationship to the total body of evidence which might be produced either to substantiate or to deny the theses outlined. On many issues, governments need not react to the attitudes of the electorate, because these are very rarely, if ever, presented as electoral demands. For example, the British parliament some years ago abolished the death penalty. Almost certainly a majority of the British population today would favour a return of the death penalty (Gallup Political Index, 201, April 1977), but parliament and its constituent parties need not react to this feeling since no election is likely to be fought on the death penalty issue and very few, if any, voters are likely to decide who to support with reference to this issue. Almost all elections are fought on economic management issues—as the Australian Labor Party discovered after its 'unconstitutional' dismissal from government in 1975. Demands relating to jobs and incomes must be respected, if not met, in electoral platforms and policies, and support sought accordingly. On other issues, parliament can lead, and to some extent ignore, the voters' views. This is particularly the case where parliamentary elections are the only form of direct popular participation in democracy; in countries which use frequent referenda, such as Switzerland and also many of the American states, the situation is somewhat different. In general terms, therefore, the models developed and examined here refer only to economic issues, on which the support for political parties is very largely based.

The evidence presented in Chapter 5–8 indicates the playing-out of political and electoral conflict on a spatial stage, and provides the basis for the case presented in Chapter 1 regarding the importance of political geography to the wider study of the geography of social well-being. A logical outgrowth of the empirical presentations is to inquire into their relevance to planning, to the development of policies and attitudes which might ameliorate, if not remove, spatial variations in social well-being. Two possible general strategies are open for consideration: the first suggests managerial changes in the operation of the systems; whereas the second suggests reforms of a more substantial nature.

Managerial changes involve the introduction of new practices within the existing structure, designed so as better to meet needs and demands. In the present context, they would involve altering the basis of political life. The most likely change would be removal of the flexibility in the operation of many government programmes so that politicians, particularly those in local governments, become much more like administrators operating within closely prescribed rules. But in almost all situations, demands exceed the resources which are made available to meet them, so that decisions have to be made regarding competing claims. In some cases, a uniform percentage cut can be applied to all demands, but in others a choice must be made. While this choice remains a political one, and while politicians are dependent on the support of certain people in certain places, the sorts of choices reported in this book are likely to continue.

In looking at reformist solutions, it is necessary to return to the discussion in Chapter 1 regarding the role of geographical analysis in the understanding of spatial variations in social well-being. The spatial structure of a society reflects its social structure (Coates, Johnston and Knox, 1977): once a spatial structure has been created, it acts to some extent as a constraint on developments in the social structure, but the fundamental laws are social, as they refer to space, and not spatial, as they refer to society. In a capitalist society the spatial structure is a mapping of class relationships, producing the spatial division of labour discussed in Chapter 1. It is upon that map that other maps are superimposed, such as those of the local government and electoral systems discussed here. If the underlying map is not going to be changed, and nor are the forces which produce it, then manipulation of the superimposed maps will at best merely disturb the edges of the problem—which is social inequality (Johnston, 1978i).

Manipulations of the spatial systems for local government and for elections are frequent and, as has been reported here, a great number of them are undertaken for sectional gain. Those which are not frequently result in sectional gain producing the situation, which Dixon (1968) has noted, that all districting is gerrymandering. Within the Anglo-Saxon ethos of private land ownership, it is impossible to produce spatial systems comprising independent territories which do not have discriminatory effects, in that some members of society are able to decide where they will live and most are constrained, to a greater or lesser extent, to certain areas only. The only 'reform' which might remove such discrimination would be to eliminate the spatial component to political activity. There would be no local government but rather all administration from one central point; and there would be a single, national constituency for elections.

Thus the evidence presented here can be interpreted in a variety of ways. It demonstrates, for example, that while there is class and political conflict played out on a spatial stage, a class or group in power is likely to manipulate some aspect of that stage for its own ends. It also indicates that politics is about short-term pragmatics, not long-term goals, and that social, and hence spatial inequality results from the pragmatic decision-making. Perhaps, then, the ultimate reformist solution is the end of politics, and the replacement of competition for the right to rule by a permanent ruling élite!

For the geographer interested in both the problems discussed here and their solution (or at least their amelioration), the outlook is somewhat pessimistic. Geographical analysis can illustrate the operation of inequitable political systems but it cannot, *qua* geographical analysis, indicate how they might be replaced. The foundations of inequality lie deeper than the spatial system, and the study of the latter is but part of a very much larger whole. Despite this general pessimism, however, the theses advanced in this book, and their illustration, provide evidence of the value of politico-geographical analyses in the understanding of the origin of inequality. Without such understanding, improvement is impossible.

Bibliography

ADAMS, R. (1965). 'On the variation in the consumption of public services', *Review of Economics and Statistics*, **47**, 400–5.

ADRIAN, C. R. (1959). 'A typology of nonpartisan elections', *Western Political Quarterly*, **12**, 449–58.

AKIN, J. S. and AUTEN, G. E. (1976). 'City schools and suburban schools: a fiscal comparison', *Land Economics*, **52**, 452–66.

ALBIN, P. S. and STEIN, B. (1971). 'Determinants of relief policy at the sub-federal level', *Southern Economic Journal*, **37**, 445–57.

ALFORD, R. (1963). *Party and Society*, Rand McNally, Chicago.

ALONSO, W. (1964), 'Location theory', in J. Friedmann and W. Alonso (eds.), *Regional Development and Planning: A Reader*, The M.I.T. Press, Cambridge, Mass., 78–106.

ALT, J. E. (1971), 'Social and political correlates of County Borough expenditures', *British Journal of Political Science*, **1**, 49–62.

ARCHER, J. C. and REYNOLDS, D. R. (1976), 'Locational logrolling and citizen support of municipal bond proposals: the example of St. Louis', *Public Choice*, **27**, 21–40.

ASHER, H. B. and VAN METER, D. S. (1974). *Determinants of Public Welfare Policies: A Causal Approach*, Sage Professional Papers in American Politics, 04–009, Sage Publications, Beverly Hills.

ASHFORD, D. E. (1974). 'The effects of central finance on the British local government system', *British Journal of Political Science*, **4**, 305–22.

—— (1975). 'Resources, spending and party politics in British local government', *Administration and Society*, **7**, 286–311.

—— BERNE, R., and SCHRAMM, R. (1976). 'The expenditure-financing decision in British local government', *Policy and Politics*, **5**, 5–24.

AXELROD, R. (1972), 'Where the votes come from: an analysis of electoral coalitions, 1952–1968', *American Political Science Review*, **66**, 11 20.

BABCOCK, R. F. (1973). 'Exclusionary zoning; a code phrase for a notable legal struggle', in L. H. Masotti and J. K. Hadden (eds.), *The Urbanization of the Suburbs*, Sage Publications, Beverly Hills, 313–28.

BANFIELD, E. C. and WILSON, J. Q. (1963). *City Politics*, Harvard University Press, Cambridge, Mass.

BANZHAF, J. F., III (1968). 'One man, 3·312 votes: a mathematical analysis of the Electoral College', *Villanova Law Review*, **14**, 304–32.

BARNETT, J. R. (undated). 'On the existence of locational bias in election campaigns.'

BARONE, M., UJIFUSA, G., and MATTHEWS, D. (1972). *Almanac of American Politics, 1972*, The Colonial Press, Clinton, Mass.

—— —— —— (1974). *Almanac of American Politics, 1974*, The Colonial Press, Clinton, Mass.

BENIGER, J. R. (1977). 'The legacy of Carter and Reagan: political reality overtakes the myth of the Presidential primaries', *Intellect Magazine*, February 1977, 234–37.

BERGMAN, E. F. (1976). *Modern Political Geography*, Wm. C. Brown, Dubuque, Iowa.

BERNSTEIN, C. and WOODWARD, B. (1974). *All the President's Men*, Quartet Books, London.

BERRINGTON, H. (1975). 'Electoral reform and national government', in S. E. Finer (ed.), *Adversary Politics and Electoral Reform*, Anthony Wigram, London, 269–92.

BERRY, B. J. L. (1970). 'The geography of the United States in the year 2000', *Transactions, Institute of British Geographers*, **51**, 21–54.

—— (ed.) (1971). *Comparative Factorial Ecology*, *Economic Geography*, **47**.

—— (1976). 'The counterurbanization process: urban America since 1970', in B. J. L. Berry (ed.), *Urbanization and Counterurbanization*, Sage Publications, Beverly Hills, 17–30.

—— and KASARDA, J. D. (1977). *Contemporary Urban Ecology*, Macmillan, New York.

—— *et al.* (1976). 'Attitudes towards integration: the role of status in community response to racial change', in B. Schwartz (ed.), *The Changing Face of the Suburbs*, University of Chicago, 221–64.

BERRY, J. M. (1974). 'Electoral economics: getting and spending', *Polity*, **7**, 120–9.

BEST, J. (1975). *The Case against Direct Election of the President: A Defense of the Electoral College*, Cornell University Press, Ithaca.

BETH, L. P. and HAVARD, W. C. (1961). 'Committee stacking and political power in Florida', *Journal of Politics*, **23**, 57–83.

BICKEL, A. M. (1971). 'The Supreme Court and reapportionment', in N. W. Polsby (ed.), *Reapportionment in the 1970s*, Univ. of California Press, Berkeley, 57–74.

BIRKE, W. (1961). *European Elections by Direct Suffrage*, Sythoff, Leyden.

BISH, R. L. (1971). *The Public Economy of Metropolitan Areas*, Markham, Chicago.

—— (1976). 'Fiscal equalization through court decisions: policy-making without evidence', in E. Ostrom (ed.), *The Delivery of Urban Services: Outcomes of Change*, Sage Publications, Beverly Hills, 75–102.

BLAIR, G. S. (1964). *American Local Government*, Harper and Row, New York.

BLALOCK, H. M. (1960). *Social Statistics*, McGraw-Hill, New York.

BLEWETT, N. (1972). 'Redistribution procedures', in H. Mayer and H. Nelson (eds.), *Australian Politics: A Third Reader*, Cheshire, Melbourne, 295–300.

—— and JAENSCH, D. (1971). *Playford to Dunstan: Politics of Transition*, Cheshire, Melbourne.

BLYDENBURGH, J. C. (1976). 'An application of game theory to political campaign decision-making', *American Journal of Political Science*, **20**, 51–65.

BOADEN, N. T. (1970). 'Central departments and local authorities: the relationship examined', *Political Studies*, **18**, 175–86.

—— (1971). *Urban Policy-Making: Influences on County Boroughs in England and Wales*, The University Press, Cambridge.

—— and ALFORD, R. R. (1969). 'Sources of diversity in English local government decisions', *Public Administration*, **47**, 203–23.

BOOMS, B. H. and HALLDORSON, J. R. (1973). 'The politics of redistribution: a reformulation', *American Political Science Review*, **67**, 924–31.

BOULDING, K. E. (1973). *The Economy of Love and Fear: A Preface to Grants Economics*, Wadsworth, Belmont, California.

—— PFAFF, M., and PFAFF, A. (eds.) (1973). *Transfers in an Urbanized Economy*, Wadsworth, Belmont, California.

BRADY, D. W. (1973). 'A research note on the impact of interparty competition on Congressional voting in a competitive era', *American Political Science Review*, **67**, 153–6.

BRAMS, S. J. (1975). *Game Theory and Politics*, The Free Press, New York.

—— and DAVIS, M. D. (1973). 'Resource-allocation models in Presidential campaigning: implications for democratic representation', *Annals of the New York Academy of Sciences*, **219**, 105–23.

—— and DAVIS, M. D. (1974). 'The 3/2s rule in Presidential campaigning', *American Political Science Review*, **68**, 113–34.

BRAND, J. (1974). *Local Government Reform in England 1888–1974*, Croom Helm, London.

BROOKES, R. H. (1959). 'Electoral distortion in New Zealand', *Australian Journal of Politics and History*, **5**, 218–23.

—— (1960). 'The analysis of distorted representation in two-party, single-member elections', *Political Science*, **12**, 158–67.

BROWN, G. (1972). *In My Way*, Penguin Books, Harmondsworth.

BRUCE, M. B. (1961). *The Coming of the Welfare State*, Batsford, London.

BRUNN, S. D. (1974). *Geography and Politics in America*, Harper and Row, New York.

—— (1975). 'Vietnam War defense contracts and the House Armed Services Committee', *East Lakes Geographer*. **10**, 17–32.

—— and HOFFMAN, W. L. (1969). 'The geography of federal grants-in-aid to states', *Economic Geography*, **45**, 226–38.

BRYCE, H. J. and MARTIN, E. (1976). 'The quality of cities with black mayors', in H. J. Boyce (ed.), *Urban Governance and Minorities*, Praeger, New York, 30–54.

BUCHANAN, C. D. (1965). *Traffic in Towns*, Penguin Books, Harmondsworth.

BUNGE, W. (1975). 'Detroit humanly viewed: the American urban present', in R. F. Abler, D. G. Janelle, A. K. Philbrick, and J. Somner (eds.), *Human Geography in a Shrinking World*, Duxbury Press, North Scituate, Mass., 147–82.

BUSHMAN, D. O. and STANLEY, W. R. (1971). 'State Senate reapportionment in the Southeast', *Annals, Association of American Geographers*, **61**, 654–70.

BUSTEED, M. A. (1975). *Geography and Voting Behaviour*, Oxford University Press, London.

BUTLER, D. E. (1963). *The British Electoral System since 1918*, Clarendon Press, Oxford.

—— and STOKES, D. (1969). *Political Change in Britain: Forces Shaping Electoral Choice*, Macmillan, London.

CAMPBELL, P. (1958). *French Electoral Systems and Elections since 1789*, Faber and Faber, London.

CANTRALL, W. R. and NAGEL, S. S. (1973). 'The effects of reapportionment on the passage of nonexpenditure legislation', in L. Papaganopoulos (ed.), *Democratic Representation and Apportionment, Annals of the New York Academy of Sciences*, **219**, 269–79.

CARALEY, D. (1976). 'Congressional politics and urban aid', *Political Science Quarterly*, **91**, 19–45.

CAREY, G. W. and GREENBERG, M. R. (1974). 'Toward a geographical theory of hypocritical decision-making', *Human Ecology*, **2**, 243–51.

CARMINES, E. G. (1974). 'The mediating influence of state legislatures in the linkage between interparty competition and welfare policies', *American Political Science Review*, **68**, 1118–24.

CHAPMAN, R. M. (1972). *Marginals '72*, Heinemann, Auckland.

CHISHOLM, M. (1975). *Human Geography: Evolution or Revolution*, Penguin Books, Harmondsworth.

CHO, Y. H. and FREDERICKSON, H. G. (1973a). *Determinants of Public Policy in the American States*, Sage Professional Papers in Administrative and Policy Studies, 03–012, Sage Publications, Beverly Hills.

—— —— (1973b). 'Apportionment and legislative responsiveness to policy preferences in the American states', in L. Papaganopoulos (ed.), *Democratic*

Representation and Apportionment, *Annals of the New York Academy of Sciences*, **219**, 247–68.

CHORLEY, R. J. and HAGGETT, P. (eds.) (1967). *Models in Geography*, Methuen, London.

CHUBB, B. (1963). 'Going about persecuting civil servants: the role of the Irish parliamentary representative', *Political Studies*, **11**, 273–86.

CION, R. M. (1971). 'Accommodation par excellence: the Lakewood Plan', in M. N. Danielsen (ed.), *Metropolitan Politics: A Reader*, Little, Brown and Company, Boston, 224-32.

CLARKE, H. D., PRICE, R. G., and KRAUSE, R. (1975). 'Constituency service among Canadian Provincial legislators: basic findings and a test of three hypotheses', *Canadian Journal of Political Science*, **8**, 520–42.

CLOTFELTER, C. T. (1975a). 'Spatial rearrangement and the Tiebout hypothesis: the case of school desegregation', *Southern Economic Journal*, **42**, 263–71.

—— (1975b). 'The effect of school desegregation on housing prices', *Review of Economics and Statistics*, **57**, 446–51.

CNUDDE C. F. and McCRONE, D. J. (1969). 'Party competition and welfare policies in the American States', *American Political Science Review*, **63**, 858–66.

COATES, B. E., JOHNSTON, R. J. and KNOX, P. L. (1977). *Geography and Inequality*, Oxford University Press, Oxford.

COBB, S. (1976). 'Defense spending and defense voting in the House: an empirical study of an aspect of the military–industrial complex thesis', *American Journal of Sociology*, **82**, 163–82.

COLEMAN, J. S. (1968). 'The marginal utility of a vote commitment', *Public Choice*, **5**, 41–56.

—— (1972). 'Control of collectivities and the power of a collectivity to act', in B. Lieberman (ed.), *Social Choice*, Gordon and Breach, New York, 269–300.

—— et al. (1966). *Equality of Educational Opportunity*, U.S. Office of Education, Washington.

CONRADT, D. P. (1970). 'Electoral law politics in West Germany', *Political Studies*, **18**, 341–56.

COWART, A. T. (1969). 'Anti-poverty expenditures in the American States: a comparative analysis', *Midwest Journal of Political Science*, **13**, 219–36.

COX, K. R. (1968). 'Suburbia and voting behavior in the London metropolitan area', *Annals, Association of American Geographers*, **58**, 111–27.

—— (1973). *Conflict, Power and Politics in the City: A Geographic View*, McGraw-Hill, New York.

CRAIN, W. M. and TOLLISON, R. D. (1976). 'Campaign expenditures and political competition', *Journal of Law and Economics*, **19**, 177–88.

CREWE, I. (1973). 'The politics of "affluent" and "traditional" workers in Britain: an aggregate data analysis', *British Journal of Political Science*, **3**, 29–52.

CRIDDLE, B. (1975). 'Distorted representation in France', *Parliamentary Affairs*, **28**, 154–79.

CROSSMAN, R. (1975). *The Diaries of a Cabinet Minister. Volume One: Minister of Housing 1964–66*, Hamish Hamilton and Jonathan Cape, London.

—— (1976). *The Diaries of a Cabinet Minister. Volume Two: Lord President of the Council and Leader of the House of Commons 1966–68*, Hamish Hamilton and Jonathan Cape, London.

CUMMINGS, M. C., JR. (1971). 'Reapportionment in the 1970s: its effects on Congress', in N. W. Polsby (ed.), *Reapportionment in the 1970s*, Univ. of California Press, Berkeley, 209–41.

CUTRIGHT, P. (1963). 'Nonpartisan electoral systems in American cities', *Comparative Studies in Society and History*, **4**, 212–26.

DANIELSON, M. N. (1976). 'The politics of exclusionary zoning in suburbia', *Political Science Quarterly*, **91**, 1–18.

DARBY, J. (1976). *Conflict in Northern Ireland*, Gill and Macmillan, Dublin.

DAVIES, B. (1968). *Social Needs and Resources in Local Services*, Michael Joseph, London.

DAVIS, O. A., DEMPSTER, A. H., and WILDAVSKY, A. (1966). 'A theory of the budgetary process', *American Political Science Review*, **60**, 529–47.

DAWSON, D. (1973). 'Revenue and equalization in Australia, Canada, West Germany and the U.S.A.', *Commission on the Constitution, Research Paper 9*, H.M.S.O., London.

DAWSON, D. A. (1976). 'Determinants of local authority expenditure', in *Report of the Committee of Inquiry into Local Government Finance (The Layfield Committee)*, Appendix 7, H.M.S.O., 1–20.

DAWSON, R. E. (1967). 'Social development, party competition, and policy', in W. N. Chambers and W. D. Burnham (eds.), *The American Party Systems: Stages of Political Development*, Oxford University Press, New York, 203–37.

—— and GRAY, V. (1971). 'State welfare policies', in H. Jacob and K. N. Vines (eds.), *Politics in the American States: A Comparative Analysis*, Little, Brown and Company, Boston, second edition, 433–76.

—— and ROBINSON, J. A. (1963). 'Inter-party competition, economic variables, and welfare policies in the American states', *Journal of Politics*, **25**, 265–89.

—— —— (1965). 'The politics of welfare', in H. Jacobs and K. N. Vines (eds.), *Politics in the American States: A Comparative Analysis*, Little, Brown and Company, Boston, first edition, 371–410.

DEAKIN, N. (1965). *Colour and the British Electorate 1964: Six Case Studies*, Pall Mall, London.

DECKARD, B. S. (1976). 'Electoral marginality and party loyalty in House roll call voting', *American Journal of Political Science*, **20**, 469–82.

DERTHICK, M. (1968). 'Intercity differences in administration of the public assistance program: the case of Massachusetts', in J. Q. Wilson (ed.), *City Politics and Public Policy*, John Wiley, New York, 243–66.

—— (1970). *The Influence of Federal Grants: Public Assistance in Massachusetts*, Harvard University Press, Cambridge, Mass.

DE RUBERTIS, W. (1969). 'How apportionment with selected demographic variables relates to policy orientation', *Western Political Quarterly*, **22**, 904–20.

DE SWAAN, A. (1973). *Coalition Theories and Cabinet Formations*, Elsevier, Amsterdam.

DICKINSON, R. E. (1964). *City and Region*, Routledge and Kegan Paul, London.

DIKSHIT, R. D. (1975). *The Political Geography of Federalism: An Inquiry into Origins and Stability*, Macmillan, New Delhi.

DIXON, R. G., JR. (1968). *Democratic Representation: Reapportionment in Law and Practice*, Oxford University Press, New York.

—— (1971). 'The court, the people, and "one man, one vote"', in N. W. Polsby (ed.), *Reapportionment in the 1970s*, Univ. of California Press, Berkeley, 7–46.

DOWNS, A. (1957). *An Economic Theory of Democracy*, Harper and Row, New York.

DREWETT, J. R., GODDARD, J. B., and SPENCE, N. A. (1976). 'Urban Britain: beyond containment', in B. J. L. Berry (ed.), *Urbanization and Counterurbanization*, Sage Publications, Beverly Hills, 43–80.

DUNCAN, O. D. (1966). 'Path analysis: sociological examples', *American Journal of Sociology*, **72**, 1–16.

DYE, T. R. (1964). 'Urban political integration: conditions associated with annexation in American cities', *Midwest Journal of Political Science*, **8**, 430–46.

—— (1965). 'State legislative policies', in H. Jacob and K. N. Vines (eds.), *Politics in the American States: A Comparative Analysis*, Little, Brown and Company, Boston, first edition.

—— (1966). *Politics, Economics, and the Public: Policy Outcomes in the American States*, Rand McNally, Chicago.

—— (1969). *Politics in States and Communities*, Prentice-Hall, Englewood Cliffs, New Jersey.

—— (1971). 'State legislative politics', in H. Jacobs and K. N. Vines (eds.), *Politics in the American States*, Little, Brown and Company, Boston, second edition, 163–209.

—— (1975). *Understanding Public Policy*, Prentice-Hall, Englewood Cliffs, New Jersey.

—— *et al.* (1963). 'Differentiation and cooperation in a metropolitan area', *Midwest Journal of Political Science*, **7**, 145–55.

EASTON, D. (1965a). *A Framework for Political Analysis*, Prentice-Hall, Englewood Cliffs, New Jersey.

—— (1965b). *A Systems Analysis of Political Life*, John Wiley, New York.

ELAZAR, D. J. (1966). *American Federalism: A View from the States*, Thomas, Y. Gowill, New York.

EULAU, H. *et al.* (1959). 'The role of the representative: some empirical observations on the theory of representation of Edmund Burke', *American Political Science Review*, **53**, 742–56.

EYRE, J. D. (1969). 'City–county territorial competition: the Portsmouth, Virginia case', *Southeastern Geographer*, **9**, 26–37.

FAIR, T. J. D. and BROWETT, J. (1979). 'The urbanization process in South Africa', in D. T. Herbert and R. J. Johnston (eds.), *Geography and the Urban Environment*, 2, Wiley, London.

FENNO, R. F. (1966). *The Power of the Purse: Appropriations Politics in Congress*, Little, Brown and Company, Boston.

—— (1973). *Congressmen in Committees*, Little, Brown and Company, Boston.

FENTON, J. H. (1960). *The Catholic Vote*, Hauser Press, New Orleans.

—— (1966). *Midwest Politics*. Holt Rinehart & Winston, New York.

—— (1966). *People and Parties in Politics*, Scott, Foresman; Glenview, Illinois.

—— and CHAMBERLAYNE, D. W. (1969). 'The literature dealing with the relationships between political processes, socioeconomic conditions and public policies in the American states: a bibliographical essay', *Polity*, **1**, 388–404.

FEREJOHN, J. A. (1974). *Pork Barrel Politics: Rivers and Harbors Legislation, 1947–1968*, Stanford University Press, Stanford.

—— (1977). 'On the decline of competition in Congressional elections', *American Political Science Review*, **71**, 166–76.

FIELD, F., MEACHER, M., and POND, C. (1977). *To Him Who Hath: A Study of Poverty and Taxation*, Penguin Books, Harmondsworth.

FIELDING, G. J. (1962), 'Dairying in cities designed to keep people out', *Professional Geographer*, **14(1)**, 12–17.

FINER, S. E. (1975). 'Adversary politics and electoral reform', in S. E. Finer (ed.), *Adversary Politics and Electoral Reform*, Anthony Wigram, London, 3–32.

FIORINA, M. P. (1974). *Representatives, Roll Calls and Constituencies*, D. C. Heath, Lexington, Mass.

—— (1977). 'The case of the vanishing marginals: the bureaucracy did it', *American Political Science Review*, 71, 177–81.

FOOT, P. (1965). *Immigration and Race in British Politics*, Penguin Books, Harmondsworth.

—— (1969). *The Rise of Enoch Powell*, Penguin Books, Harmondsworth.

FORREST, J., MARJORIBANKS, E., and JOHNSTON, R. J. (1977). 'Local effects at New Zealand local elections', in R. J. Johnston (ed.), *People, Places and Votes: Essays on the Electoral Geography of Australia and New Zealand*, Department of Geography, University of New England, Armidale, New South Wales, 35–50.

FRANKLIN, S. H. (1975). 'Regional development—and growth—in New Zealand', *Pacific Viewpoint*, 16, 143–58.

FREEMAN, T. W. (1968). *Geography and Regional Administration in England and Wales: 1830–1868*, Hutchinson, London.

FRIED, R. C. (1971). 'Communism, urban budgets, and the two Italies: a case study in comparative urban government', *Journal of Politics*, 33, 1008–51.

—— (1974). 'Politics, economics, and federalism: aspects of urban government in Austria, Germany and Switzerland', in T. N. Clark (ed.), *Comparative Community Politics*, Sage Publications, Beverly Hills, 313–50.

—— (1975). 'Comparative urban policy and performance', in F. I. Greenstein and N. W. Polsby (eds.), *Policies and Policy-making*. Handbook of Political Science 6, Addison-Wesley, Reading, Mass., 305–80.

—— (1976). 'Party and policy in West German cities', *American Political Science Review*, 70, 11–24.

FROST, R. T. (1961). 'Stability and change in local government', *Public Opinion Quarterly*, 25, 221–35.

FRY, B. R. and WINTERS, R. F. (1970). 'The politics of redistribution', *American Political Science Review*, 64, 508–22.

GARNER, B. J. (1975). 'The effect of local government reform on access to public services: a case study from Denmark', in R. F. Peel, M. Chisholm, and P. Haggett (eds.), *Processes in Physical and Human Geography: Bristol Essays*, Heinemann, London, 319–38.

GELFAND, M. I. (1975). *A Nation of Cities: The Federal Government and Urban America, 1933–1965*, Oxford University Press, New York.

GILBERT, C. E. (1975). 'Welfare policy', in F. I. Greenstein and N. W. Polsby (eds.), *Policies and Policy-making*, Handbook of Political Science 6, Addison-Wesley, Reading, Mass., 111–240.

GLADFELTER, D. D. (1971). 'The political separation of city and suburb: water for Wauwatosa', in M. N. Danielsen (ed.), *Metropolitan Politics: A Reader*, Little, Brown and Company, Boston, 75–85.

GLASSBERG, A. (1973). 'The linkage between urban policy outputs and voting behavior: New York and London', *British Journal of Political Science*, 3, 341–361.

GOSS, C. (1972). 'Military committee membership and defense-related benefits in the House of Representatives', *Western Political Quarterly*, 25, 215–33.

GRAHAM, B. D. (1962). 'The choice of voting method in federal politics, 1902–1918', *Australian Journal of Politics and History*, 8, 164–82.

GRANT, D. R. (1965). 'A comparison of predictions and experience with Nashville "Metro"', *Urban Affairs Quarterly*, 1, 34–54.

GRAY, V. (1973). 'Innovation in the states: a diffusion study', *American Political Science Review*, **67**, 1174–85.
—— (1976). 'Models of comparative state politics: a comparison of cross-sectional and time series analyses', *American Journal of Political Science*, **20**, 235–56.
GREENE, K. V., NEENAN, W. B., and SCOTT, C. D. (1974). *Fiscal Interactions in a Metropolitan Area*, D. C. Heath, Lexington, Mass.
GREENSTONE, J. D. and PETERSON, P. E. (1968). 'Reformers, machines and the war on poverty', in J. Q. Wilson (ed.), *City Politics and Public Policy*, John Wiley, New York, 267–92.
GREER, A. L. and GREER, S. (1976). 'Suburban political behavior: a matter of trust', in B. Schwartz (ed.), *The Changing Face of the Suburbs*, University of Chicago Press, Chicago, 203–20.
GRUMM, J. G. (1971). 'The effects of legislative structure on legislature performance', in R. I. Hofferbert and I. Sharkansky (eds), *State and Urban Politics: Readings in Comparative Public Policy*, Little, Brown and Company, Boston, 298–322.
GUDGIN, G. and TAYLOR, P. J. (1974). 'Electoral bias and the distribution of party voters', *Transactions, Institute of British Geographers*, **63**, 53–73.
—— —— (1978). *The Spatial Organization of Elections*, Pion, London.
GUTERBOCK, T. M. (1976). 'The push hypothesis: minority presence, crime, and urban deconcentration', in B. Schwartz (ed.), *The Changing Face of the Suburbs*, University of Chicago Press, Chicago, 137–62.

HALL, P. G. (1971). 'Spatial structure of metropolitan England and Wales', in M. Chisholm and G. Manners (eds), *Spatial Policy Problems of the British Economy*, Cambridge University Press, Cambridge, 96–125.
—— et al. (1973). *The Containment of Metropolitan England*, George Allen and Unwin, London.
HAMPTON, W. A. (1970). *Democracy and Community*, Oxford University Press, London.
Hansard Society for Parliamentary Government (1976). *Report of the Hansard Society Commission on Electoral Reform*, The Hansard Society, London
HANSEN, T. and KJELLBERG, F. (1976). 'Municipal expenditures in Norway: autonomy and constraints in local government activity', *Policy and Politics*, **4**, 25–50.
HANSON, R. A. and CREW, R. E. (1973). 'The policy impact of reapportionment', *Law and Society Review*, **5**, 69–93.
HARVEY, D. W. (1973). *Social Justice and the City*, Edward Arnold, London.
—— (1975). 'The political economy of urbanization in advanced capitalist societies. The case of the United States', in G. Gappert and H. M. Rose (eds.), *The Social Economy of Cities*, Sage Publications, Beverly Hills, 119–64.
HAWKINS, B. W. (1968). 'Reapportionment aids Georgia's urban bills', *National Civic Review*, **57**, 153–6.
—— (1971). 'Consequences of reapportionment in Georgia', in R. I. Hofferbert and I. Sharkansky (eds.), *State and Urban Politics: Readings in Comparative Public Policy*, Little, Brown and Company, Boston, 273–98.
—— and DYE, T. R. (1970). 'Metropolitan fragmentation: a research note', *Midwest Review of Public Administration*, **4**, 17–24.
—— and WHELCHER, C. (1968). 'Reapportionment and urban representation in legislative influence positions: the case of Georgia', *Urban Affairs Quarterly*, **3**, 69–80.
HAWKINS, R. B., JR. (1976). 'Special districts and urban services', in E. Ostrom (ed.),

The Delivery of Urban Services: Outcomes of Change, Sage Publications, Beverly Hills, 171–88.

HAWLEY, A. H. (1951). 'Metropolitan population and municipal government expenditures in central cities', *Journal of Social Issues*, 7,

—— and ZIMMER, B. G. (1961). 'Resistance to unification in a metropolitan community', in M. Janowitz (ed.), *Community Political Systems*, The Free Press, Glencoe, Illinois, 146–84.

—— —— (1970). *The Metropolitan Community*, Sage Publications, Beverly Hills.

HEADLAM-MORLEY, A. (1929). *The New Democratic Constitutions of Europe*, Oxford University Press, London.

HEARD, A. (1960). *The Costs of Democracy*, University of North Carolina Press, Chapel Hill.

HEARD, K. A. (1974). *General Elections in South Africa, 1943–1970*, Oxford University Press, Cape Town.

HERBERT, D. T. and JOHNSTON, R. J. (1978). 'Geography and the urban environment', in D. T. Herbert and R. J. Johnston (eds.), *Geography and the Urban Environment*, Wiley, London, 1–30.

HILL, D. M. (1974). *Democratic Theory and Local Government*, George Allen and Unwin, London.

HINCKLEY, B. (1976). 'Seniority 1975: old theories confront new facts', *British Journal of Political Science*, 6, 383–99.

HIRSCH, W. Z. (1970). *The Economics of State and Local Government*, McGraw-Hill, New York.

HIRSCHMAN, A. O. (1970). *Exit, Voice and Loyalty: Responses to Decline in Firms, Organizations and States*, Harvard University Press, Cambridge, Mass.

HOFFERBERT, R. I. (1966). 'The relation between public policy and some structural and environmental variables in the American states', *American Political Science Review*, 60, 73–82.

HOFFMAN, H. (1976). 'The democratic response of urban governments: an empirical test with simple spatial models', *Policy and Politics*, 4, 51–74.

HOOSON, D. J. M. (1960). 'The distribution of population as the essential geographical expression', *Canadian Geographer*, 4, 10–20.

HOTELLING, H. (1929). 'Stability in competition', *Economic Journal*, 39, 41–57.

HUGHES, C. A. (1977). 'Malapportionment and gerrymandering in Australia', in R. J. Johnston (ed.), *People, Places and Votes: Essays on the Electoral Geography of Australia and New Zealand*, Department of Geography, University of New England, Armidale, New South Wales, 93–110.

—— and AITKIN, D. (1970). 'The Federal redistribution of 1968: a case study in Australian political conflict', *Journal of Commonwealth Political Studies*, 8, 18–39.

ISSERMAN, A. M. (1976). 'Interjurisdictional spillovers, political fragmentation and the level of local public services: a re-examination', *Urban Studies*, 13, 1–12.

JACKSON, K. T. (1972). 'Metropolitan government versus political autonomy: politics on the crabgrass frontier', in K. T. Jackson and S. K. Schultz (eds.), *Cities in American History*, A. A. Knopf, New York, 442–62.

JACKSON, W. K. (1973). *New Zealand: Politics of Change*, Reed Education, Wellington.

JAENSCH, D. (1970). 'A functional gerrymander—South Australia, 1944–1970', *Australian Quarterly*, 42, 96–101.

JENKINS, M. A. and SHEPHERD, J. W. (1972). 'Decentralizing high school administration in Detroit: an evaluation of alternative strategies of political control', *Economic Geography*, 48, 95–106.

JEWELL, M. E. (1962). 'Political patterns in apportionment', in M. E. Jewell (ed.), *The Politics of Reapportionment*, Atherton Press, New York, 1–48.

JOHNSON, R. W. and SCHOEN, D. (1976). 'The "Powell effect": or how one man can win', *New Society*, **37**, 22 July 1976, 168–72.

JOHNSTON, R. J. (1974a). 'Regional development and regional planning: a New Zealand debate', *Town and Country Planning*, **42**, 363–9.

—— (1974b). 'Local effects in voting at a local election', *Annals, Association of American Geographers*, **64**, 418–29.

—— (1976a). 'Resource allocations and political campaigns: notes towards a methodology', *Policy and Politics*, **5**, 181–99.

—— (1976b). 'Geography and an alternative electoral system', *Globe*, **49**, 3–13.

—— (1976c). 'Observations on accounting procedures and urban-size policies', *Environment and Planning*, **A 8**, 327–40.

—— (1976d). 'Population distributions and the essentials of human geography', *South African Geographical Journal*, **58**, 93–106.

—— (1976e). *The World Trade System*, G. Bell and Sons, London.

—— (1976f). 'Spatial structure, plurality systems and electoral bias', *Canadian Geographer*, **20**, 310–28.

—— (1976g). 'Parliamentary seat redistribution: more opinions on the theme', *Area*, **8**, 30–4.

—— (1977a). 'The electoral geography of an election campaign', *Scottish Geographical Magazine*, **93**, 98–108.

—— (1977b). 'National sovereignty and national power in European institutions', *Environment and Planning*, **A 9**, 569–77.

—— (1977c). 'The compatability of spatial structure and electoral reform: observations on the electoral geography of Wales', *Cambria*, **4**, 125–51.

—— (1977d). 'Regarding urban origins, urbanization and urban patterns', *Geography*, **62**, 1–8.

—— (1977e). 'Population distributions and electoral power: preliminary investigations of class bias', *Regional Studies*, **11**, 309–21.

—— (1978a). *Multivariate Statistical Analysis in Geography: A Primer on the General Linear Model*, Longman, London.

—— (1978b). 'Politics and social well-being: an essay on the political geography of the welfare state', in M. Busteed (ed.), *Developments in Political Geography*, Academic Press, London.

—— (1978c). 'People, places and votes: an introduction', in R. J. Johnston (ed.), *People, Places and Votes: Essays on the Electoral Geography of Australia and New Zealand*, Department of Geography, University of New England, Armidale, New South Wales, 1–10.

—— (1978d). 'Political geography and welfare: observations on interstate variations in AFDC programs', *Professional Geographer*, **29**, 347–52.

—— (1978e). 'Environment, elections and expenditures: analyses of where governments spend', *Regional Studies*, **11**, 383–94.

—— (1978f). 'The electoral base to public policy: some introductory explorations', in R. J. Johnston (ed.), *People, Places and Votes: Essays on the Electoral Geography of Australia and New Zealand*. Department of Geography, University of New England, Armidale, New South Wales, 133–50.

—— (1978g). 'The allocation of federal money in the United States: aggregate analysis by correlation', *Policy and Politics*, **6**, 279–97.

—— (1978h). 'Political spending in the United States: analyses of political influences on the allocation of federal money', *Environment and Planning*, A10, 691–704.

—— (1978i). 'Class conflict and political and electoral geography', *Antipode*.

—— and HUNT, A. J. (1977). 'Voting power in the E.E.C.'s Council of Ministers: an essay on method in political geography', *Geoforum*, **8**, 1–9.

KASPERSON, R. E. (1969). 'Ward systems and urban politics', *Southeastern Geographer*, **9**, 27–35.

KAVANAGH, D. (1970). *Constituency Electioneering in Britain*, Longman, London.

KEECH, W. R. (1968). *The Impact of Negro Voting: The Role of the Vote in the Quest for Equality*, Rand McNally, Chicago.

KELLY, J. R. (1971). 'Vote weightage and quota gerrymanders in Queensland, 1931–1971', *Australian Quarterly*, **43**, 38–54.

KENDALL, M. G. and STUART, A. (1950). 'The law of the cubic proportion in election results', *British Journal of Sociology*, **1**, 183–96.

KESSEL, J. H. (1962). 'Government structure and political environment', *American Political Science Review*, **56**, 615–20.

KEY, V. O., JR. (1949). *Southern Politics in State and Nation*, A. A. Knopf, New York.

KINCAID, J. S. (1973). *Poverty and Inequality in Britain*, Penguin Books, Harmondsworth.

KING, D. N. (1973). 'Financial and economic aspects of regionalism and separatism', *Commission on the Constitution, Research Paper 10*, H.M.S.O., London.

KNIGHT, B. B. (1976). 'The states and reapportionment: one man, one vote reevaluated', *State Government*, **49**, 155–60.

KNIGHT, D. B. (1977). *A Capital for Canada: Conflict and Compromise in the Nineteenth Century*. University of Chicago, Department of Geography, Research Paper 182, Chicago.

KNOX, P. L. (1974). 'Level of living: a conceptual framework for monitoring regional variations in well-being', *Regional Studies*, **8**, 11–19.

LADD, E. C., JR. and HADLEY, C. D. (1976). 'Transformation of the American party system', *Dialogue*, **9(4)**, 15–24.

LAKEMAN, E. (1974). *How Democracies Vote*, Faber and Faber, London.

LAVER, M. (1976). 'Strategic campaign behaviour for electors and parties: the Northern Ireland Assembly Election of 1973', in I. Budge, I. Crewe, and D. Fairlie (eds.), *Party Identification and Beyond*, John Wiley, London, 315–34.

LEHNE, R. (1972). 'Population change and congressional representation', Commission on Population Growth and the American Future; Research Reports, Volume 4, *Governance and Population: The Governmental Implications of Population Change*, Government Printer, Washington, 83–98.

—— (1975). 'Suburban foundations of the new Congress', *Annals, American Academy of Political and Social Sciences*, **422**, 141–51.

LENGLE, J. I. and SHAFER, B. (1976). 'Primary rules, political power, and social change', *American Political Science Review*, **70**, 25–40.

LEVY, F., MELTSZER, A. J., and WILDAVSKY, A. (1974). *Urban Outcomes: Schools, Streets and Libraries*, University of California Press, Berkeley.

LINEBERRY, R. L. (1977). *Equality and Urban Policy*, Vol. 39, Sage Library of Social Research, Sage Publications, Beverly Hills.

—— and FOWLER, E. P. (1968). 'Reformism and public policies in American cities', in J. Q. Wilson (ed.), *City Politics and Public Policy*, Wiley, New York, 97–123.

—— and SHARKANSKY, I. (1974). *Urban Politics and Public Policy*, Harper and Row, New York.

Local Government Finance (England and Wales) (1975). *The Rate Support Grant Order 1975*, H.M.S.O., London.

LOCKARD, D. S. (1959). *New England State Politics*, Princeton University Press, Princeton.

LONGLEY, L. D. and BRAUN, A. G. (1972). *The Politics of Electoral College Reform*, Yale University Press, New Haven.

LOOSEMORE, J. and HANBY, V. J. (1971). 'The theoretical limits of maximum distortion: some analytic expressions for electoral systems', *British Journal of Political Science*, 1, 467–77.

LYONS, W. E. (1969). 'Legislative redistricting by independent commissions: operationalizing the one man—one vote doctrine in Canada', *Polity*, 1, 428–59.

McDONALD, G. T. (1976). 'Rural representation in Queensland state parliament', *Australian Geographical Studies*, 14, 33–42.

MACRAE, D., JR. (1952). 'The relation between roll-call votes and constituencies in the Massachusetts House of Representatives', *American Political Science Review*, 46, 1046–55.

MANLEY, J. (1970). *The Politics of Finance: The House Committee on Ways and Means*, Little, Brown and Company, Boston.

MARANDO, V. L. and WHITELEY, C. R. (1972). 'City–county consolidation: an overview of voter response', *Urban Affairs Quarterly*, 8, 181–203.

MASSAM, B. H. (1973). 'Forms of local government in the Montreal area, 1911–71: a discriminant approach', *Canadian Journal of Political Science*, 6, 243–53.

—— (1975). *Location and Space in Social Administration*, Edward Arnold, London.

MASTERS, N. S. (1961). 'Committee assignments in the House of Representatives', *American Political Science Review*, 55, 345–57.

MAY, R. J. (1972). 'Federal finance: politics and gamesmanship', in H. Mayer and H. Nelson (eds.), *Australian Politics: A Third Reader*, Cheshire, Melbourne, 237–56.

MAY, J. D. (1974). 'Democracy and rural over-representation', *Australian Quarterly*, 46, 52–6.

—— (1975). 'Rural over-representation: pros and cons in recent Australian debate', *Journal of Commonwealth and Comparative Politics*, 13, 132–45.

MAYHEW, C. (1976). *The Disillusioned Voter's Guide to Electoral Reform*, Arrow Books, London.

MAYHEW, D. R. (1971). 'Congressional representation: theory and practice in drawing the districts', in N. W. Polsby (ed.), *Reapportionment in the 1970s*, University of California Press, Berkeley, 249–85.

MERCER, J. (1974). 'City manager communities in the Montreal metropolitan area', *Canadian Geographer*, 18, 352–66.

MILIBAND, R. (1969). *The State in Capitalist Society*, Weidenfeld and Nicolson, London.

MILLS, E. S. (1972). *Urban Economics*, Scott, Foresman; Glenview, Illinois.

MOORE, B. and RHODES, J. (1976). 'The relative needs of local authorities: the "standard expenditure" approach as an alternative to regression analysis in determining the needs element of the rate support grant', in *Report of the Committee of Inquiry into Local Government Finance (The Layfield Committee)*, Appendix 7, H.M.S.O., London, 93–145.

MORRILL, R. L. (1973). 'Ideal and reality in reapportionment', *Annals, Association of American Geographers*, 63, 463–77.

—— (1976). 'Redistricting revisited', *Annals, Association of American Geographers*, 66, 548–56.

MULLER, P. O. (1976). *The Outer City: Geographical Consequences of the Urbanization of the Suburbs*, Resource Paper 75–2, Commission on College Geography, Association of American Geographers, Washington.

MUMPHREY, A. J. and WOLPERT, J. (1973). 'Equity considerations and concessions in the siting of public facilities', *Economic Geography*, **49**, 109–21.

MUNNS, J. M. (1975). 'The environment, politics, and policy literature: a critique and reformulation', *Western Political Quarterly*, **28**, 646–67.

MUSGRAVE, P. (1977). *The General Theory of Gerrymandering*, Sage Professional Papers in American Politics, 04–034, Sage Publications, Beverly Hills.

MUSGRAVE, R. A. (1969), *Fiscal Systems*, Studies in Comparative Economics series No. 10, Yale University Press, New Haven & London.

NATHAN, R. P. (1976). 'Methodology for monitoring revenue sharing', in C. O. Jones and R. D. Thomas (eds.), *Public Policy Making in a Federal System*, Sage Publications, Beverly Hills, 65–9.

—— and ADAMS, C. (1976). 'Understanding central city hardship', *Political Science Quarterly*, **91**, 47–62.

NEENAN, W. B. (1972). *Political Economy of Urban Areas*, Markham, Chicago.

—— (1973). 'Suburban–central city exploitation thesis: one city's tale', in K. E. Boulding, M. Pfaff, and A. Pfaff (eds.), *Transfers in an Urbanized Economy*, Wadsworth, Belmont, California, 10–38.

NELSON, H. J. (1952). 'The Vernon area, California—a study of the political factor in urban geography', *Annals, Association of American Geographers*, **42**, 177–91.

NEWTON, K. (1976a). 'Community performance in Britain', *Current Sociology*.

—— (1976b). *Second City Politics*, Oxford University Press, London.

—— and SHARPE, L. J. (undated). 'Service output in local government: some reflections and proposals', unpublished manuscript.

NICHOLSON, R. J. and TOPHAM, N. (1971). 'The determinants of investment in housing by local authorities: an econometric approach', *Journal, Royal Statistical Society A*, **134**, 273–320.

—— —— (1972). 'Investment decisions and the size of local authorities', *Policy and Politics*, **1**, 23–44.

—— —— (1973). 'Step-wise regression and principal components analyses in estimating a relationship in an econometric model', *Manchester School*, 187–205.

—— —— (1975). 'Urban road provision in England and Wales 1962–68', *Policy and Politics*, **5**, 3–29.

—— —— and WATT, P. A. (1975). 'Housing investment by different types of local authority', *Bulletin of Economic Research*, **27**, 65–86.

NIE, N. H., VERBA, S., and PETROCIK, J. R. (1976). *The Changing American Voter*, Harvard University Press, Cambridge, Mass.

NORAGON, J. L. (1973). 'Redistricting, political outcomes, and gerrymandering in the 1960s', in L. Papaganopoulos (ed.), *Democratic Representation and Apportionment, Annals of the New York Academy of Sciences*, **219**, (314–33.

OFFE, C. (1975). 'The theory of the capitalist state and the problem of policy formulation', in L. N. Lindberg, R. Alford, C. Crouch, and C. Offe (eds.), *Stress and Contradiction in Modern Capitalism*, Lexington Books, Lexington, Mass., 125–44.

O'LEARY, C. (1961). *The Irish Republic and its Experiment with Proportional Representation*, University of Notre Dame Press, Notre Dame, Indiana.

—— (1962). *The Elimination of Corrupt Practices in British Elections 1868–1911*, Clarendon Press, Oxford.

—— (1975). 'Ireland: the North and the South', in S. E. Finer (ed.), *Adversary Politics and Electoral Reform*, Anthony Wigram, London, 153–84.

OLIVER, F. R. and STANYER, J. (1969). 'Some aspects of the financial behaviour of county boroughs', *Public Administration*, **47**, 169–84.

O'ROURKE, T. B. (1972). *Reapportionment: Law, Politics, Computers*, American Enterprise Institute, Washington.

ORR, D. M., JR. (1969). 'The persistence of the gerrymander in North Carolina Congressional redistricting', *Southeastern Geographer*, **9**, 39–54.

OSTROM, E. and PARKS, R. B. (1973). 'Suburban police departments: too many and too small?', in L. H. Masotti and J. K. Hadden (eds.), *The Urbanization of the Suburbs*, Sage Publications, Beverly Hills, 367–402.

OZBUDUN, E. (1970). *Party Cohesion in Western Democracies: A Causal Analysis*, Sage Professional Papers in Comparative Politics, 01–006, Sage Publications, Beverly Hills.

PADDISON, R. A. (1976). 'Spatial bias and redistricting in proportional representation election systems: a case-study of the Republic of Ireland', *Tijdschrift voor Economische en Sociale Geografie*, **67**, 230–40.

PALDA, K. S. (1973). 'Does advertising influence votes? An analysis of the 1966 and 1970 Quebec elections', *Canadian Journal of Political Science*, **6**, 638–55.

PARRY, G. (1973). 'How the South went sour', in B. Edwards (ed.), *Right Out*, Reed, Wellington, 223–37.

PENNIMAN, C. (1971). 'The politics of taxation', in H. Jacob and K. N. Vines (eds.), *Politics in the American States: A Comparative Analysis*, Little, Brown and Company, Boston, second edition, 520–55.

PHILLIPS, K. P. (1969). *The Emerging Republican Majority*, Arlington House, New Rochelle, New York.

PIERCE, N. R. (1968). *The People's President: The Electoral College in American History and the Direct-Vote Alternative*, Simon and Schuster, New York.

PORTER, D. O. (1976). 'Federalism, revenue sharing and local government', in C. O. Jones and R. D. Thomas (eds.), *Public Policy Making in a Federal System*, Sage Publications, Beverly Hills, 81–101.

—— et al. (1973). *The Politics of Budgeting Federal Aid: Resource Mobilization by Local School Districts*, Sage Professional Papers in Administrative and Policy Studies, 03–003, Sage Publications, Beverly Hills.

PRED, A. R. (1967). *Behavior and Location*, Volume I, C. W. K. Gleerup, Lund.

—— (1977). *City Systems in Advanced Economies*, Hutchinson, London.

PRICE, H. D. (1962). 'Florida: politics and the "pork choppers"', in M. E. Jewell (ed.), *The Politics of Reapportionment*, Atherton Press, New York, 81–97.

PULSIPHER, A. G. and WEATHERBY, J. L., JR. (1968). 'Malapportionment, party competition and the functional distribution of government expenditure', *American Political Science Review*, **62**, 1207–19.

QUAIFE, G. R. (1969). 'Make us roads, no matter how', *Australian Journal of Politics and History*, **15**, 47–54.

RAE, D. W. (1971). *The Political Consequences of Electoral Laws*, Yale University Press, New Haven, second edition.

—— (1972). 'An estimate for the decisiveness of election outcomes', in B. Lieberman (ed.), *Social Choice*, Gordon and Breach, New York, 379–92.

RAFFEL, J. A. (1977). 'Political dilemmas of busing: a case study of interdistrict metropolitan school desegregation', *Urban Education*, **11**, 375–95.

RAKOFF, S. H. and SCHAEFER, G. F. (1970). 'Politics, policy and political science: theoretical alternatives', *Politics and Society*, **1**, 51–77.

RANNEY, A. (1965). 'Parties in State politics', in H. Jacob and K. N. Vines (eds.), *Politics in the American States: A Comparative Analysis*, Little, Brown and Company, Boston, first edition, 61–100.

RHODES, G. (1970). *The Government of London: The Struggle for Reform*, Weidenfeld and Nicolson, London.

—— (1972). 'The new government of London: an appraisal', in G. Rhodes (ed.), *The New Government of London: The First Five Years*, Macmillan, London, 457–96.

—— (1976). 'Local government finance, 1918–1966', in *The Relationship between Central and Local Government: Evidence and Commissioned Work*, being Appendix 6 to the *Report of the Committee of Inquiry into Local Government Finance (The Layfield Committee)*, H.M.S.O., London, 102–72.

RICHARDS, P. G. (1968). *The New Local Government System*, Allen and Unwin, London.

RIEW, J. (1970). 'Metropolitan disparities and fiscal federalism', in J. P. Crecine (ed.), *Financing the Metropolis: Public Policy in Urban Economics*, Sage Publications, Beverly Hills, 137–61.

RIMMER, P. J. (1975). 'Politicians, public servants and petitioners: aspects of transport in Australia 1851–1901', in J. M. Powell and M. Williams (eds.), *Australian Space, Australian Time: Geographical Perspectives*, Oxford University Press, Melbourne, 182–225.

RIPLEY, R. *et al.* (1973). *Structure, Environment and Policy Actions*, Sage Professional Papers in American Politics, 04–006, Sage Publications, Beverly Hills.

ROBERTSON, D. (1971). 'The content of election addresses and leaders' speeches', in D. E. Butler and M. Pinto-Duschinsky, *The British General Election of 1970*, Macmillan, London, 437–45.

—— (1976). *A Theory of Party Competition*, John Wiley, London.

ROGALY, J. (1976). *Parliament for the People: A Handbook of Elecotral Reform*, Maurice Temple Smith, London.

ROSE, R. (1976a). 'Models of change', in R. Rose (ed.), *The Dynamics of Public Policy: A Comparative Analysis*, Sage Publications, Beverly Hills, 1–34.

—— (1976b). *The Problem of Party Government*, Penguin Books, Harmondsworth.

ROSSI, P. H. and CUTRIGHT, P. E. (1961). 'The impact of party organization in an industrial setting', in M. Janowitz (ed.), *Community Political Systems*, The Free Press, Glencoe, Illinois, 81–116.

ROWLEY, G. (1970). 'Elections and population changes', *Area*, **3**, 13–18.

—— (1975). 'Electoral change and reapportionment: prescriptive ideals and reality', *Tijdschrift voor Economische en Sociale Geografie*, **66**, 108–20.

Royal Commission on Local Government in England (1968). *Local Government in South East England*, Research Studies, 1, H.M.S.O., London.

Royal Commission on Local Government in England 1966–1969 (1969a). *Volume I. Report*, H.M.S.O., London.

Royal Commission on Local Government in England 1966–1969 (1969b). *Volume III. Research Appendices*, H.M.S.O., London.

RUNDQUIST, B. S. and FEREJOHN, J. (1976). 'Observations on a distributive theory of policy-making: two American expenditure programs compared', in C. Liske, W. Lock and J. McCamart (eds.) *Comparative Public Policy*, Wiley, New York, 87–108.

RYDON, J. (1968). 'Malapportionment—Australian style', *Politics*, **3**, 133–47.

SANDFORD, C. T. (1977). 'Growth and control of public expenditure', in C. T. Sandford, M. S. Bradbury, and Associates, *Case Studies in Economics: Economic Policy*, Macmillan, London, 150–78.

SARKISSIAN, W. (1976). 'The idea of social mix in town planning: an historical review', *Urban Studies*, **13**, 231–46.
SCAMMON, R. (1974). *America Votes*, Congressional Quarterly Inc., Washington.
SCHNORE, L. F. (1965). *The Urban Scene: Human Ecology and Demography*, The Free Press, New York.
—— (1972). *Class and Race in Cities and Suburbs*, Markham, Chicago.
—— ANDRE, C. D., and SHARP, H. (1976). 'Black suburbanization, 1930–1970', in B. Schwartz (ed.), *The Changing Face of the Suburbs*, University of Chicago Press, Chicago, 69–94.
SCHUMACHER, E. F. (1973). *Small is Beautiful: A Study of Economics as if People Mattered*, Abacus, London.
SCOTT, S. and CORZINE, J. (1971). 'Special districts in the San Francisco Bay Area', in M. N. Danielsen (ed.), *Metropolitan Politics: A Reader*, Little, Brown and Compnay, Boston, 201–14.
SCOTT, T. M. (1973) 'Suburban governmental structures', in L. H. Masotti and J. K. Hadden (eds.), *The Urbanization of the Suburbs*, Sage Publications, Beverly Hills, 213–38.
SELF, P. (1957) *Cities in Flood*, Faber and Faber, London.
SENIOR, D. (1969). *Memorandum of Dissent*, Volume II of Royal Commission on Local Government in England 1966–1969 (The Maud Committee), H.M.S.O., London.
SHANNON, W. W. (1968). *Party, Constituency and Congressional Voting*, Louisiana State University Press, Baton Rouge.
SHARKANSKY, I. (1968). *Spending in the American States*, Rand McNally, Chicago.
—— (1969). *The Politics of Taxing and Spending*, Bobbs-Merrill, Indianapolis.
—— (1970a). *Regionalism in American Politics*, Bobbs-Merrill, Indianapolis.
—— (1970b). *The Routines of Politics*, van Norstrand Rheinhold, New York.
—— (1970c). 'Environment, policy, output and impact: problems of theory and method in the analysis of public policy', in I. Sharkansky (ed.), *Policy Analysis in Political Science*, Markham, Chicago, 61–79.
—— (1971a). 'Economic theories of public policy: resource policy and need-policy linkages between income and welfare benefits', *Midwest Journal of Political Science*, **15**, 722–40.
—— (1971b). 'Economic development, representative mechanisms, administrative professionalism and public policies: a comparative analysis of within-state distributions of economic and political traits', *Journal of Politics*, **33**, 112–32.
—— (1972). *The Maligned States*, McGraw-Hill, New York.
—— and HOFFERBERT, R. I. (1971). 'Dimensions of state policy', in H. Jacob and K. N. Vines (eds.), *Politics in the American States: A Comparative Analysis*, Little, Brown and Company, Boston, second edition, 315–53.
SHARPE, L. J. (1976). 'The role and functions of local government in modern Britain', in *The Relationship between Central and Local Government: Evidence and Commissioned Work*, being Appendix 6 to the *Report of the Committee of Inquiry into Local Government Finance (The Layfield Committee)*, H.M.S.O., London, 203–20.
SIMMONS, R. C. (1976). *The American Colonies*, Longman, London.
SINGHAM, A. W. (1965). 'Immigration and the election', in D. E. Butler and A. King, *The British General Election of 1964*, Macmillan, London, 360–8.
SLEEMAN, J. F. (1973). *The Welfare State: Its Aims, Benefits and Costs*, George Allen and Unwin, London.
SLOAN, L. (1969). '"Good government" and the politics of race', *Social Problems*, **17**, 161–75.

SMALLWOOD, F. (1965). *Greater London: The Politics of Metropolitan Reform*, Bobbs-Merrill, Indianapolis.

SMITH, D. M. (1975). 'Mapping human well-being', *International Social Science Journal*, **27**, 364–71.

SMITH, H. R. and HART, J. F. (1955). 'The American tariff map', *Geographical Review*, **45**, 327–46.

SOFEN, E. (1971). 'Reflections on the creation of Miami's Metro', in M. N. Danielsen (ed.), *Metropolitan Politics: A Reader*, Little, Brown and Company, Boston, 285–95.

SOKOLOW, A. D. (1973). 'Legislative pluralism, committee assignments and internal norms: the delayed impact of reapportionment in California', in L. Papaganopoulos (ed.), *Democratic Representation and Apportionment*, *Annals of the New York Academy of Sciences*, **219**, 291–313.

SOPER, C. S. and RYDON, J. (1958). 'Under-representation and electoral prediction', *Australian Journal of Politics and History*, **4**, 94–106.

SPILERMAN, S and DICKENS, D. (1975). 'Who will gain and who will lose influence under different electoral rules', *American Journal of Sociology*, **80**, 443–77.

STANYER, J. (1975). 'On the study of urban electoral behaviour', in K. Young (ed.), *Essays on the Study of Urban Politics*, Macmillan, London, 25–51.

STAVE, B. M. (ed.) (1976). *Socialism and the Cities*, Kenniket Press, Fort Washington, New York.

STEED, M. (1969). 'Callaghan's gerrymandering', *New Society*, 26 June 1969, 996–7.

—— (1971). 'The results analysed', in D. E. Butler and M. Pinto-Duschinsky, *The British General Election of 1970*, Macmillan, London, 386–415.

—— (1974). 'The results analysed', in D. E. Butler and D. Kavanagh, *The British General Election of February 1974*, Macmillan, London, 313–39.

—— (1975). 'The evolution of the British electoral system', in S. E. Finer (ed.), *Adversary Politics and Electoral Reform*, Anthony Wigram, London, 35–54.

STETZER, D. F. (1975). *Special Districts in Cook County: Toward a Geography of Local Government*, Research Paper 169, Department of Geography, University of Chicago, Chicago.

STUART, B. C. (1972). 'The impact of Medicaid on interstate income differentials', in K. E. Boulding and M. Pfaff (eds.), *Redistribution to the Rich and the Poor: The Grants Economics of Income Distribution*, Wadsworth Publishing Company, Belmont, California, 149–68.

SULLIVAN, J. L. (1972). 'A note on redistributive politics', *American Political Science Review*, **66**, 1301–6.

TAPER, B. (1962). *Gomillion versus Lightfoot*, McGraw-Hill, New York.

TATALOVICH, R. (1975). '"Friends and neighbours" voting: Mississippi, 1943–73', *Journal of Politics*, **37**, 807–14.

TAYLOR, A. H. (1972). 'The effect of party organization: correlation between campaign expenditure and voting in the 1970 election', *Political Studies*, **20**, 329–31.

TAYLOR, G. (1971). 'North and south: the education split', *New Society*, 4 March 1971, 346–7.

TAYLOR, P. J. (1977). 'Apolitical geography', *Progress in Human Geography*, 1, 130–5.

—— and GUDGIN, G. (1975). 'A fresh look at the Parliamentary Boundary Commissions', *Parliamentary Affairs*, **28**, 405–15.

—— —— (1976a). 'The myth of non-partisan cartography: a study of electoral biases in the English Boundary Commission's Redistribution for 1955–1970', *Urban Studies*, **13**, 13–25.

TAYLOR, P. J. (1976b). The statistical basis of decision-making in electoral districting', *Environment and Planning*, **A 8**, 43–58.

——— ——— (1977). 'Antipodean demises of Labour', in R. J. Johnston (ed.), *People, Places and Votes: Essays on the Electoral Geography of Australia and New Zealand*, Department of Geography, Univeristy of New England, Armidale, New South Wales, 111–20.

——— and JOHNSTON, R. J. (1978). 'Population distributions and political power in the European Parliament', *Regional Studies*, **12**, 61–8.

——— ——— (1979). *Geography of Elections*, Penguin Books, Harmondsworth.

TIEBOUT, C. M. (1956). 'A pure theory of local expenditures', *Journal of Political Economy*, **64**, 416–24.

TOLCHIN, M. and TOLCHIN, S. (1971). *To the Victor ... Political Patronage from the Clubhouse to the White House*, Random House, New York.

TOMPKINS, G. L. (1975). 'A causal model of state welfare expenditures', *Journal of Politics*, **37**, 392–416.

TRESCH, R. W. (1975). 'State governments and the welfare system: an econometric analysis', *Southern Economic Journal*, **42**, 33–43.

TUFTE, E. R. (1973). 'The relationship between seats and votes in two-party systems', *American Political Science Review*, **67**, 540–54.

TULLOCK, G. (1976). '*The Vote Motive*, Institute of Economic Affairs, London.

TYLER, G. and WELLS, D. I. (1962). 'New York: constitutionally Republican', in M. E. Jewell (ed.), *The Politics of Reapportionment*, Atherton Press, New York, 221–47.

——— ——— (1971). 'The new gerrymander threat', *American Federationist*, **78**, 1–7.

United States Department of Commerce (1974). *Statistical Abstract of the United States*, Government Printer, Washington.

VILE, M. J. C. (1976). *Politics in the U.S.A.*, Hutchinson, London.

WALKER, J. L. (1969). 'The diffusion of innovations among the American states', *American Political Science Review*, **58**, 880–9.

WALLACE, R. A. (1960). *Congressional Control of Federal Spending*, Wayne State University Press, Detroit.

WARNER, S. B. (1968). *The Private City*, University of Pennsylvania Press, Philadelphia.

WAY, H. F. (1962). 'California: brutal butchery of the two-party system', in M. E. Jewell (ed.), *The Politics of Reapportionment*, Atherton Press, New York, 249–64.

WELCH, W. P. (1974). 'The economics of campaign funds', *Public Choice*, **20**, 83–97.

——— (1976). 'The effectiveness of expenditures in State legislature races', *American Politics Quarterly*, **4**, 333–56.

WESTERGAARD, J. H. and RESLER, H. (1976). *Class in a Capitalist Society*, Penguin Books, Harmondsworth.

WILLIAMS, P. M. (1966). 'Two notes on the British electoral system', *Parliamentary Affairs*, **20**, 13–30.

WILSON, H. (1974). *The Labour Government 1964–70: A Personal Record*, Penguin Books, Harmondsworth.

WILSON, J. Q. and BANFIELD, E. C. (1964). 'Public-regardingness as a value premise in voting behavior', *American Political Science Review*, **58**, 876–87.

WIRT, F. M. (1973). 'Financial and desegregation reform in suburbia', in L. H. Masotti and J. K. Hadden (eds.), *The Urbanization of the Suburbs*, Sage Publications, Beverly Hills, 457–88.

WISTRICH, E. (1972). *Local Government Reorganisation: The First Years of Camden,* London Borough of Camden, London.

WOHLENBERG, E. H. (1976a). 'Interstate variations in AFDC programs', *Economic Geography,* **52**, 254–66.

—— (1976b). 'Public assistance effectiveness by states', *Annals, Association of American Geographers,* **66**, 440–50.

—— (1976c). 'An index of eligibility standards for welfare benefits', *Professional Geographer,* **28**, 381–4.

WOLFINGER, R. E. and HEIFETZ, J. (1965). 'Safe seats, seniority, and power in Congress', *American Political Science Review,* **59**, 337–49.

WOOD, R. C. (1961). *1400 Governments: The Political Economy of the New York Metropolitan Region,* Harvard University Press, Cambridge, Mass.

WRIGHT, G. C. (1975). 'Interparty competition and state social welfare policy', *Journal of Politics,* **37**, 796–803.

YOUNG, K. (1976). 'The conservative stategy for London, 1855–1975', *London Journal,* **2**, 56–81.

YUNKER, J. H. and LONGLEY, L. D. (1976). *The Electoral College: Its Biases Newly Measured for the 1960s and 1970s,* Sage Professional Papers in American Politics, 04–031, Sage Publications, Beverly Hills.

ZIMMER, B. G. (1976). 'Suburbanization and changing political structures', in B. Schwartz (ed.), *The Changing Face of the Suburbs,* Univeristy of Chicago Press, Chicago, 165–202.

ZOLOTH, B. S. (1976). 'Alternative measures of school segregation', *Land Economics,* **52**, 278–98.

Index